A GUIDE TO
KENTUCKY
OUTDOORS

A GUIDE TO KENTUCKY OUTDOORS

By Arthur B. Lander, Jr.

MENASHA RIDGE PRESS

HILLSBOROUGH
North Carolina

Copyright © 1978 by Arthur B. Lander, Jr.
All rights reserved
Printed in the United States of America
Published by Menasha Ridge Press
Route 3, Box 58G
Hillsborough, North Carolina 27278
ISBN 0-89732-001-8
Library of Congress card number 78-71189

Library of Congress Cataloging in Publication Data

Lander, Arthur B.

A Guide to Kentucky Outdoors.

1. Outdoor recreation—Kentucky—Guide-books.
2. Parks—Kentucky—Guide-books. 3. Lakes—Kentucky—
Recreational use—Guide-books. 4. Kentucky—Description
and travel—1951-   —Guide-books.   I. Title.
GV191.42.K4L36   917.69'04'4   78-26510
ISBN 0-89732-001-8 pbk.

In Memory of Genie and Arthur, My Loving Parents

2

Acknowledgements

Thanking all the persons and agencies who helped in the compilation of material for a reference book of this size is almost as great a task as the writing of the book itself. First of all, I would like to thank L. Darryl Armstrong and Rebecca Bruce of TVA at Land Between the Lakes; Mary Ellen Bickett of the Kentucky Department of Parks; and Charles Manning, Mimi Lewis, Dan Mangeot, and Gerald White of the Kentucky Department of Public Information. My sincere thanks also to the rangers of the United States Forest Service and National Park Service, to the resource managers of the U.S. Army Corps of Engineers, and to Karen Cissell and her staff at Kentucky Western Waterlands for their help in research.

I would also like to thank Ramona Marsh for her unit on bicycling and *Courier-Journal* staffer Jim Strader for his work on the hunting and fishing chapters. My personal thanks also go to my typist, Debi Spitznagel, who does such neat and efficient work. My deepest personal thanks go to my close friends who put up with the day-to-day roller-coaster of emotions that every writer must endure when facing a task of such magnitude. Last of all and most, I would like to express my deepest appreciation to Dick Wood, my publisher, who took me into his stable of writers and had faith in my ability from the very start and all throughout the project.

Contents

I   Introduction   1

II   National and State Parks   5

    Introduction   5

    Kentucky's National Parks   6

        Mammoth Cave National Park   7

        Cumberland Gap National Historical Park   12

    The Kentucky State Park System   16

        Big Bone Lick State Park   17

        Carter Caves State Resort Park   18

        Columbus-Belmont Battlefield State Park   20

        Cumberland Falls State Resort Park   21

        Fort Boonesborough State Park   22

        General Butler State Resort Park   24

        John James Audubon State Park   24

        Levi Jackson Wilderness Road State Park   25

        My Old Kentucky Home State Park   27

        Kentucky Horse Park   28

        Blue Licks Battlefield State Park   29

        Natural Bridge State Resort Park   31

        Pine Mountain State Resort Park   32

        Pennyrile Forest State Resort Park   33

        Breaks Interstate Park   34

        Louisville-Jefferson County Metropolitan Park   36

        Otter Creek Park   37

III   Land Between the Lakes   41
      Introduction   41
      History   43
      Camping   47
      Backpacking and Day-Hiking Trails   57
      Resource Management   62
      Environmental Education and Special Activities and Areas   71
IV   Major Lakes; Their Parks, Marinas, and Campgrounds   81
      Introduction   81
              Dale Hollow Lake   83
              Cave Run Lake   85
              Nolin River Lake   86
              Barren River Lake   88
              Laurel River Lake   90
              Rough River Lake   92
              Green River Lake   93
              Lake Cumberland   95
              Lake Barkley   103
              Kentucky Lake   111
V   Selected Small Lakes; Their Parks, Marinas, and Campgrounds   123
              Herrington Lake   123
              Williamstown Lake   126
              Grayson Lake   127
              Bullock Pen Lake   128
              Guist Creek Lake   128
              Dewey Lake   129
              Beaver Lake   132
              Carr Fork Lake   132
              Buckhorn Lake   133
              Kincaid Lake   135
              Lake Malone   135
              Greenbo Lake   136
              Fishtrap Lake   137

	Mauzy Lake	138
	Oxbow Lakes-Ballard County Wildlife Management Area	138
VI	State and National Forests	141
	Introduction	141
	Kentucky's State Forests	142
	Tygarts and Olympia State Forests	142
	Knobs State Forest	143
	Pennyrile State Forest	143
	Six Mile Island State Forest	144
	Kentucky Ridge and Kentenia State Forest	144
	Dewey State Forest	144
	Daniel Boone National Forest	145
	Morehead Ranger District	145
	Stanton Ranger District	146
	Berea Ranger District	150
	Somerset Ranger District	151
	London Ranger District	154
	Stearns Ranger District	155
	Redbird Purchase Ranger District	157
VII	Nature and Science Areas	159
	Introduction	159
	Lilley Cornett Woods	160
	Berea College Forest	162
	Clyde E. Buckley Wildlife Sanctuary	163
	Bernheim Forest	165
	Murphy's Pond	166
	Reelfoot Lake	167
	Spencer-Morton Preserve	171
VIII	Special Interest Recreational Activities	173
	Introduction	173
	Snow Skiing	173
	Scuba Diving	174

Hang-Gliding   175
Sport Parachuting   177
Bicycling   178
    History   179
    Bicycling Organizations   179
    Tours   182
    Bikeways   187
    Louisville Area   187
    Lexington Area   189
    Bikecentennial Trail   189

IX Fishing   195
  Introduction   195
    Largemouth Bass   195
    Spotted Bass   198
    Smallmouth Bass   199
    Bluegill   200
    Crappie   202
    Rockfish   204
    Sauger and Walleye   205
    White Bass   207
    Rainbow Trout   209
    Brook Trout   211
    Muskellunge   212
    Catfish   214
    Rough Fish   215
    Rock Bass   216
    Gar, Bowfin, Flier, and Chain Pickerel   216
    Frog Gigging   217
    Trotlines   218
    License Fees, Creel, and Size Limits   220
    Rainbow Trout Streams   221
    Trout Stocking in Lake Tailwaters   226

Trout Stocking in Daniel Boone National Forest   226

Muskellunge Streams   228

X   Hunting   235

Introduction   235

Whitetail Deer   236

Wild Turkey   238

Waterfowl   240

Cottontail Rabbit   242

Swamp Rabbit   243

Gray and Fox Squirrel   244

Bobwhite Quail   246

Ruffed Grouse   246

Mourning Dove   248

Raccoon   249

Furbearers and Varmints   250

Best Wildlife Management Areas For Waterfowl Hunting   250

Best Wildlife Management Areas For Deer Hunting   253

Best Wildlife Management Areas For Wild Turkey Hunting   254

Best Wildlife Management Areas For Small Game Hunting   256

Kentucky Lake shoreline at Land Between the Lakes. Photograph by Kentucky Department of Public Information.

1
Introduction

Welcome to Kentucky's outdoors!

Forested mountains, spectacular natural rock arches, cascading waterfalls, ferns and blooming wildflowers, vast underground caverns, broad shimmering lakes, the whisper of wings through the fog as a flock of mallards sails overhead, the thrash of a chunky largemouth struggling to throw the spinnerbait hooked in his lip—Kentucky's outdoor recreation potential is unparalleled for a midwestern state.

The 40,395 square miles of land stretching 400 miles from the Cumberland Plateau to the Mississippi River is varied in landscape, and each of the Commonwealth's five geographic regions has its own brand of outdoor recreation. Fishing, hunting, camping, nature study, boating, and sightseeing in the outdoors beckon millions of persons to Kentucky each year from surrounding states. Kentuckians as well enjoy life in the outdoors and constitute the largest group of visitors to the state's outdoor recreation areas.

The purpose of *A Guide to Kentucky Outdoors* is to identify and describe all the recreational opportunities in Kentucky. This recreation guide is the product of months and months of telephone interviewing, tedious organization of information, and hundreds of miles of travel across Kentucky. An attempt has been made to organize the material in "recreational clusters." The material is presented in a narrative format, rather than by means of the static charts and listings that characterize regional guides and state publications, in hopes that readers will be better able to grasp the magnitude of Kentucky's outdoor resources. Every effort has been made to be as comprehensive and accurate as possible. If any inaccuracies, omissions, or new facility developments are noted by readers, we would appreciate knowing about them, so that corrections can be made in future editions. Write in care of Menasha Ridge Press, Route 3, Box 58G, Hillsborough, North Carolina, 27278.

Arthur B. Lander, Jr.
St. Matthews, Kentucky
April, 1978

Kentucky State Parks

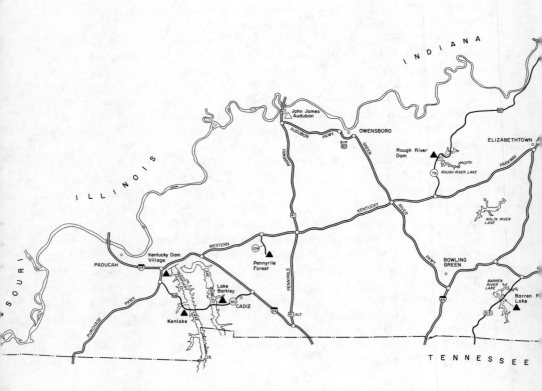

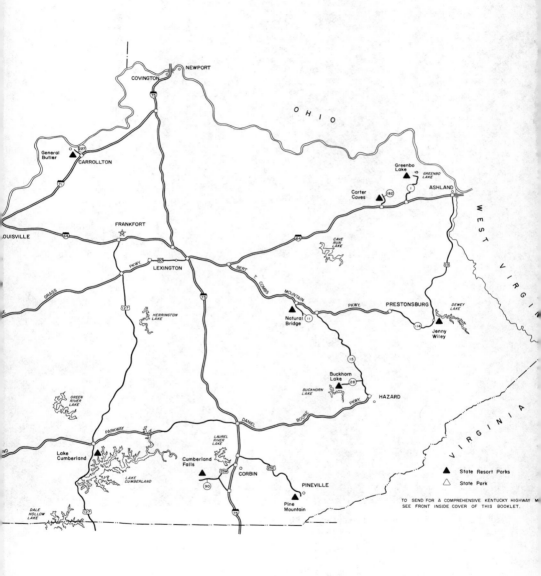

OHIO

NEWPORT

COVINGTON

General
Butler ▲ CARROLLTON

227

71

FRANKFORT ☆

LOUISVILLE 64

LEXINGTON

PKWY.

BERT T. COMBS MOUNTAIN

GRASS

127

HERRINGTON
LAKE

75

Natural ▲
Bridge 11

PKWY.

Greenbo
Lake ▲

GREENBO
LAKE

Carter ▲
Caves 182

ASHLAND

WEST VIRGINIA

64

CAVE
RUN
LAKE

23

PRESTONSBURG

DEWEY
LAKE

114 ▲ Jenny
Wiley

15

Buckhorn
Lake ▲
BUCKHORN 28
LAKE

HAZARD

BOONE PKWY.

GREEN
RIVER
LAKE

DANIEL

PARKWAY

Lake ▲
Cumberland

LAKE
CUMBERLAND

LAUREL
RIVER
LAKE

Cumberland ▲
Falls 25W

CORBIN

25E

90

75

PINEVILLE

Pine ▲
Mountain

127

DALE
HOLLOW
LAKE

VIRGINIA

▲ State Resort Parks
△ State Park

TO SEND FOR A COMPREHENSIVE KENTUCKY HIGHWAY M
SEE FRONT INSIDE COVER OF THIS BOOKLET.

Cumberland Gap National Historical Park. Photograph by Kentucky Department of Public Information.

2
National and State Parks

Introduction

Kentucky's parks are places where people go to camp, fish, sightsee, swim, sunbathe, water ski, sail, commune with nature, explore underground caverns, bird-watch, study wildflowers, backpack—or simply relax and take it easy.

Blessed by living in a state with more than its share of charming countryside, sprawling azure lakes, forested mountains, and interesting historical sites, Kentuckians should count themselves lucky that their park administrators through the years have been concerned with preserving these features for vacationers. The success of Kentucky's park system hasn't happened overnight; it has taken immense foresight, years of planning, and vigorous legislative action. The tradition of fine hospitality and common courtesy is not the only reason for the popularity of traveling in Kentucky.

Kentuckians take their parks and outdoor recreation as seriously as they do bourbon whiskey and thoroughbred horseracing. In 1976, for example, 31 million persons visited Kentucky's state parks. Another 4 million spent time at the two national parks in Kentucky, Cumberland Gap National Historical Park and Mammoth Cave National Park. Visitors came from almost every state in the union, and a surprising number from Europe as well. The largest number of visitors at Kentucky parks is native Kentuckians, followed by persons from the neighboring states of Ohio, Indiana, Illinois, Michigan, Tennessee, Missouri, and West Virginia.

In this chapter we will discuss Kentucky's national parks and those state parks which include campgrounds. Water-oriented state parks and their recreation potential and facilities will be discussed in the chapters on lakes.

Kentucky's National Parks

There are thirty-eight national parks in America, the core of a system of some 250 areas administered by the National Park Service, an agency created by Congress in 1916. Today, more than sixty years later, the National Park Service is a huge, multifaceted unit of the Department of the Interior that oversees the management of twenty-seven million acres, areas of priceless natural and historic character. These areas are the crown jewels, the holy land of outdoor recreation in America—snow-capped peaks above timberline, deserts, seashores, vast underground caverns, and sweeping forestlands. Within the system are millions of acres of roadless, true "wilderness"—by definition, lands unaltered by man. In an era when mankind seems determined to continue the all-out attack on nature by indiscriminate pollution—endless cutting of forests, draining of wetlands, widespread use of chemical poisons, and degradation of air and water— our national parks are perhaps the only areas in this country where we can get a true picture of the majesty that once spread from coast to coast. The parks are a heritage of wild lands, of plant and animal communities— "untamed ecosystems that we need to learn more about, to respect and preserve for the enjoyment of future generations." Perhaps our national parks can instill in all of us the realization that these natural systems play an integral role in the survival of our total supporting environment, and ultimately of mankind.

Kentucky is most fortunate in that it has one national park and one national historical park, both of which are superlative in their respective categories. Mammoth Cave, the largest cave known to man, is certainly the best known of the two major caves in the national park system, a geological masterpiece researched by scientists from all over the world. Cumberland Gap National Historical Park, the largest in terms of acreage of the national historical parks in America, memorializes the "Gateway to the West," the mountain pass through which pioneers first crossed the westernmost part of the Appalachian mountain ranges.

These two parks offer unparalleled opportunities for wilderness-type recreation—backpacking, trout fishing, nature photography, canoeing, rock climbing, and spelunking. Yet they are also great places for the less strenuous challenges of camping, natural history study, and informal family day outings. And there's enough room for everybody to explore and find his own little corner in the backcountry, a place he can thrill in "discovering."

Mammoth Cave National Park
Mailing address: Mammoth Cave, Kentucky, 42259
Telephone: (502) 758-2251

Indians of the pre-Columbian era were probably the first persons to venture into Mammoth Cave. With reed torches as a light source, they explored the main passageways of the vast underground world. These prehistoric explorers left behind evidence which archaeologists pieced into a picture of primitive man—piles of ashes, wooden bowls, flint tools, chipped gypsum deposits, blackened ceilings, and the mummified remains of those who became lost or trapped and died, their clothing and bones preserved by the constant temperature and humidity.

With the coming of the white man in the eighteenth century, the story of Mammoth Cave began to unfold. A hunter trailing a wounded bear is credited with finding the cave's main entrance, known today as the "historic entrance," in 1798. There is some reason to believe, however, that passageways and sinks, later substantiated to be part of the Mammoth Cave and Flint Ridge Cave systems, may have been inspected superficially by white "long hunters" in the 1770s.

The nineteenth century brought private ownership of the cave and surrounding lands. The discovery of saltpeter, mixed in with the fine, dry cave dirt, was perhaps responsible for the initial interest in the Mammoth Cave. The embargo imposed by Britain during the War of 1812 made it necessary to mine domestically the nitrates needed in the manufacturing of gun powder, as foreign sources were shut off. The saltpeter mining operation in Mammoth Cave brought attention to the unique natural attraction and fostered the idea of promoting it as a money-making proposition. That possibility materialized in 1816 when commercially guided tours began, although it was not until 1838 that a daring black guide named Stephen Bishop crossed Bottomless Pit, opening the way to discovery of points of interest that would make Mammoth Cave a world-renowned tourist attraction.

The increased explorations spawned a period of scientific research in Mammoth Cave. The first blind cave animal, the Mammoth Cave blindfish (*Amblyopsis spelaea*), a small, colorless fish lacking pelvic fins, was captured from Echo River by the ichthyologist De Kay in 1838. Dr. John Locke of the Ohio Medical College published the first description of gypsum cave formation, which opened discussions in the scientific community about the other minerals found in the cave and their possible uses. The stable environmental conditions inspired Dr. John Croghan, master of Locust Grove Plantation in Louisville, to attempt to establish the cave as a health spa and sanatorium for persons suffering from consumption. The experiment failed, despite the fact that the air in Mammoth Cave was pure and highly oxygenated.

The grandeur of the cave awed visitors, and the word soon spread around the world. Dignitaries, performers, and evangelists flocked to see the magnificent corridors, underground rivers, and crystalline formations. Grand Duke Alexis of Russia dined in the banquet hall in 1872; "the Swedish Nightingale," Jenny Lind, broke the mysterious silence, her voice ringing like a golden chime through nature's greatest opera house. Billy Sunday, moved by a visit to Mammoth Cave, wrote, "I felt smaller today than I ever did in my life; there is only one word in the language to describe Mammoth Cave, and that is Mammoth."

Geologists tell us that the process that formed Mammoth Cave began millions of years ago. As is the case in virtually all limestone caves, subterranean water dissolving porous rock is responsible for both the caverns and the formations. Rainwater containing small amounts of carbonic acid seeped through sinkholes and joints (fractures in rock layers), eventually cutting passageways at multiple levels. The upper levels dried out. Then the seepage, a drop at a time, deposited limestone which became travertine (cave onyx), the mineral of which the stalagmites, stalactites, draperies, and cascading flowstone are composed. The trickles of water finally converged into underground rivers such as Echo and Roaring rivers.

Mammoth Cave was the first cave known to contain gypsum, which is formed in the drier passageways of the upper levels by the slow leaching of calcium sulfate through porous limestone. The gypsum crystals form beautiful patterns which crust the ceilings of the cave. In other areas, the roof has collapsed, forming sinks; in lower passageways, the collapsed roof is seen as convex "domes," or deep pits between parallel passageways. Unique formations that occur in Mammoth Cave include helictites, a form of stalactite which turns up at the tip; lily pads, an irregular deposit around a pool of standing water; and gypsum crusts of "flowers," as found in the Snowball Dining Room.

The most famous and earliest tavern for guests touring Mammoth Cave was Bell's Tavern, where virtually all the famous visitors stayed. It was the social center of the community and was renowned for fine food, lodging, imported brandy, and locally-made whiskey and beer. In addition to Bell's Tavern, accommodations were available at the old Mammoth Cave Hotel, which grew steadily from a nucleus of a few small log cabins built during the mining days in 1812.

The ballroom of the Mammoth Cave Hotel was the scene of many a gala dance and dinner. But, on the night of December 9, 1916, the grand old hotel with its wide verandas and spacious rooms caught fire and burned to the ground in a matter of minutes. It was not until 1925 that a major reconstruction of the hotel was completed. Meanwhile, in 1923, the Mammoth Cave Development Company built a 25-room hotel, appropriately named in honor of the cave's premier feature, Frozen Niagara. The new, modern Mammoth Cave Hotel was built in 1965.

The years of private ownership of Mammoth Cave were not to the liking of many individuals who argued that property mismanagement and a complex trustee arrangement of ownership were responsible for decreased visitation after the turn of the century. As early as 1905, the matter was taken up with the Department of Interior through requests that the area become a national park. It was not until 1923, however, that a survey and discussion within the agency as to the feasibility of such a park actually began. In July 1925, the park's spearhead group, the Mammoth Cave National Park Commission, was incorporated. By May 1934, the condemnation and purchase of lands for the park had begun, and two years later the park came under jurisdiction of the National Park Service. Mammoth Cave National Park was formally declared open to visitors on September 18, 1946, when it officially became the nation's twenty-sixth national park. Since almost half the land consisted of cleared fields and eroded soil banks, a complete reforestation plan was inititated, with a major portion of the work done by the Civilian Conservation Corps (CCC).

Today, Mammoth Cave National Park is reborn with vast forests like those which crowned the rolling hills a century ago. The National Park Service has done a remarkable job of making the park one of Kentucky's true showplaces. Interpretive activities at Mammoth Cave National Park include six cave tours, nature walks, boat trips on the Green River, the Joppa Ridge Motor Trail, evening slide presentations, informal programs, and children's naturalist trips through Mammoth Cave and surface backcountry areas.

The Historic Tour is a two-mile tour beginning at the Historic Entrance and featuring the War of 1812 mining operation, Indian artifacts, Fat Man's Misery, Mammoth Dome, a talk on cave formations, and a torch-throwing demonstration. The least strenuous of the cave tours, the Frozen Niagara, features an impressive hour-and-one-half walk through a garden of stalagmites, stalactites, flowstone, and draperies.

Narrow winding cave passages, steep hills, domes, pits, gypsum flowers, and other cave formations are included in the four-mile, four-and-one-half-hour Half Day Scenic Tour. An hour and a half into the tour there is a visit to the Snowball Dining Room, 276 feet underground. Food is available at extra cost.

Before the invention of the electric light, cave guides used lanterns to see in the darkness. The Lantern Tour is a nostalgic journey back to this era. The three-mile tour, which includes one-half mile of the Historic Tour route, passes the War of 1812 mining operation, Mummy Ledge, tuberculosis huts, the largest cave rooms, excavations of Indian artifacts, and a torch-throwing demonstration. The Great Onyx Tour, which features cave formations exclusively, is the tour for those interested in learning about Mammoth Cave's complex geology. Departing from the Visitor's Center, the three-hour tour begins with a three-mile bus ride with an interpretive talk on surface aspects along the way.

If you really want to capture the spirit of spelunking and the early exploration fever which has carried over to our generation, the Wild Cave Tour is just such an adventure. The rugged, six-hour tour is limited to 14 persons 16 years of age or older, and reservations are advised, since the tour is offered only on weekends and is often booked months in advance. Much of the tour involves unimproved trails and crawlways; participants should be in excellent physical condition. Old clothes and hiking boots or leather work boots are suggested, as well as gloves. Hard hats, headlamps, and knee pads are provided. Reservations may be made by telephone at (502) 758-2251 from 8:00 a.m. to 4:30 p.m., central standard time. Ask the operator for the Wild Cave Tour clerk. In contrast, there is also a special tour for the handicapped in wheelchairs and their attendants.

The Historic, Frozen Niagara, Half Day (Scenic) and Physically Handi-capped Tours are held daily and on weekends throughout the year except Christmas Day. The Wild Cave and Lantern Tour are held on weekends only. The Great Onyx Tour is held during the summer season (June to Labor Day) only. The costs for all the cave tours range from 50¢ for children under 16 years of age to $3.50 for persons on the Wild Cave Tour.

The temperature of Mammoth Cave is approximately 54 degrees Fahrenheit year-round, and persons on cave tours should wear sweaters or light jackets. All cave tours depart from the Visitor's Center, and are on a first-come, first-served basis. Individual reservations are accepted only for the Wild Cave Tour and Trog, a three-hour children's naturalist program held in the summer that features surface interpretation as well as cave touring. Trog is open to children ages 8 to 12 years.

The seasonal programs above ground are primarily guided woodland walks and evening programs. Insect repellent is recommended for all walks to ward off ticks and chiggers. The Green River Bluffs walk is about a mile in length and explores the woodlands atop bluffs overlooking the Green River, one of the deepest rivers for its width in the world. The River Styx Walk, named for one of the five rivers surrounding Hades in Greek mythology, is a leisurely stroll through forestlands to where the river emerges from Mammoth Cave. Both the Green River Bluffs and River Styx nature walks begin at the Visitor's Center.

Two other guided walks are Cedar Sink and Beaver Pond. The exploration of a huge sinkhole containing a disappearing stream, massive bluffs, and dense woodlands, is part of this two-and-one-half-hour trip which begins at the Cedar Sink parking area off highway Ky-422. The Beaver Pond walk explores the fringes of a pond where a colony of beavers once lived. Talks on aquatic systems and the changing ecology of the area highlight this informal walk which begins at Sloan's Crossing parking area.

The evening programs in the main campground, park amphitheater, and Houchins Ferry campground stress local history, folklore, and music. Slide shows are given occasionally by park naturalists and persons doing research in the cave. There is a cutback in these nightly events during the spring and fall seasons, and they are not held in the winter.

The Joppa Ridge Motor Trail is a unique automobile route through ridgetop and valley woodlands. Beginning near the Green River west of the Visitor's Center, it is a two-mile, one-way road with numbered stops along the way. At each stop there are areas in different stages of plant succession—grass and weed fields, shrubs and small cedars, cedar forests, cedar forests with deciduous understory, and deciduous forests. At each station along the way there's a chance of seeing different animal life; be alert for beautiful song birds, hawks, foxes, squirrels, and whitetail deer. The drive features beautiful stands of hardwoods and evidence of homesites that existed on the ridge when the park lands were under private ownership.

The *Miss Green River II*, a 63-foot diesel-powered cruiser, makes four trips daily during the summer on the historic river, recalling steamboat days when paddle-wheelers plied their trade after the lock and dam system was completed in 1906. Today's scenic boat trip which lasts an hour and costs less than $2 for adults and $1 for children, is a brief glimpse into this romantic means of travel of another era which inspired Horace Hovey to write at the turn of the century, "No more delightful river ride than this can be found in the middle west, or more diversified by frown cliffs, wild forests, opening amphitheaters that smile in summer with rustling fields of corn, with here and there attractive villages and flourishing cities."

The park's main campground is on highway Ky-70/255, within walking distance of the Visitor's Center, Historic Entrance to Mammoth Cave, and the nature program amphitheater. There are 145 sites for tents or RVs. Facilities and services include drinking water, flush toilets, dumping station, seasonal grocery, ice, coin laundry, picnic tables and shelters, grills, and firewood.

The cost for camping is $3 per night, with a limit of 14 days. Pets are allowed but must be leashed. The Service Center, located next to the campground, has a post office, service station, showers, and store for campers' supplies. The store, laundry, and showers are closed from Thanksgiving to Easter week and are open only on weekends, including Fridays, in spring and fall. No reservations are accepted for campsites.

In season, all facilities and services at Mammoth Cave National Park are jammed with visitors, and finding a campsite may be next to impossible. An alternative is the free campsite at Houchins Ferry, open to primitive camping only, 12 sites, no RVs.

The National Park Concessions, Inc., operates the Mammoth Cave Hotel, Sunset Point Motor Lodge, the hotel annex, and seasonal woodland cottages with full-service accommodations for park visitors. A dining room and coffee shop, a craft shop featuring demonstrations of broom-making and weaving by Berea College students, the Visitor's Center exhibit room, and the service center for campers are all conveniently located together. Reservations for rooms and cottages and inquiries about rates can be made by writing to Mammoth Cave Hotel, Mammoth Cave, Kentucky, 42259, or by calling (502) 758-2225.

The popularity of Mammoth Cave has grown tremendously through the years. Because of the park's location in the Midwest and its proximity to major population centers and to Interstate-65, a major north-south route just a few miles from the park's entrance, visitation has mushroomed in recent years at a rate of 30,000 additional persons each year. Visitor impact has caused pollution problems, traffic jams, overuse of facilities and services, and damage to the cave. As a result, under a recently devised plan which will be implemented over the next 10 to 20 years, a number of changes in visitor use will take place to relieve the environmental ills described above. The master plan for Mammoth Cave National Park emphasizes diversification of park use.

Actions planned for the near future include expanding the number and variety of cave tours; creating a new staging area at the park's periphery from which visitors would be transported to the Visitor's Center, thereby reducing automobile pollution and congestion; phasing out existing facilities; modifying intrapark road circulation; establishing a trail system; and increasing the number of backcountry campsites for fishermen and backpackers.

Mammoth Cave is Kentucky's foremost tourist attraction and ranks as one of the world's great wonders. With the 1972 discovery by a team from the National Cave Research Foundation of a passageway connecting Mammoth Cave and the Flint Ridge Cave system, the combined system is now by far the longest in the world, totaling more than 144 miles.

Cumberland Gap National Historical Park
Mailing address: P.O. Box 840, Middlesboro, Kentucky, 40965
Telephone: (606) 248-2818

On April 13, 1750, the land west of the Alleghenies was opened to extensive exploration and eventual settlement, ultimately clearing the way for the establishment of America's fifteenth state—Kentucky. On that date Dr. Thomas Walker, who had been employed by the Loyal Land Company of Virginia to seek out a site for future settlement beyond the mountains, discovered a great pass with an Indian road leading through it, which later became the main artery of westward migration. Walker named the pass in honor of the Duke of Cumberland.

Following the termination of the French and Indian War (1754–60) which had temporarily postponed exploration, hunters passed through the gap in large numbers to venture deep into the fabulously rich land they had heard about from Walker and his men. Some established trade with the Shawnee and Cherokee Indians who visited Kentucky to hunt in the lowlands along Warrior's Path, the footpath which led from Cumberland Gap northward to the Ohio River.

Perhaps the most famous of these frontiersmen was Daniel Boone, who with his brother Squire learned more about Kentucky than anyone else while hunting and exploring for two years between 1769 and 1771. By 1773 he had convinced his family and four other families to move from their homes in Yadkin Valley, North Carolina, to Kentucky. Just before they reached the gap, however, Boone's son James and several others were killed during an Indian attack. As a result of this tragedy, they returned to North Carolina. But Boone was not easily discouraged and two years later he returned with a party of axemen and began cutting the Wilderness Road. The successful establishment of Fort Boonesborough at the trail's northern terminus was the realization of Daniel Boone's life-long dream. It was a personal victory for Boone, settling in an unspoiled land where game was plentiful and the soil was rich for farming.

In the years following the establishment of Fort Boonesborough and the American revolution, the number of settlers passing through Cumberland Gap steadily increased. By 1800, it was estimated that of the approximately 400,000 who had gone west, 75 percent had used the Cumberland Gap route. By that time the trail through the gap had been widened to accommodate wagons.

This floodtide of immigration soon brought cattle drives, stagecoaches, and a new importance to Cumberland Gap. As the storm clouds gathered for the greatest of America's internal challenges, the Civil War, the strategic value of the gap was quickly recognized, and the area figured prominently in the opening action in the western theatre of operations—for whoever occupied the great pass state of Kentucky would also control the rebel states of Virginia and Tennessee. Even more important, they would control the railroad between Tennessee and Virginia.

The gap was occupied initially by the Confederates under the command of Brigadier General Felix K. Zollicoffer, who was later killed during an offensive campaign that ended in defeat and lost the gap to Federal forces. Eventually, after a series of capture and recapture by both the Federals and the Confederates, Cumberland Gap was permanently occupied by Union forces from the fall of 1863 until the close of the war. By 1865, the once heavily wooded hillsides of the gap and the adjacent mountains lay wasted, studded with stumps, pocked with entrenchments, and scarred by deeply rutted supply roads. It was ravaged and deserted.

Interest in the gap returned again in the mid-1880s when geologists investigating the area found rich deposits of coal and iron. An industrial scheme was based on these discoveries; huge sums of money were invested by an English syndicate in railroads, coal mines, and iron furnaces. The resulting industrial boom gave birth to the city of Middlesboro, Kentucky, in the wide basin just north of the gap. During the Panic of 1893, however, financial reverses caused the boom to collapse, although limited prosperity continued due to substantial investments by northern capitalists.

By the turn of the century the renewed growth of trees had restored much of the scenic beauty of the gap and the surrounding mountains. The area's historic and scenic qualities encouraged many people to begin talking about the establishment of a park. Public recognition of these qualities at the 1922 Appalachian Logging Conference in Cincinnati led to the introduction in 1923 of two bills calling for the establishment of a park, but final Congressional designation of the area as a park did not come until June 11, 1940, 18 years later.

Cumberland Gap National Historical Park was formally dedicated on July 4, 1959, and is the largest of the national historical units in the National Park System. The 20,194-acre park straddles the crest of Cumberland Mountain, running southwestwardly for a distance of 17½ miles from a point on the Kentucky-Virginia boundary near Ewing, Virginia, to the Tennessee-Kentucky corner, with an average width of only one and two-thirds miles.

Cumberland Gap National Historical Park is a favorite with hikers, and rightly so, as it is a park of precipitous mountains clothed with dense deciduous hardwood forests. A 14½-mile section of the park along the crest of Cumberland and Brush Mountains is roadless, an area of rocky cliffs (shale, limestone, sandstone, and conglomerate), high mountain valleys, and plateau land, with many commanding views of the valleys below and distant mountain ranges. On the crest of Powell Mountain is Goose Nest Sink, a huge saucer-shaped depression that was formed as the result of the collapse of a cave ceiling.

There are four major streams in the park. Two of the streams, Shillalah and Martin's Fork of the Cumberland River, one of Kentucky's Wild Rivers, are especially beautiful. A virgin stand of hemlocks guards its headwaters, and the stream rolls through narrow rock valleys canopied with heavy stands of rhododendron and mountain laurel, which bloom in the spring.

Wildflowers and ferns thrive along the creek's moss-covered banks. Special trout fishing seasons are held in Cumberland Gap National Historical Park; season dates are May 15 to September 1, weather permitting. Access to these streams requires long cross-country hikes.

Cumberland Gap National Historical Park is rich in plants and wildlife. The 52 species of mammals that have been identified by the park's biologist include the commonly encountered chipmunk, gray squirrel, raccoon, opossum, whitetail deer, and red fox.

From March to October the moist mountainside valleys are carpeted with ferns and wildflowers that include the early blooming trailing arbutus, dwarf crested iris, and painted trillium. Warmer weather brings out May apples, the rare Turk's cap lily, Indian pipe, and yellow adder's-tongue. Because the altitude of the park ranges from 1,300 to 3,513 feet above sea level, there is a diverse distribution of shrubs and evergreens, as well as herbaceous ground plants.

If you're a hiker who enjoys bird-watching, you'll find the park has an abundance of birdlife, as has most of the Appalachian region. There are 115 species from 31 families known to be either residents or transient visitors. Seasonal visitors include the endangered bald eagle; a lesser-known bird of prey, the marsh hawk; and a meadow dweller, the blue-winged warbler. Perhaps the game bird most often sighted is the ruffed grouse. It is not uncommon to hear them "drumming" their wings during the annual spring mating season.

Wilderness Road Campground, near the trailhead of Ridge Trail, is the park's only campground. There are 165 sites for tents or RVs. Open April to October, the campground is on Highway US-58 on the Virginia side of Cumberland Gap and can be reached via US-25E. Facilities and services include flush toilets, drinking water, picnic tables, and grills. Groceries and ice are available nearby at Cumberland Gap, Tennessee. Campsites are $2 per night, with a limit of 14 days. Reservations are accepted for groups only.

Cumberland Gap National Historical Park is a hiker's paradise, with more than 30 miles of trails. One road is open to four-wheel-drive vehicles and provides good access to backcountry areas of the park. The three-mile road, which connects Cubbage, Kentucky, with Hensley Settlement, a restored mountain village atop Brush Mountain, is extremely steep and narrow but passable by four-wheel-drive vehicle. The road, which is also used by hikers, is reached via highways Ky-988 (Sugar Run Road) and Ky-217 from the Visitor's Center on US-25E. Cubbage Road ends near the Martin's Fork backcountry camp. A fire road which leads eastward atop Brush Mountain in the opposite direction from Hensley Settlement is ideal for foot access to prime fishing spots on Martin's Fork of the Cumberland River. The road is not marked and is closed to auto traffic by a gate.

During the summer National Park Service personnel present a number of interpretive programs for visitors. A schedule of these events is available at the Visitor's Center, one mile south of Middlesboro, Kentucky, near the northern entrance to Cumberland Gap on highway US-25E. Museum exhibits on the natural history of the region, its earliest inhabitants, and the pioneer era, and a 10-minute slide program on the history of the gap itself, have been prepared for those seeking general orientation at the administrative headquarters. There is also a number of publications on various subjects on sale at the information desk.

The interpretive programs in recent years have included campfire sessions in the rustic setting of the outdoor amphitheater at Wilderness Road Campground, programs of mountain music such as ballads and bluegrass and discussions on the evolution of these forms, guided hikes to such points of interest as Sand Cave and Hensley Settlement, and two-hour walks on day-hiking trails near the campground, Visitor's Center, and Sugar Run picnic area. These leisurely strolls with park naturalists are accompanied by informal lectures on such topics as local flora and early settlers and their way of life. Additional activities include exploration of limestone caves in Lewis Hollow, mountain crafts demonstrations, lectures on local Civil War action, and an after-dinner "snipe hunt."

A point of major importance near the Visitor's Center and administrative offices is the Pinnacle, an overlook on the crest of Cumberland Mountain. Indian chiefs were said to have used the breathtaking lookout point as a sacred council grounds where tribal policies were discussed. The Pinnacle is reached via a paved road from the park's Visitor's Center.

Since there are no food concessions or lodge accommodations in Cumberland Gap National Historical Park, visitors must either camp or lodge at nearby motels and parks. Lodging is available in Middlesboro, Kentucky; Cumberland Gap, Tennessee; or Pine Mountain State Resort Park, 16 miles north in Pineville, Kentucky.

The Kentucky State Park System

In May of 1974, the Kentucky State Park System celebrated its fiftieth anniversary. In just half a century, the dream of a few ambitious persons has materialized into one of the nation's most respected state park systems. Tourism is a billion-dollar business in Kentucky and the state parks are a major contributing factor.

In this chapter, we will discuss the state parks not located on lakes, Louisville's metro parks, and Kentucky's only interstate park. These parks are located throughout the state in prime vacation regions. Fifteen of Kentucky's state parks are complete "resort" parks with luxurious lodge accommodations, restaurants, housekeeping cottages that often overlook sprawling lakes or forested mountains, campgrounds, marinas, swimming pools, and complete recreational facilities (golf courses, trap ranges, horseback riding stables, tennis courts, and indoor gamerooms).

The campground services and facilities in the Kentucky State Park System are generally consistent throughout, the only exception being that the most popular park campgrounds have a greater number of sites with electrical and water hookups. No reservations are taken at any Kentucky state park campground and visits are limited to 14 days. Strict leash rules for pets are in effect throughout the system. Senior citizens receive discounts on campground fees at all Kentucky state parks.

Kentucky's state parks have traditionally enjoyed the reputation of being "family parks," with recreational opportunities for children as well as adults. Five of the parks have outdoor amphitheaters where period dramas and musicals are presented during the summer. No alcoholic beverages are served in Kentucky state parks (an interesting irony, since Kentucky produces more bourbon than any other state in America—and where else would Bourbon County be dry and Christian County be wet!).

Lodge rooms feature wall-to-wall carpeting, tub and shower, individual temperature controls, television, and maid service. Ten of the state resort parks are open year-round and feature off-season rates. Reservations should be made well in advance since the parks are jammed during the summer, especially on holidays.

Reservations may be made over a toll-free line if you're calling from Alabama, Ohio, Indiana, Illinois, Missouri, Tennessee, Georgia, South Carolina, Virginia, or West Virginia. The number is 1-800-626-2911. The number for calls from anywhere in Kentucky is 1-800-372-2961. American Express, Visa, and MasterCharge cards are accepted for lodging, meals, and gift shop purchases at all Kentucky state resort parks.

Big Bone Lick State Park
Mailing address: Union, Kentucky 41091
Telephone: (606) 384-3522

Thousands of years ago during the Pleistocene Epoch (Ice Age), enormous herds of mastodons, mammoths (elephant-like creatures), giant ground sloths, bison, musk ox, and numerous other prehistoric mammals were driven southward by the advance of glaciers. The animals' craving for salt led them to Big Bone Lick, where there were large deposits caused by numerous sulfur springs. But in the marshy quagmire surrounding the springs, the huge animals became trapped and died. Centuries later, in 1739, their fossilized bones were found by a French-Canadian explorer, Charles de Longueil, who is thought to be the first white man ever to see the area.

Big Bone Lick was later extensively explored by Daniel Boone. Records from explorations during the Revolutionary War period indicate that the huge backbones of the fossilized animals were used as seats and the ribs were long enough for tent poles. Ten-pound teeth with grinding surfaces of 75 square inches were found. Later, in 1807, President Thomas Jefferson sent a party of explorers to collect fossils from the site. They were displayed in the White House and later given to a natural history museum in Paris, France.

Until the mid-1800s Big Bone Lick was a fashionable spa where wealthy people went to "take the waters." The 512-acre park along the Ohio River at Union, Kentucky, was added to the state system in 1960. Big Bone Lick can be reached via the Walton exit on Interstate-75. Follow Ky-1292 four and one-half miles west, then proceed three miles on Ky-338. The park grounds and outdoor museum are open year-round, and the campground, indoor museum, and gift shop are open April 1 through October 31. The outdoor museum features a fascinating recreation of the time when the huge creatures found the salt licks, and includes interpretive plaques and awesome, life-size models of the prehistoric mastodons and bison. The campground has 62 sites for either tents or RVs, all with electrical hookups. The campground's facilities and services include showers, drinking water, flush toilets, dumping station, grocery, ice, picnic tables and shelter, grills, firewood, and swimming pool (open in season).

Carter Caves State Resort Park
Mailing address: Olive Hill, Kentucky, 41164
Telephone: (606) 286-4411

This northeastern Kentucky park in Carter County can be reached by driving five miles east on highway US-60 from Olive Hill, Kentucky, then three miles north on Ky-182. The thousand-acre park is noted for the cave system which honeycombs the hills, the splendid woodlands, and nearby Tygart's Creek, a fine canoeing and fishing stream.

Opened in the 1940s, Carter Caves State Resort Park has a full menu of recreational pastimes, including four cave tours. Tickets for the X Cave and Saltpeter Cave tours can be purchased at the park's Trading Post, open

9:00 a.m. to 7:00 p.m. daily. Prices range from 35¢ to $1 and group rates are available. Tickets for the Cascade Cavern Tour can be purchased at the Cascade Visitor's Center, open from 9:00 a.m. to 5:00 p.m. daily. Tour costs for adults and children are less than $1.

Cascade Cavern Tours are offered seven times daily. The hour-long leisurely walk includes the Counterfeiters Room, "Hanging Gardens of Solomon," and numerous formations typical of limestone caves. The Salt-peter Cave Tour, held only on weekends, is a forty-five minute, one-mile tour. Highlights include, in addition to a discussion of the 1812 saltpeter mining operations, Indian Princess Grave, the Legend of the Lost Miner, and "Devil's Dome."

The X Cave gets its name from an unusual X-shaped formation of stalactites, stalagmites, and flowstone curtains. The easy tour lasts only 40 minutes and is about a quarter of a mile long.

The two strenuous tours offered at Carter Caves State Resort Park are the Bat Cave Tour and the Laurel Cave-Horn Hollow Cave Tour. The Bat Cave Tour is offered by reservation only on Tuesdays, Wednesdays, Saturdays, and Sundays. The two-hour tour covers about two miles, with extended stooping and squatting required. During the tour, participants must wade in water; flashlights, old clothes, sturdy shoes, and jackets are advised. Children under 16 must be accompanied by adults. The highlight of the tour is discussion and observation of a colony of rare bats.

The Laurel Cave-Horn Hollow Cave Tour departs from the Trading Post at 2 p.m. on Thursdays only and includes one and one-half miles overland hiking and one-half mile in caves. The tour lasts about two hours and is the only tour at Carter Caves State Resort Park that is free of charge. Since the tour involves wading in deep water and extended stooping and crawling, preschool children are not permitted. Sturdy shoes, flashlight, and warm clothes are advised.

In season, park naturalists conduct canoeing trips on Tygart's Creek, a smooth water Class I stream bordered by dense woodlands and farmlands and known for good fishing for muskellunge, smallmouth bass, and panfish. The canoe trips are free and reservations are required. The informal, unscheduled trips are limited to persons 14 years old and older, and those under 16 years of age must be accompanied by an adult. Canoe trips are limited to 10 persons. There's a good chance of sighting wildlife—kingfishers, turtles, wood ducks, and maybe even a deer.

The lodge, swimming pool for guests only, 45-acre land and beach house, nature center (with interpretive exhibits on geology, plants, and animals), and cave tours are open seasonally, April 1 to October 31; the housekeeping cottages and campground are open year-round. The campground's services and facilities include showers, flush toilets, dump stations, ice, playground for youngsters, picnic and shelter houses, and firewood.

Columbus-Belmont Battlefield State Park
Mailing address: Columbus, Kentucky, 42032
Telephone: (502) 677-2327

In September of 1861 a garrison of more than nineteen thousand Confederate troops set to work fortifying the bluffs overlooking the Mississippi River at Columbus, Kentucky. An extensive network of trenches and breastworks was built, and 140 heavy guns, mostly 32- and 64-pounders, were positioned to guard against attack on both the river and inland fronts. Further fortified by floating batteries and a huge, mile-long chain stretched across the river to prevent Union gunboats from penetrating this all-important route to the heart of the South, the outpost became known as the "Gibraltar of the West."

Successfully defended in the Battle of Belmont on November 7, 1861, and during flanking skirmishes on the Kentucky side of the river, the position finally had to be abandoned the next spring, when the Confederates were flanked by Grant's troops. The Union army moved into Tennessee with the capture of Fort Donelson and Fort Henry, on the Tennessee and Cumberland rivers. Columbus was then occupied by Union forces who held it for the remainder of the Civil War.

Today, the battleground is a Kentucky State Park. Civil War cannons and a wrought iron fence surrounding an old cemetery where many of the battle's dead are buried are the first things visitors see when they arrive at 156-acre Columbus-Belmont State Park.

Columbus-Belmont's most interesting attraction to history buffs is likely to be a section of the chain Confederate forces stretched across the Mississippi and the giant anchor used to secure it to the bluffs on the Kentucky side. Each link in the chain weighs 15 pounds and is more than a foot long. That would make the entire weight of the chain in excess of 39 tons.

The story of Columbus-Belmont's fortification and the battle in 1861 is told by numerous historical markers on the grounds and a diorama in the park's museum. Displays of Indian relics—birdstones, skinstones, arrow points, and other artifacts recovered from Indian campsites unearthed locally—are featured in the three-room museum, which is housed in a circa 1852 home where the mayor of Columbus once lived. Personal correspondence between a Union officer and his commander and sketches of the fortifications published in *Harper's Weekly* during the Confederate occupation are displayed alongside powder flasks, cannonballs, canister shot, and glass enclosed cases filled with flintlock and percussion cap rifles and shotguns. Minie balls, bullet molds, and an interesting collection of ordnance found in 1916 by Alfred A. Scott are on exhibit, as well as a Union officer's dress uniform, a medical kit, and a hospital scene. Admission to the museum is 50¢ for adults and 25¢ for children.

Picnickers will find tables and grills around the park and three shelter houses for eating outside during inclement weather. There are swings, monkey bars, and sand pits for the children, and a railing around the steep bluff from which barges may be seen negotiating the bend at Wolfe Island, downstream from the Columbus ferry that shuttles the historic Mississippi.

Open seasonally, April 1 to October 31, Columbus-Belmont Battlefield State Park is located in Hickman County, Kentucky, at Columbus, on highway Ky-80. The campground, adjacent to the cemetery where those who lost their lives in the Battle of Columbus-Belmont were laid to rest, has 24 sites equipped with electrical hookups for either tents or RVs. The campground's services and facilities include drinking water, showers, flush toilets, and picnic tables and shelter.

Cumberland Falls State Resort Park
Mailing address: Corbin, Kentucky, 40701
Telephone: (606) 582-4121

A $400,000 bequest in the will of Senator T. Coleman DuPont, a former Kentuckian, made possible the 1931 purchase of 500 acres adjacent to Cumberland Falls and the establishment of one of Kentucky's foremost state parks. Today, Cumberland Falls State Resort Park is a showplace in the system. Plummeting 67 feet into a rocky gorge, Cumberland Falls is nicknamed "Niagara of the South" beause it is the highest falls in the eastern United States south of Niagara. A moonbow, unique in the western hemisphere, appears in the mist of the thundering waterfall when the moon is full. The only other such moonbow in the world occurs at Victoria Falls in Africa.

The 1,794-acre park is in southeastern Kentucky's Whitley County in Daniel Boone National Forest off Interstate-75 (from the Corbin and Williamsburg interchange), eight miles south on highway US-25W, then seven or eight miles west on Ky-90. The park is open all year and the lodge, woodland suites, and cottages have both heat and air conditioning for year-round comfort.

Cumberland Falls State Resort Park is one of the few parks with planned recreational programs even in the winter. Seasonal programs highlight the park's 15 miles of day-hiking trails and natural history. Other activities include seminars on nature photography, special horseback rides, demonstrations of mountain crafts, and square dancing at an outdoor pavilion.

The Cumberland River flows through the wooded plateau land and is a

white water river, one of Kentucky's Wild Rivers protected from development by law. Downstream from Cumberland Falls the river is constricted
into narrow chutes over rock shoals. It is considered to be one of the most
difficult and dangerous canoeing streams in the state.

There are two campgrounds with a total of 73 sites with electrical
hookups for either tents or RVs. Dump stations are available at both areas;
water is not available in the winter. The grocery and laundry facilities are
open from April 1 to October 31.

Fort Boonesborough State Park
Mailing address: Route 5, Richmond, Kentucky, 40475
Telephone: (606) 527-3328

In April of 1775 a band of rugged frontiersmen began building a wooden
stockade near the confluence of the Kentucky River and Otter Creek in
modern-day Madison County, Kentucky. The journey through the wilds of
Kentucky to the spot chosen for Fort Boonesborough had been a long and
arduous one. The party of axemen moved crosscountry, hacking their way
through miles of thick canebrakes and brush. They forded both the Rockcastle and Cumberland rivers after passing through Cumberland Gap, and
trudged for miles over hard-packed buffalo traces. Making their way in
close proximity to the Warrior's Path, a north-south foot trail heavily traveled by Shawnee Indians, they had to be constantly alert for sudden bloody
ambushes, which plagued the expedition's progress and morale for nearly
the entire trip.

The original Fort Boonesborough was established at the northern terminus of this first trans-Appalachian route, the Wilderness Road. But as history proves, Kentucky was not easily won. The late 1770s were filled with
uncertainty and peril for Boone, his family, and the close-knit band of
settlers at Fort Boonesborough.

Two centuries later, when a new Fort Boonesborough opened its gates
to visitors for the first full season on April 1, 1975, it signaled a recreation
of the time and spirit of the original settlement. The Fort Boonesborough of
today, albeit safe and secure from Indian attack, remains busy with the
ways of pioneer life. Craftsmen demonstrate the spinning of wool into yarn,
yarn dyeing, pottery making, chair caning, basketmaking, and cabinetmak-
ing, in the atmosphere of a primitive Kentucky settlement. A blacksmith
hammers away at a glowing, red-hot horseshoe he holds to the anvil with a
pair of long-handled tongs. His shop, complete with antique tools of the
trade, is housed in a log shelter in the middle of the fort's enclosed yard.

In the yard, a long-skirted young woman carefully mixes herbs in a kettle of boiling water until the desired color is reached. Then the yarn, which has been carded and spun from raw wool by another of Boonesborough's craftsmen, is dipped and dipped again, and hung out to dry in the sun. The brightly colored yarns, woven on antique looms, will soon be sewn into bedspreads and quilts.

In a nearby cabin, a cabinetmaker is fitting together a hutch of early American design, which is held together without the aid of glue or nails. Its metal hinges have been handmade by the settlement's blacksmith. Next door, earthenware pottery—tableware, mugs, candle holders, and crocks—is being fashioned by the skilled hands of a potter.

A reproduction of a ladderback chair owned by Boone is being hand-caned by a nimble craftsman. "Basket oak," half-inch-wide strips of wood that have been soaked in water to make them more pliable, is woven into an egg basket of the style that rested across the neck of a market-bound horse in the days of produce and poultry trading in the Cumberlands.

Cabin 15 is the soapmaking cabin, and visitors may be surprised to know that this crudely made lye soap is mild enough for linens and delicate wools. The mixture is boiled in a huge kettle and poured into molds to "set up." Women in calico sunbonnets, artisans of a craft taught to the settlers by Indians, are making folk toys such as the cornshuck dolls that little girls played with in pioneer days.

Three cabins in Fort Boonesborough are furnished as if pioneers had arranged things: a rope bed in the corner, a spinning wheel at the hearth, candle holders on the mantel, and fire dogs supporting a heap of blazing logs in the fireplace. A blockhouse at one corner of the fort is a storehouse for barreled goods—flour, powder, and pickles—as well as hides, saddles, and farming implements. On occasion, Fort Boonesborough rings with the volleys of black powder fired in long rifles by frontiersmen clad in buckskins.

The fort is open seasonally April 1 to October 31, and admission is charged for tours. Group rates are available. Seasonal recreation facilities include a beach, swimming area, and bathhouse on the Kentucky River. River tours on the stern-wheeler *Dixie Belle* are held daily during the summer.

Open all year, Fort Boonesborough State Park is one mile north of Boonesboro, Kentucky, in Clark County on highway Ky-388, just off Ky-627, eight miles off Interstate-75. In driving time, it's just two hours south of Cincinnati (some 100 miles). The riverside campground has 187 sites for either RVs or tents, all with water and electricity. Showers, flush toilets, dumping station, grocery, ice, coin laundry, playground, picnic tables and shelters, grills, firewood, and beach are near the campground.

General Butler State Resort Park
Mailing address: Carrollton, Kentucky, 41008
Telephone: (502) 732-4384

General Butler State Resort Park, one mile north of Interstate-71 at Carrollton, in Carroll County, was named in honor of native Kentuckian William
Orlando Butler (1791–1880) who served in the War of 1812 and was a
member of Congress (1839–43) and a general in the Mexican War (1848).
In August of 1931, General Butler's 300-acre estate was presented to the
state. Butler's mansion, which sits on the western fringes of the 809-acre
park, is now open to touring. The mansion is furnished in the style of the
period in which it was built. The lodge accommodations are open seasonally, the cottages year-round.

Recreation at General Butler State Resort Park is limited to playground-
type recreation such as golf, tennis, horseback riding, swimming, and miniature golf. A game and picnic area and miniature railroad are located next
to highway Ky-227 by 30-acre Butler Lake. Across the lake is the campground, open year-round. The 135 campsites, all with electrical hookups
for tents or RVs, are located along a series of looping roads. Facilities
include showers, flush toilets, dumping station, ice, coin laundry, picnic
tables and shelter, and grills.

John James Audubon State Park
Mailing address: Henderson, Kentucky, 42420
Telephone: (502) 826-2247

The John James Audubon State Park in western Kentucky memorializes the
nineteenth-century naturalist who roamed the backwoods of the American
frontier and became one of the great animal and birdlife artists. During his
lifetime (1785–1851), Audubon spent a total of 14 years in Kentucky. He
lived in Louisville and in Red Banks (later named Henderson), where he
was a partner in a store and grist mill. A woodsman, hunter, and naturalist
first, Audubon took little interest in business affairs and spent much time
afield. His knowledge of the techniques of art was acquired through his
own experimentation, with only limited instruction.

The print collection of the John James Audubon Memorial Museum
includes 126 of the original paintings from *The Birds of America*, his
best-known work. The folio edition was published in England from 1827 to
1838. Its aquatint engravings were made from copper plates and the im-

pressions were then water-colored by hand. The four-volume set sold for $1,000, and fewer than two hundred sets were completed.

The exhibits in the castle-like museum are based largely on three of Audubon's published works, *The Birds of America, The Ornithological Biography,* and *The Quadrupeds of North America.* In addition to prints and oil paintings of birds and animals, exhibits include family mementos such as watches, antique jewelry, silver spoons, forks, and candleholders; an oil portrait of Audubon by Nicola Marchall; pewter teapots and plates; a riverboat "captain's chair"; a beaded deerskin shirt believed to have been worn by Audubon during his Missouri expedition in 1843; manuscripts and journals; and a portrait of Daniel Boone by Audubon.

John James Audubon State Park is in Henderson, Kentucky, on highway US-41. Added to the Kentucky State Park System in 1934, the park was originally located on 275 acres of land purchased by the community as a memorial to the wildlife artist whose works have never been equaled. Today, the park consists of 692 acres of heavily forested, hilly woods with two small lakes of 28 and 12 acres, respectively. The park is a nature lover's paradise, as there are extensive stands of beech, hickory, and oak trees, and scattered wetlands. Birdlife, small mammals, and a few deer inhabit the park. There are eight day-hiking trails: Museum, King Benson, Kentucky Coffee Tree, Lake Overlooks, Wilderness Lake, Woodpecker, Cardinal, and Back Country Trail, comprising a total of approximately nine miles of footpaths. A ninth day-hiking trail, the Audubon Trail, built by a local Boy Scout troop, is a continuous route around the park, utilizing very little of the park's trail system. Audubon Trail participants must register at the park office; there is a small fee charged to insure the trail is maintained properly. The four-hour hike which begins and ends at the museum is marked with white flags.

The rental cottages and museum are open daily from May 1 to October 31 and on Saturdays and Sundays from November 1 to April 30. The swimming lake, snack bar, and golf course are open seasonally, as well (May 1 to October 31). The campground of 58 sites with electrical hookups is open all year. Drinking water, showers, flush toilets, a picnic grounds and shelter, ice, and dumping station are nearby.

Levi Jackson Wilderness Road State Park
Mailing address: London, Kentucky, 40741
Telephone: (606) 864-5108

In the late eighteenth century, a buckskin-clad frontiersman emerged from the wilderness to direct the white man's settlement of Kentucky. The land

west of the Appalachians, deeded from the Cherokee Indians, was to become America's fifteenth state, and Daniel Boone's name was destined to
be ineradicably linked with Kentucky's. A trapper, market hunter, farmer,
and land surveyor by vocation, Daniel Boone was perhaps the most important leader of pioneer settlers who journeyed from the Carolinas and Virginia to the game-rich land beyond the Cumberlands.

In the 1760s Kentucky was the hunting preserve of Shawnee and
Cherokee Indians. White hunters who violated the ancestral rights of the
Indians took their lives in their hands. Any white man found to be killing
elk, deer, or buffalo in Kentucky, or trapping beaver, was stripped of his
horse, gun, and traps—and left to the merciless wilderness.

Boone's early expeditions into Kentucky, during which he passed
through the mountains at Cumberland Gap, fared no differently. On one
occasion, Boone's hunting partner, Benjamin Cutbirth, was shot and be-
headed by Shawnee furious at the increasing number of "long hunters"
encroaching on their hunting lands. A Shawnee named Captain Will is said
to have warned Boone that if he were ever captured in Kentucky, he would
be killed.

Boone's many brushes with death at the hands of the Shawnee proved
to be the foundation of an interesting relationship he developed with his
red brothers over the years. His ability to avoid capture by hiding in the
woods, his knowledge of the terrain, and his general woodsmanship made
his entrapment a grand occasion. In fact, the Shawnee felt that capturing
Boone by outsmarting him in the woods was an honor. Many times he
escaped being taken prisoner by simply extending common courtesy, shak-
ing their hands and acknowledging his surprise at being caught. Colonel
Boone, as he was called in later years, was a celebrity of sorts; and if they
had wanted to kill him, there was more than one occasion when they had
him defenseless. His very name, and the legends that sprang from his
adventures, took root in Kentucky, where they grew into indelible addi-
tions to the history of the Commonwealth.

Levi Jackson Wilderness Road State Park, two miles south of London
on US-25, is located on a section of the path followed by Boone in 1775
from Cumberland Gap to the confluence of Otter Creek and the Kentucky
River, where a wooden stockade, named Fort Boonesborough in his honor,
was built. The 815-acre park, open year-round, is approximately 54 miles
south of Fort Boonesborough State Park, as the crow flies.

The Mountain Life Museum, open from 9:00 a.m. to 5:00 p.m. May 1
to November 30, is one of the main attractions at the park. The museum is
a group of hewn-log cabins furnished with authentic antiques. A two-room
cabin once used as a schoolhouse is now filled with Indian artifacts and
pioneer era guns. The household furnishings of early settler Levi Jackson
are displayed in another cabin. Other interesting features are the Bald Rock

Chapel, complete with collection plate, original pulpit, and 200-year-old rosewood piano, and the blacksmith's cabin with the original tools, anvil, and bellows. Admission is less than $1 for both adults and children.

The recreational facilities at the park include a field archery range; three miles of day-hiking trails on "Boone's Trace," which passes McHargue's water mill on the Little Laurel River; a horseback riding stable; swimming pool (open Memorial Day to Labor Day); bathhouse; and snack bar.

A gift shop and grocery, at the entrance to the campground, are open May through November. The campground at Levi Jackson Wilderness Road State Park is one of the finest in the system, with 200 paved sites, 125 of which are equipped for RVs. All sites have electrical outlets and water hookups. Three central service buildings with flush toilets, showers, laundry facilities, and a TV room serve the campers.

My Old Kentucky Home State Park
Mailing address: Bardstown, Kentucky, 40004
Telephone: (502) 348-3502

Bardstown is the county seat of Nelson County, in the western half of the Bluegrass Region. William Bard, who was born in Pennsylvania, settled near where Bardstown is today on a 1000-acre tract of land issued to him in 1775 by the Assembly of Virginia. David Bard, one of William's sons, later donated two acres of this land for the site of a county courthouse, and so, in 1782, the Salem community became known as Bardstown.

During the last two decades of the eighteenth century, Bardstown grew from a small crossroads settlement to a frontier town. Because of its location at the center of travel routes linking the southeastern part of Kentucky where settlers came through Cumberland Gap and the northern reaches of the Ohio River at the falls where flatboats converged, Bardstown's growth was boosted by America's westward expansion. Manufacturing and trade flourished.

By the early 1800s, Bardstown was one of the most populated towns in Kentucky and on its way to becoming an educational center. With its many fine homes, inns, and exuberant hospitality, Bardstown was known throughout the South as a town of wealth, refinement, and beauty. The atmosphere surrounding its educational facilities and the many learned men in various professions who lived there earned for the town the title "Athens of the West," a sobriquet it shared with Lexington.

Many of the homes of Georgian and Greek revival architecture that were built by the town's foremost early citizens still stand. Their weathered brick, carved paneling, high-ceilinged rooms, and magnificent spiral stairways are reminders of the era when the great homes were occupied by Kentucky governors, lawyers, senators, and statesmen.

The most famous of the old estates in Bardstown is Federal Hill, "My Old Kentucky Home." Built between 1795 and 1797 by Judge John Rowan, Federal Hill was often filled with politicians, artists, and intellectuals of the era. Henry Clay and James Monroe are among the famous persons who were entertained there. Late in the summer of 1852, young Stephen Collins Foster from Pittsburgh visited his Rowan cousins and was inspired to compose the beloved ballad, "My Old Kentucky Home."

In 1922 Mrs. Madge Rowan Frost sold Federal Hill to the state so that it could become My Old Kentucky Home State Park. The mansion, filled with period furniture, priceless heirlooms, and rare old portraits, has been restored and is open to touring.

My Old Kentucky Home State Park is located 33 miles south of Louisville on highway US-31E and Ky-150. Federal Hill mansion is, of course, the main attraction, but the 235-acre park is also known for the acclaimed outdoor musical "The Stephen Foster Story," a colorful, rollicking production held nightly except Mondays during the summer season (mid-June through Labor Day) in the park's outdoor amphitheater.

The park is open all year except Mondays in December, January, and February. Tours of My Old Kentucky Home are conducted from 9:00 a.m. to 7:30 p.m. mid-June through Labor Day, and 9:00 a.m. to 5:00 p.m. the rest of the year. The cost of the guided tour is less than $1 for both adults and children.

A nine-hole golf course, pro shop, seasonal picnic grounds, and full-time seasonal recreational program, as well as a shady campground with 40 electrical hookups, are part of the park's facilities and services. Primitive camping in the off-season is allowed by permission of the park office; the campground has showers, flush toilets, dumping station, grills, and firewood. Grocery, ice, and laundry are nearby.

Kentucky Horse Park
Mailing address: Iron Works Pike, Lexington, Kentucky, 40505
Telephone: (606) 252-0220

A new concept in state parks, the Kentucky Horse Park, due to open in September 1978, will honor not only the thoroughbred but the harness racer, and will focus attention on the unique relationship between man and all equines. The $25-million park on Iron Works Pike between Newton Pike and Interstate-75 is located on land purchased from Walnut Hall Stud Farm, more than a thousand acres of prime Bluegrass countryside. Construction has been underway since early 1977, and 23 structures will be built. Several stables of unique architecture are being renovated for use by visiting horsemen during equine events at the park. A two-story museum, located near the entrance to the park, and the Visitor's Center will feature exhibits on the development of different breeds of horses and their uses throughout the centuries, and will explain the many contemporary equine sports. A walking tour of the Kentucky Horse Park will allow the visitor to observe horses being trained, a farrier and harness maker at work, and the daily "backside" routine of mucking stalls and the grooming of thoroughbreds.

A 256-site campground with full electrical and water hookups and a service center (dump station, grocery store, laundry facilities, bath house, swimming pool, and tennis courts) are under development, as is a fast-food restaurant operated by the Kentucky Department of Parks.

The restaurant will be located near the one-quarter-mile oval where several exhibitions of harness and thoroughbred racing will be conducted daily. The track is in the shadow of the statue of Man o' War, perhaps the greatest Kentucky thoroughbred ever to race. The gravesite statue, one-and-one-quarter times Man o' War's actual size, is a tribute to a game runner who, in two seasons on the track, won 20 of 21 starts, his only loss coming to a horse ironically named Upset.

In 1974 when the U.S. Equestrian Team won the world championship, it also won the right to hold the international competition for the first time in America. The Kentucky Horse Park was selected as the site for this competition, the 1978 World Championship Three-Day Event, which was held on September 14–17, 1978. The activities for the three days included dressage, stadium jumping, and cross country. Representatives from fifteen nations competed. Other events to be held at the Kentucky Horse Park include field trials, horse shows, a steeplechase race meet, and hunter and jumper events.

Blue Licks Battlefield State Park
Mailing address: Maysville Road, Carlisle, Kentucky, 40311
Telephone: (606) 289-5507

Despite the fact that Cornwallis's defeat at Yorktown on October 19, 1781, signaled an end to armed confrontation on the eastern seaboard, the Revolutionary War beyond the Appalachians blazed on for more than 13 months. Raiding parties of Shawnee, Wyandot, and Mingo led by British officers crossed the Ohio River and laid siege to the widely-scattered outposts of Kentucky's wilderness frontier. One such raid on Bryan's Station set the stage for the last engagement of the American Revolution in Kentucky—the Battle of Blue Licks.

The angry frontiersmen at Bryan's Station wanted revenge for their burned crops and slaughtered cattle; and so, on August 17, 1782, in the company of Daniel Boone, they rode northeast in hot pursuit of the British-led marauders—the likes of Simon Girty, cutthroat renegade who five years before in the "bloody year of the three sevens," had helped Shawnee chief Blackfish direct the siege of Fort Boonesborough.

Upon reaching the Licking River, Daniel Boone warned that the enemy was more than likely waiting in ambush ahead. The most knowledgeable of the frontiersmen, Boone knew every creek and ravine in that part of the wilderness and, an expert hunter and woodsman, was wise in the ways of the Indian.

But Boone's suggestions were not heeded. An overzealous major from the Lincoln County militia, out to disprove comments about his bravery, rallied the frontiersmen, calling out as he waded across the Licking River, "All those who are not damned cowards follow me, and I'll soon show you the Indians." The men were ambushed in a narrow ravine near Blue Licks Spring. Sixty Kentuckians died, among them Israel Boone, and the defeat would haunt Daniel Boone for the rest of his life.

Mineral springs in the area drew wild game in pioneer days—buffalo, elk, and deer. In January 1778, Daniel Boone and a group of men from Boonesborough were captured by Chief Blackfish while making salt at the mineral springs. In the late nineteenth century the springs were the site of a fashionable spa and hotel, and water was bottled and shipped across America from the springs, which eventually went dry.

Today, 193 years after the Battle of Blue Licks, the countryside is made up of farms and woods along the Licking River. The spot where Kentucky's sons fell is marked by a stone monument that stands as the focal point at Blue Licks Battlefield State Park off highway US-68 at Blue Licks Spring, south of Mount Olivet.

The 100-acre park, on the Robertson-Nicholas county line, was opened in 1926. Operating seasonally from April 1 to October 31, the park offers 15 sites for tent or trailer camping, a community swimming pool, shaded picnic grounds with stone barbecue grills, playgrounds, a gift shop, and a museum of pioneer Kentucky, now under restoration.

Established in 1926 with Indian artifacts excavated by archaeologist W. J. Curtis, the cedar-and-fieldstone museum has a wide variety of displays. Butter churns, spinning wheels, leather trunks, looms, and fireplace cookware such as waffle irons and meat broilers are included in the pioneer home furnishings. Whiskey bottles circa 1840 bearing "E.C. Booz manufacturer" (from which the slang term "booze" for liquor came) are on exhibit with a collection of bitters bottles. Other frontier household goods include a spoon mold, flax cord, wooden keys, a candle mold, and a coffee roaster. Early farm tools—hemp hackle, wooden pitchforks, corn planter, and lantern—are on the first floor of the museum. A diorama with sound recording details the Battle of Blue Licks.

Downstairs are Indian relics recovered from the nearby Fox Field Indian burial grounds. Pottery, beads, skulls, bear teeth, arrow points, and bone needles dating from 8000 B.C. to A.D. 1300 are on display.

Admission to the museum is 50¢ for adults and 25¢ for children. Blue Licks Museum, like the state park, is open from April 1 through October 31.

Natural Bridge State Resort Park
Mailing address: Slade, Kentucky, 40376
Telephone: (606) 663-2214

In 1926, the L & N Railroad donated 137 acres to the Commonwealth of Kentucky for a state park at the site of Natural Bridge, a natural rock arch 80 feet long and 65 feet high on the middle fork of the Red River in Powell and Wolfe counties. The scenic area had been a whistlestop since the 1890s when the Kentucky Union Railroad Company first laid tracks into the mountains. Natural Bridge State Resort Park is south of the Mountain Parkway at the Slade, Kentucky, exit on highway Ky-11. Open year-round, the 1,899-acre park has full facilities—lodge, cottages, 175-capacity dining room, meeting rooms, nature center, and a calendar of entertainment and recreation events. The 35-room Hemlock Lodge is equipped with air conditioning, wall-to-wall carpeting, telephone, color TV, and private balcony. All rooms have either two double beds or a double bed and a studio couch. Daily maid service is available to lodge guests.

There are six efficiency cottages, all fully furnished with cooking utensils and linens, air conditioning, color TV, telephone, and electric heat. These cottages have a combination living room-bedroom, kitchen, and bath. The four one-bedroom cottages also have kitchens, living room, and bath.

The lodge gift shop has the largest selection of American Indian turquoise jewelry in Kentucky's state park system. The lodge rooms overlook 54-acre Mill Creek Lake and Hoedown Island and are open from Memorial Day to Labor Day. Square dancing is held nightly. The park's activity center, open seasonally, houses the nature center. Interpretive guided tours of nearby Red River Gorge Geological Area are held during the summer. Other seasonal activities include horseback riding, skylift, community pool (free to lodge and cottage guests), and planned recreation programs. A canoe and paddle boat rental service is available daily and on weekends in the spring and fall.

There are six day-hiking trails through the woodlands and rock formations. Plantlife includes hemlock, beech, tulip poplar, oaks, and pine trees, spring blooming rhododendron, mountain laurel, and magnolias. As many as 75 species of birds have been identified in the park in a single day. Wildflower buffs flock to the park in March, April, and May for the annual appearances of jack-in-the-pulpit, May apples, bloodroot, pink lady's slipper, and countless varieties of ferns. Occasionally foxes, deer, raccoons, and other mammals are seen.

The geology of the park is similar to that of the entire Cumberland plateau region, with deep ravines, high-walled cliffs, and towering rock formations of conglomerate sandstone, claystones, and silt stones. A folding of the earth's crust raised many of these layers of material off the bottoms of inland seas; gradually, the layers were eroded by rainfall and the freezing and thawing action of dramatic seasonal upheavals. The interesting geological formations of Natural Bridge State Resort Park are Pivot Rock, Balancing Rock, Battleship Rock, Profile Rock and Owl's Window, Devil's Gulch, Lookout Point, Lover's Leap, and the towering Natural Bridge.

The park's campground, open year-round, has 95 sites, all with water and electrical hookups. Drinking water, flush toilets, showers, RV dump station, ice, playground, and picnic tables are available at the campground.

Pine Mountain State Resort Park
Mailing address: Pineville, Kentucky, 40977
Telephone: (606) 337-3066

Pine Mountain State Resort Park, Kentucky's first state park, is sandwiched between Kentucky Ridge State Forest and the town of Pineville along the Cumberland River. In 1924, citizens of Pineville secured a 2000-acre tract of mountainous woodlands and offered it to the state for a recreation and conservation area, which was known as Cumberland Park until 1938. There was little development of facilities at the park in the early years. In 1933, the first real improvements were initiated by the Emergency Conservation Work Program through the Civilian Conservation Corps (CCC). The CCC laborers built roads, trails, picnic tables, shelters, cabins, foot bridges, and a road leading to the top of Pinnacle Point. They also built an amphitheater which was filled with 6,000 persons for the inaugural Mountain Laurel Festival held on May 31, 1935. This festival has become an annual event, held each spring when the mountain laurel is in bloom.

The 2500-acre mountain park is 36 miles southeast of Corbin, Kentucky (off Interstate-75), on US-25 E at Pineville in Bell County. Open year-round, Pine Mountain State Resort is a perennial favorite with nature lovers. The 30 lodge rooms (each with modern conveniences, two double beds, wall-to-wall carpeting, air conditioning, electric heat, full bath and shower, and private balcony), overlook some of the most magnificent scenery in the Cumberland Mountains. From April 1 to November 15, rental accommodations are available, including seven rustic log cabins with combination living room-bedroom, kitchen, and bath, and three one-bedroom cottages with living room, kitchen, and bath. Ten two-bedroom cottages with living room, kitchen, and bath are available year-round. All cottages have telephone, television, air conditioning and electric heat, tableware, cooking utensils, and linens, and range in price from $18 to $38 a night.

The Middlesboro-Bell County Airport is one mile west of Middlesboro, 12 miles from the park. Transportation to and from the unlighted, paved 3,650-foot landing strip can be arranged by park managers. Fuel and tie-downs are available at the landing strip.

A dining room which overlooks the mountains is open daily for breakfast from 7:00 to 10:30 a.m., lunch from 11:30 a.m. to 2:30 p.m., and dinner from 5:30 to 9:00 p.m. Other park facilities include a craft/gift shop, meeting room, lodge, swimming pool (guests only), horseback riding stables (seasonal), indoor recreation room, playground, and day-hiking trails.

The campground at Pine Mountain State Resort Park, open from April 1 to October 31, has 36 sites, all with electricity. Drinking water, flush toilets, and showers are available at the central service building. In July and August, "The Book of Job," a religious choral drama, is presented in the Laurel Cove Amphitheater (daily except Sundays). Other entertainment includes singing groups, square dancing, arts and crafts fairs, guided nature walks, and special interest programs (nature photography, floral arrangements, wildlife seminars). A 35-acre lake, nature museum, and wildflower garden are on the grounds.

Pennyrile Forest State Resort Park
Mailing address: Dawson Springs, Kentucky, 42408
Telephone: (502) 797-3421

In June of 1946, the United States Department of Agriculture transferred 15,200 acres of land in Christian and Caldwell counties to the Commonwealth of Kentucky. The hilly woodlands became a state forest, and a tract of 435 acres was eventually developed into Pennyrile Forest State Resort Park.

Open May 27 through October 31, Pennyrile Forest State Resort Park is located on Ky-109, 12 miles northwest of Hopkinsville, Kentucky. The park has a 24-room lodge; each room is equipped with two double beds, television, telephone, private bath, and balcony or patio. Additional accommodations include 15 housekeeping cottages: three are efficiencies, three have one bedroom, and nine have two bedrooms. All cottages have television, telephone, air conditioning, electric heat, tableware, cooking utensils, and linens. Lodge accommodations range from $16 to $24 per night; the cottages rent for $22 to $35 a night.

The dining room serves breakfast from 7:00 to 10:30 a.m., lunch from 11:30 a.m. to 2:30 p.m., and dinner from 7:30 to 9:00 p.m.. A gift shop housed in the lodge offers Kentucky handicrafts, prints, books and souvenirs, and a recreation room (foosball, table tennis, and video games). The seasonal outdoor recreational facilities, offered from Memorial Day to Labor Day, include horseback riding, swimming pool for lodge and cottage guests, and rental rowboats ($4 a day) and paddle boats ($3 an hour) at the 55-acre lake on the park grounds. The sand beach and bathhouse complex are open seasonally. A nine-hole golf course is open April 1 to October 31.

The park's campground, open April 1 to October 31, has 68 campsites, all with water and electrical hookups. Facilities include flush toilets, showers, drinking water, RV dump station, grocery, picnic tables, grills, shelter, and playground.

Breaks Interstate Park
Mailing address: Breaks, Virginia, 24607
Telephone: (703) 865-4413

Breaks Interstate Park, straddling the Kentucky-Virginia border, encompasses 2,860 acres of skyscraping mountain scenery, woodlands, and rock cliffs. Nestled in the hills of eastern Kentucky's Pike County and Virginia's Wise County in the Jefferson National Forest, the park is located just over 170 miles southwest of Lexington via the Mountain Parkway to Prestonsburg, then southeast on Ky-23/460 to Elkhorn City. The park's past is woven of legends: the Hatfield-McCoy feud, tales of sacred Indian grounds, the exploits of explorer/settler Daniel Boone. One story tells of vast fortunes in silver hidden in the hills by Englishman John Swift.

Breaks Interstate Park was created by joint action of the Kentucky and Virginia legislatures in 1951. Development of facilities began in 1958. The central attraction at the park is Breaks Canyon, a five-mile-long, 1,600-foot horseshoe-shaped chasm. Russell Fork of the Big Sandy River, a raging white water river, cuts through the narrow gorge; forestlands and an imposing rock knob called the Towers overlook the river's twisting path. Geologists believe that the rock formations are of the Pennsylvanian, late Paleozoic era.

Breaks Interstate Park is open year-round; the lodge and restaurant are open seasonally, April 1 to October 31. The 30 units in the motor lodge rent for $16 single occupancy, $19 double. All rooms have two double beds. There are four two-bedroom housekeeping cottages (open year-round) that may be rented on a weekly basis, $25 per night. The Rhododendron Lodge houses the gift shop and restaurant.

The park's campground, also open seasonally, has 44 RV sites with water and electical and sewer hookups, 20 sites for tents only, and 85 sites with water hookups only. All campsites include picnic tables and grills. Flush toilets, showers, and drinking water are available at the campground's bathhouse. There are five picnic shelters on the grounds. During the summer, outdoor dramas and special programs such as nature slide shows are held in the park's amphitheater.

The recreational facilities include an Olympic-size swimming pool (open Memorial Day to Labor Day), 12-acre Laurel Lake (paddle boat rentals available), horseback riding, interpretive nature programs, and nature walks. There are approximately 10 miles of day-hiking trails in the park. The Prospector's Trail leads from the Russell Fork overlook on Va-647 to its intersection with the River Trail, which descends with numerous switchbacks to the bank of the Russell Fork. The Laurel Branch Trail also intersects with the Prospector's Trail near the state line overlook. The Ridge Trail and Geological Trail intersect the Laurel Branch Trail at the Notches, a rock formation. The Center Creek Trail and Grassey Creek Trail intersect Ky-80 on the Kentucky-Virginia line at the north end of the park. There are no established day-hiking trails in the vicinity of the Lover's Leap, Mill Rock Point, or the Towers, but there are footpaths along the canyon rim. The Chestnut Ridge Nature Trail incorporates sections of the Ridge, Geological, and Laurel Branch trails, and is a self-guided nature/geological interpretive trail with 27 numbered stops. A booklet available at the Visitor's Center/Nature Museum explains the forest types, the predominant species of shrubs and wildflowers, and the origins of rock formations in the park. Exhibits of area history (antiques, moonshine stills, farm implements), plant and animal communities, an audio-visual birdsong display, and a park facilities map are located in the Visitor's Center.

Louisville-Jefferson County Metropolitan Parks
Mailing address: Metropolitan Park and Recreation Board, P.O. Box 13334, 1297 Trevilian Way, Louisville, Kentucky, 40213
Telephone: (502) 459-0440

General George Rogers Clark, a Revolutionary War hero, is considered to be the founder of Louisville. After building a stockade on Corn Island in the Ohio River, General Clark marched off to victorious campaigns in the Northwest. When he returned, he prompted the building of a full-scale city on the southern banks of the Falls of the Ohio. The city was named for King Louis XVI of France, who had helped the American Revolutionary cause with much-needed money and war materials.

When Louisville was mapped out, General Clark suggested a local parks system; he believed that "greens" should be located every three blocks throughout the city. This noble idea was never adopted, but by 1890 an act of the Kentucky Legislature had commissioned Boston architect Frederick Olmstead to draw up plans for the first three city parks, which were to be located at the end of scenic tree-lined parkways. The parks were named Shawnee, Cherokee, and Iroquois for Indian tribes that had once roamed Kentucky.

In 1940, a "sister" system of county parks was created. The two systems merged in 1968, and the Metropolitan Parks and Recreation Board was given title to the 166 parks (approximately 7,000 acres), so that politics would not enter into their management.

Eight of the Louisville metro parks are open to camping from April 1 to November 1, weather permitting. All campsites are primitive and permits are required for overnight stays. The permits are free but must be picked up at the offices of the Metropolitan Park and Recreation Board, 1297 Trevilian Way, during business hours (8:30 a.m. to 4:30 p.m., Monday through Friday only). The permits are not available at the individual parks.

The following regulations apply to all metro parks with campgrounds: all parks are closed between 1:00 a.m. and 6:00 a.m., to keep the traffic noise from disturbing campers; alcoholic beverages are not permitted; pets must be leashed at all times; electric motors are allowed on fishing lakes in the parks, but gasoline motors are not; and the Metropolitan Park and Recreation Board will not be responsible for lost articles.

Forest View Park is located on 585 acres of hilly woods on Holsclaw Hill Road in Fairdale, a surburban community of Louisville off Outer Loop Exit of Interstate-65 South. The facilities include a 10-mile hiking/horseback riding trail, picnic tables, shelter, drinking water, and pit toilets.

McNeely Park, six and one-half miles off Interstate-65 South via Preston Highway exit (Ky-61), then three miles east on Cooper Chapel Road, is an 83-acre park with tennis courts, baseball/softball diamond, picnic tables, grills, drinking water, and flush toilets. A 76-acre fishing lake is located on the grounds.

Tom Wallace Park is located south of Louisville on Ky-907 to Fairdale, then three-fourths of a mile south on Mitchell Hill Road. The park consists of 204 acres (including a seven-acre lake) with picnic table, grills, playground, shelter, and archery range.

Fisherman's Park is located on Old Heady Road off Ky-155 (Taylorsville Road). The 65-acre park has six small fishing lakes, pit toilets, playground, and picnic table.

Long Run Park is located three miles northeast of Eastwood off US-69 (Shelbyville Road). The 452-acre park has flush toilets, picnic tables, grills and shelter, tennis courts, playground, a nine-hole golf course, and a 40-acre lake.

Chenoweth Park is located two miles south of Jefferstown on Mary Dell Lane off Billtown Road. The 282-acre park has picnic tables, grills, shelter, playground, a three-acre lake, a nine-hole golf course, a 21-station exercise course, drinking water, and flush toilets.

Waverly Park is located two and one-half miles off US-31W (Dixie Highway) on Arnoldtown Road in Pleasure Ridge Park. The 302-acre park has picnic tables, grills, playground, archery range, drinking water, and flush toilets.

Sun Valley Park is located one mile off US-31W (Dixie Highway) on Bethany Lane in Valley Station. Facilities include 30 RV sites, picnic tables, grills, shelter, swimming pool (open June 10 to August 20), tennis courts, baseball/softball diamond, recreation center, playground, drinking water, and pit toilets.

Otter Creek Park
Mailing address: Route #1, Vine Grove, Kentucky, 40175
Telephone: (502) 583-3577

Otter Creek Park, five miles west of Muldraugh, Kentucky, on Ky-1638, is owned by the City of Louisville, but not managed by the Metropolitan Park and Recreation Board. Open March 15 to December 31, the 2,000-acre park along the Ohio River is approximately 25 miles southwest of Louisville. There are four campgrounds (all open April 1 to November 1). The largest campground has 150 campsites, all with water and electrical hookups (16 also have sewer hookups). Other facilities include flush toilets, showers, drinking water, grocery, ice, picnic tables, grills, boat launching ramp on the river, four swimming pools (open Memorial Day to Labor Day), RV dump station, and laundry; 25 miles of hiking trails in a "wilderness area"; Visitor Center with local flora, fauna, and geology exhibits (closed Mondays); and playground with basketball and tennis courts and miniature golf courses. One campground is reserved for tents; all sites are primitive. Two of the campgrounds are for groups of more than 50 persons on a weekly basis only; the fee is $12.50 per person per week.

Accommodations at the park include twelve lodges: six two-family lodges that sleep up to 12 persons each and rent for $32.50 per night Monday through Friday, $37.50 per night on weekends; four family-size lodges that rent for $20 per night Monday through Friday, $25 per night on weekends; and two large lodges for groups up to 30 people that rent for $3.50 per person Monday through Friday and $4 per person on weekends.

There are three picnic areas, all with flush toilets, grills, tables, and shelters.

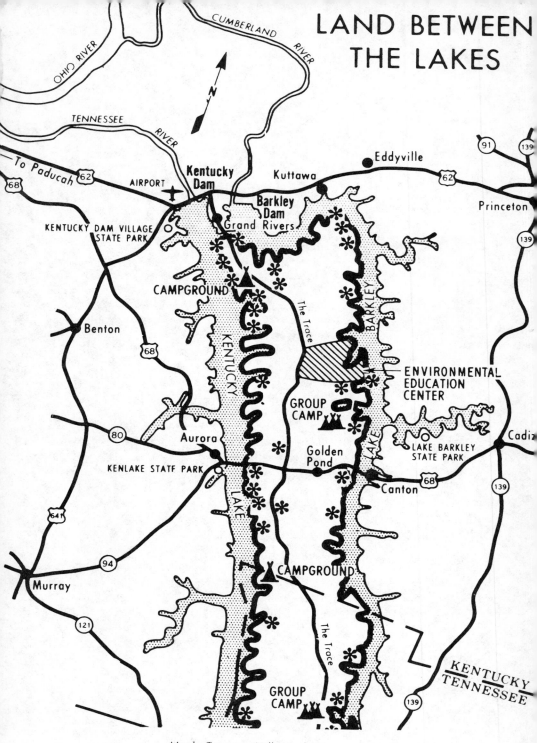

LAND BETWEEN THE LAKES

CUMBERLAND RIVER

OHIO RIVER

TENNESSEE RIVER

91
139

To Paducah
62
68

AIRPORT

Kentucky Dam

Kuttawa

Eddyville

62

Princeton

139

Barkley Dam

Grand Rivers

KENTUCKY DAM VILLAGE STATE PARK

CAMPGROUND

Benton

68

Kentucky

BARKLEY

The Trace

ENVIRONMENTAL EDUCATION CENTER

80

Aurora

GROUP CAMP

Cadiz

LAKE BARKLEY STATE PARK

Golden Pond

LAKE

KENLAKE STATE PARK

Canton

68

139

64

94

Murray

LAKE

CAMPGROUND

121

The Trace

KENTUCKY
TENNESSEE

GROUP CAMP

139

Map by Tennessee Valley Authority.

3
Land Between the Lakes

Introduction

A bowhunter waits in a tree stand beside a clearing at sunrise, his heart pounding in his chest as a stocky 10-point whitetail suddenly appears from dense cover, the soft rays of the morning sun backlighting his massive antlers and the frost-tinged broomsage. A small girl giggles with delight as she pets a bleating nanny goat, while nearby a man confined to a wheelchair explores on a paved nature trail. A party of backpackers relaxing after a hard day on the trail sips cups of hot tea after dinner around a glowing campfire; gusting wind and a spectacular display of lightning in the distance herald the approach of a thunderhead across Kentucky Lake.

The Land Between the Lakes experience. More than a vast outdoor playground, national demonstration area, and model recreational unit, Tennessee Valley Authority's 170,000-acre wooded peninsula in western Kentucky and Tennessee is an encounter session with Nature, a living classroom for people of all ages, walks of life, and levels of environmental awareness—birdwatchers, botanists, hunters, history buffs, Boy Scouts, inner city or handicapped children, ORV four-wheelers, backpackers, and campers. Land Between the Lakes is a showcase of aggressive but responsible management of natural resources, a testing grounds for innovative recreation programs and environmental education facilities, and an exemplification of the co-existence of radically different outdoor lifestyles. Land Between the Lakes (LBL) is a demonstration of the richness of this country's resources and the feasibility of their renewal and utilization—the embodiment of the idealism set forth by the late President John F. Kennedy when he authorized the project in June 1963.

The multiple-use concept, in which an area is managed for timber, wildlife, and outdoor recreation, did not begin with LBL. The concept has been faithfully championed by the National Forest Service (NFS), whose roots date back to the establishment by Congress of the Department of Agriculture's Division of Forestry in 1886. The significant point that must be made here is that LBL is a redefinition of the concept, unique in both purpose and scope. Flanked by man-made impoundments, and effectively isolated from the stumbling blocks to successful multiple-use management that plague other state- or Federally-owned areas not only in Kentucky, but in the whole country—private land holdings, poaching, packs of roaming dogs, court battles over timber cutting and mining entreats—LBL's success has been astounding.

Land acquisition was completed on July 1, 1969. Today, almost 10 years later, most of the signs of human habitation have all but disappeared. Former homesites and farm buildings have been removed, and eroded fields have been reforested. A comprehensive land use program that plans all recreational developments, manages timberlands, and will improve wildlife habitat was undertaken. Today, 85 percent of LBL is oak-hickory hardwood forest.

The character of the land is that of rugged, hilly forestlands with very little flat land. A program of sharecropping produces almost 4,000 acres of food for wildlife each year. One main paved highway, the Trace, formerly Ky-453/Tn-49, stretches the length of the isthmus from the Barkley Canal at Grand Rivers, Kentucky, to highway US-79 at Dover, Tennessee. The area's other major paved road, Old Ferry Road, is perpendicular to the Trace and connects Birmingham Ferry on Kentucky Lake and Kuttawa Landing on Lake Barkley, both of which are now lake access points. There are no private inholdings of land, no hotels, gas stations, or other commercial establishments in LBL—just campgrounds, historical/scenic visitor areas, and miles of gravel roads which crisscross the wooded hills and creekbottoms.

LBL's past is as interesting as its future is promising. Prehistoric Indians, pioneer homesteaders, loggers, iron makers, and moonshiners of the Prohibition era are all part of the region's colorful past. Restorations and special weekend events explore these chapters in the region's history. A variety of camping facilities is available—group camps for underprivileged children, the handicapped, Scouts, backwoods skills schools, civic and religious groups, family campgrounds for RVs and tent camping, informal lake access campgrounds, and backcountry camps for persons who seek complete solitude.

Interpretation of the natural, scenic, and historic aspects of LBL is also provided through hiking trails and visitor points of interest: Center Station; Empire Farm; the Youth Station; Silo Overlook; Buffalo Range; Wrangler's Camp, a horseback riding area; and Hematite Lake. Recreation, though, is the main reason for the 2.3 million recorded visits to LBL in 1976. Hunting is a major activity. Waterfowl, whitetail and fallow deer, rabbit, quail, squirrel, dove, and wild turkey were sought by hunters during special fall, winter, and spring seasons.

One day's drive from 76 million people, LBL is increasingly popular and may someday prove to be one of the Midwest's primary outdoor recreation areas. Its management concept is unique, offering a broader scope of recreational opportunities than either our national parks or our national forests. If nothing else, LBL has earned a niche as a recreational alternative for an American populace with more and more hours of leisure time each year, and has succeeded in bringing the outdoor environment closer to a people more dependent on urban ways.

History

The history of the region that is now Land Between the Lakes is as interesting to contemplate as the matter of how the Tennessee and Cumberland rivers, both major waterways of the mid-South, were formed so that they parallel each other for nearly 40 miles. The unique geological beginnings seem appropriate for the fascinating region.

It is speculated that shifts in the earth's crust during glacial periods millions of years ago brought the two rivers close together, a hogback of land the only thing keeping them from flowing into one another. The two mighty rivers flow on a northward course into the Ohio, not far from where she empties into the Mississippi.

With "twin" rivers guarding the eastern approaches, it's not surprising that the first white explorers and settlers to reach the isolated triangle of land known today as "The Purchase" came by boat rather than overland. The region had been occupied intermittently by people of the Mississippian culture, whose tools and weapons—points, scrapers, knives, and hand tools—were fashioned from chert, a colored rock. Their civilization thrived in the region for several hundred years until 1500.

These prehistoric Indians, called Mound Builders, lived in fortified villages and practiced agriculture. The transition to the Woodland, nomadic culture was due primarily to the development of sophisticated hunting methods which freed them to wander in search of game. The Mound Builder culture is the opening chapter in a region whose colorful past includes French explorers, determined settlers, pig iron magnates, a cigar-chomping, whiskey-drinking Civil War general, and the moonshiners whose white lightning made Golden Pond famous.

A French trader named Jean Charleville, on his way up the Mississippi from New Orleans, is thought to be one of the first European visitors to the area between the Cumberland and Tennessee rivers. In March of 1780 the region was explored by two overland survey parties, one headed by Dr. Thomas Walker of Cumberland Gap fame, the other by Col. Richard Henderson who had commissioned Daniel Boone to explore eastern Kentucky in the 1770s for a future settlement site for Transylvania Land Company. But settlement couldn't wait for statehood; by 1800 the first homesteaders were pouring in, hacking out small farms from the towering forests. Only the soil in the narrow floodplains was rich enough for farming, so the mainstay of the pioneer diet was wild game—buffalo, deer, wild turkey, small game— and whatever corn and salted pork they could pack in or barter for. Corn and hogs eventually became the major agricultural products.

Many of the first settlements were on the western bank of the Tennessee River and eastern bank of the Cumberland River. Eddyville, on Eddy Creek of the Cumberland River, was an early river port and trading center. The region took on the frontier flavor, never developing into a southern plantation-style agricultural society.

Perhaps the most important economic development in the region during the nineteenth century was the mining of low-grade iron ore and its conversion into pig iron in rock furnaces fueled by charcoal. During this period, Kentucky became a leading state in iron production in the South and Midwest; yet the tragic by-product was the large-scale cutting of the region's extensive stands of timber to the point of laying the area to waste. Iron making required enormous amounts of charcoal made from hardwoods—some 2,000 bushels were needed to fuel a furnace for one 24-hour period, and often as many as 12 furnaces were in operation at one time.

The charcoal was made by a primitive and tedious method in which 50 cords of wood were stacked in a circular hearth or "coal pit," 30 feet in diameter and 8 feet high. The amount of charcoal produced depended on the skill of the workers and their ability to keep the pit from going up in smoke. Layers of wet leaves and clay were placed over the wood, and a chimney was left open in the center for ventilation.

To light the pit a man climbed to the top of the stacked wood and opened up the "crow's nest," or chimney, stuffed it with kindling, and set it afire. The top of the pit was recovered and holes were cut in the side of the stack to control the amount of air reaching the fire. The entire process had to be attended 24 hours a day for up to 14 days by colliers, as the charcoal pit attendants were called. The seven-man crew often had three to five pits going at one time. The color of the smoke coming from the chimney told skilled attendants if there was too little or too much air and when the charcoal was ready to be drawn. Using a long-handled shovel, the "coal drawer" removed the charcoal from a cut in the base of the stack. After being wetted down with water to put out the fire, the charcoal was hauled in baskets to the furnace. The amount of charcoal produced per stack varied greatly; 1,650 bushels per stack was considered good. Thus, one crew's three pits could yield a maximum of approximately 5,000 bushels in 14 days. In that same time, however, each furnace consumed 28,000 bushels of charcoal!

Not only did the industry tax the region's resources but it drew a large labor force, mostly slaves, the first large numbers of them to be imported to the area between the rivers. Chinese coolies are also said to have been used, as were local farmers. It took a work force of 250 to 300 men to operate the largest furnaces.The wages were meager, as the profit margin in iron making was slim.

The iron-making boom that began in the 1820s tailed off after the Civil War, ending finally in 1912. The last furnace in the area was built in 1855.

Center Furnace was one of the largest and longest operating of all the furnaces in the area. Its name probably came from the fact that it was built halfway between Fulton and Empire furnaces, both of which were built in partnership by iron magnate Daniel Hillman.

The preparation of the ore and the actual iron-making process were fairly simple, but demanded constant attention and back-breaking work. Prior to the Civil War, slaves were used to dig the ore out of surrounding hills with picks and shovels. Impurities were burned off on cordwood fires and dust and dirt were sifted off with a screen.

The process by which pig iron was made differed little from the methods employed during colonial times. The furnace had to be located in front of a hill so that the heavy ore could be loaded by gravity from an ore box rolling over a trolley track. The ore was mixed with charcoal and limestone and dumped into the furnace from above. During the course of one blast cycle (9 to 11 months), the furnace operated 24 hours a day, six days a week. The workers rested on Sundays, but even then the fire was never allowed to go out. The "tapping" or "casting," pouring of the molten iron, was done every 12 hours; the maximum yield for one pouring was about eight tons (84 bars weighing 150 pounds each). During one blast cycle, 10,000 cords of wood were used. One useful by-product from iron making was the blue-greenish slag, a glassy substance that was broken up with sledge hammers after it cooled and used to gravel roads.

The pig iron was sorted into grades after it cooled and hauled by wagon to the Cumberland River where it was shipped downriver to the railroad at Kuttawa. Some of the iron was made into implements by local blacksmiths, but most was hauled by rail to Pittsburgh where it was sold by commissioned agents.

The one lasting contribution of the iron age between the rivers is William Kelly's process by which cold air was injected into molten iron to make steel. The air-blast process heralded the "Age of Steel" and enabled America to become one of the foremost producers of steel and a highly industrialized power in the world.

Kelly came to the region by way of Pittsburgh, married into a prominent family in Eddyville, and, with his father-in-law's help, went into the iron-making business. His trial-and-error experiments earned him laughs and ridicule from local skeptics who refused to believe that "air is fuel." Using an adaptation of a crude bellows, Kelly perfected the process but failed to patent his invention. An Englishman, following his progression of experiments at the furnace, carried Kelly's secret to England. Kelly later identified this man by photographs as Henry Bessemer, who tried to patent Kelly's process in November 1856. Kelly sued and won, but the court suits and the disruption of his finances cost Kelly his iron furnace business in Eddyville and kept him in debt until the 1870s when royalties from his process began to roll in as steel making became big business in Pittsburgh. And unfortunately, Bessemer is remembered as the original inventor.

The Civil War brought a divison of loyalties between the people of the region, as it did all across Kentucky. The iron industry between the rivers was slowed by the conflict, as many of the furnaces were shut down, destroyed, or abandoned. The region's main strategic importance was not in its iron production but in the fact that the Tennessee and Cumberland rivers, gateways to the South, were located there. Early in the war, the Confederates closed off the Mississippi River to the Union gunboats by fortifying the bluffs and stretching a chain across the river. Late in 1861, the Union commander in St. Louis, Gen. Henry H. Halleck, sent orders to Ohio-born, West Point-educated Ulysses S. Grant in Cairo, Illinois, to march his troops southward. Grant's ultimate mission was to engage the Confederates on the Tennessee and Cumberland Rivers. On January 30, 1862, the order was given to move on Fort Henry on the Tennessee River.

The river was at floodstage, Fort Henry was nearly underwater, and the Union army, by employing ground troops on the bluffs and gunboats in the river, easily overtook the Confederate outpost. Grant's next move did not meet with as much success. The Confederates routed the Union troops; but when Grant heard of the losses, he ordered a fierce counterattack. His persistence won in the end. Fort Donelson and upwards of 10,000 men were captured when the Confederates agreed to unconditional surrender. The victory earned Grant the nickname of "Unconditional Surrender Grant," by which he was known throughout the rest of his lifetime.

The bold move into the Confederacy was one of the earliest actions in the war, an important series of battles that won control of the mid-South for the Union, and greatly influenced the career of U.S. Grant, a man Abraham Lincoln later defended as a "fighter." The remaining years of the war in western Kentucky and Tennessee were relatively calm except for the nuisance of raider desperadoes, masquerading as Confederate cavalry, who scoured the countryside.

From the post-Civil War Reconstruction period until the early twentieth century, the major events in the area between the Cumberland and Tennessee rivers were the tobacco wars and the further decline of the pig iron industry due to labor shortages and outdated equipment. The people of the isolated region clung to oldtime ways, resisting change and modernization. Privately-financed land and development schemes failed, and the region went into general economic decline until an age-old tradition of whiskey making surfaced with Prohibition, and Golden Pond white lightning became the vogue in northern speakeasies. The Scotch-Irish immigrants that settled between the rivers were the first to distill whiskey there. All the raw materials of the art were readily available—corn, firewood, spring water, and plenty of white oak wood for barrels.

The economics of the situation were attractive, as well. The average still produced about 100 gallons of whiskey every three or four days. The illegal whiskey cost about $1 a gallon to make and the distiller sold it for $2.50 to $4 at the still.

Federal agents like "Big Six" Henderson and John Bays were legendary in their pursuit of the illegal whiskey makers. In one year Bays was in on the capture of mash and whiskey that, if taxed, would have totaled three million dollars in revenue to the Federal government. The revenue officers found the stills either by "bird dogging"—that is, tracking them down either by smell or by following streams—or by someone's squealing to the authorities. The average jail term for conviction was usually "a year and a day." Only in cases of repeated offenses or the use of force or guns in apprehension was the sentence longer. First time offenders were probated.

Although the Depression and Prohibition years marked the time when illegal whiskey making was first begun on a large scale, moonshining continued throughout the 1950s. In fact, it is estimated that the production of whiskey at that time had reached a level of 450 gallons a day. At the Federal tax rate of $10.50 per gallon, the U.S. government was losing about $47,000 a day. At that, western Kentucky ranked only tenth among producers of illegal whiskey, but the region was famous for the quality of its product.

The late fifties signaled the beginning of a period of expansion for the future. With the development of the Land Between the Lakes area, tourism began to rear its head as a business of growing importance to the region.

Camping

Camping is one of the most popular outdoor pastimes at Land Between the Lakes. There are 29 camping areas in all, 21 of which are informal use areas. The others include four group camps, three family campgrounds, and one new innovative backcountry camp. The three family campgrounds and the informal use campgrounds are equipped with basic facilities and operate on a first-come, first-served basis. Reservations are accepted at all group campgrounds and the backcountry campground. Camping is not allowed at any of the nine day-use areas.

Rules for the family and group campgrounds, as set forth by TVA, are as follows:

1. Use numbered campsites only. Select a site and report the number to the campground attendant at the gate; or, in the case of reservations, use only those sites you have reserved.

2. Place tents, truck campers, motor homes, trailers, etc., on prepared gravel camp pads or driveways. Do not park on grass areas.

3. Camping stay is limited to 14 days.

4. Checkout time is 4 p.m.

5. All pets must be tied or chained securely. Dogs must have current inoculation for rabies as prescribed by state of origin.

6. Pets are prohibited at swimming areas.

7. Fires are allowed only at campsites and must be attended at all times.

8. Do not cut, damage, pull up, or drive nails into trees or shrubs.

9. Hang lanterns on hangers provided, on clothesline suspended from or between trees, or place them on top of your table. Never hang a lantern directly against the side of a tree.

10. Place all garbage and refuse in trash cans.

11. Keep noise to a minimum, especially from 11 p.m. to 7 a.m.; be considerate of others.

12. Firearms and fireworks are prohibited.

13. Camping equipment left unattended overnight without authorization from gate personnel may be moved at owner's expense.

14. Licensed motorcycles with licensed drivers may enter and leave the campground by riding directly to and from their campsite on maintained roads. All other motorbikes are prohibited.

15. Visitors to registered campers are permitted provided the campground is not full. Visiting hours are from 7 a.m. to 10 p.m. The basic camping fee will be charged after 10 p.m.

16. Report any loss, theft, accident, or disturbance to the main gate. Turn in all found articles to the gate. TVA reserves the right to request campers and visitors failing to observe these regulations to leave the campground in the interest of the enjoyment of others.

17. Reservations should be made through the main offices of Land Between the Lakes, TVA-US, Golden Pond, Kentucky, 42231. Telephone: (502) 924-5602.

Family Campgrounds

Hillman Ferry is the largest of the three family campgrounds at LBL. Located half a mile south of the intersection of the Trace and the Old Ferry Road on Pisgah and Moss bays of Kentucky Lake in northern LBL, Hillman Ferry Campground is open year-round. The sprawling campground is divided into five units, with a total of 260 sites with electrical hookups (no sewer or water hookups) and 130 primitive sites. All sites are graveled. A 32-foot maximum length for motorhomes and travel trailers is suggested.

There are two launching ramps in the campground, three swimming areas/beaches on the lake, an archery range, dumping station, sports equipment checkout building, picnic tables, shelters and grills, paved courts for volleyball and basketball, a softball field, a bicycle skills course, a campfire theater, and plenty of open spaces for a rousing game of touch football. Flush toilets, showers, and sink facilities are spaced throughout the campground, as are faucets for drinking water.

A public telephone is available at the campground's entrance building. The campground rates for Hillman Ferry are $3 from May 15 to September 15 and $2 from September 16 to May 14. There's an extra 50¢ charge for electrical hookups.

Rushing Creek Campground, flanked by the Rushing Creek and Jones Creek embayments of Kentucky Lake, straddles the Kentucky-Tennessee border. The 400-acre family campground, open from May through September, was the first such facility in LBL (June 1, 1964). Rushing Creek Campground is reached via the Trace, formally Ky-453/Tn-49, and a paved approach road. To encourage use, the camping rates have been reduced to $2 a night by TVA; an additional 50¢ is charged for electrical hookups. During the summer, as in all of the family campgrounds, college students majoring in recreation conduct activities such as movies, campfires, singalongs, skits, arts and crafts sessions, guided hikes, contests for children, softball, volleyball, basketball, and horseshoe pitching. Nondenominational worship services are held at the campfire theater each Sunday morning during the summer.

There are fifty primitive campsites in Skunk Hollow and 60 electrically-equipped sites on Bobcat Ridge overlooking the lake. An overflow visitors area is adjacent. Other facilities include flush toilets, drinking water, ice, showers, picnic shelters, tables and grills, two scenic overlooks, launching ramp, day-hiking trails, beach, playcourts, and two RV dump stations. All campsites are graveled; a 21-foot maximum length for travel trailers and motorhomes is suggested.

Piney Campground is located three miles north of the southern boundary of LBL on highway US-79 in Stewart County, Tennessee, off Fort Henry Road. Open year-round, Piney Campground has 200 campsites, all with electricity. The campground is on the south shore of the Piney Creek embayment of Kentucky Lake. From May 15 to September 15 the cost per night is $3; from September 16 to May 14, $2, with an additional charge of 50¢ for electrical hookups. Drinking water, dump station, shower/toilet facilities, launching ramp, campfire theater, beach, children's playground, athletic fields, archery range, bird study area, minibike trails, hiking trails, and fishing pier are available at Piney Campground.

Backcountry Camp

Ginger Ridge Backcountry Camp in Tennessee, a 700-acre unit opened August 1, 1975, is LBL's answer to the lure of complete solitude and offers the back-to-nature atmosphere that increasing numbers of Americans are seeking. The unique primitive camp is in southern LBL on Kentucky Lake's Ginger Bay, approximately four miles west of the Buffalo Range off the Trace on Ginger Creek Road. Available by reservation only from April 1 to November 1, the Ginger Ridge Backcountry Camp has 13 unimproved sites scattered throughout the woodlands for complete privacy. Persons with reservations receive keys to the central "control gate," locked at all times to insure that campers won't be disturbed. The campground's user fee is $1 a day. Facilities include centrally located chemical toilets, drinking water, lake access, and trash cans. During the summer months campers may register and pick up their keys at the Rushing Creek Campground; at all other times campers register at the Golden Pond Information Center off US-68 or at Piney Campground, north of US-79. There is a limit of 10 people, four vehicles, and 14 days occupation per visit at each site.

Group Campgrounds

LBL's four group campgrounds are perhaps the most innovative recreational facilities in any major public outdoor area in this country. The newest of these areas is at Colson Hollow in the Kentucky portion of southern LBL, near Redd Hollow Informal Campground on Kentucky Lake. The Colson Hollow Group Camp is the upcoming area for special activities use—National Hunting and Fishing Day, craft fairs, ORV rallies, reunions, and camporees. The camping facilities are basic with chemical toilets, drinking water, and picnic tables. Colson Hollow is slowly replacing Pond Hollow Bivouac Area, LBL's first group campground that is now being used as a visitor overflow area. Camping at Pond Hollow is free, by permit only. Facilities include picnic tables, grills and drinking water, and unimproved sites.

Perhaps the most sophisticated of the four group camps is Brandon Springs in the Tennessee portion of LBL on Bards Lake, a 320-acre subimpoundment of Lake Barkley. When one considers the remote location of the camp, the facilities are astounding—radical design dormitories accommodating 128 people, cafeteria-style dining, sundecks, ultra-modern bathrooms and showers, boat dock, day-hiking trail system, nature interpretive area, meeting rooms, swimming pool, play fields, and indoor recreation facilities. Brandon Springs is ideally suited for the aged, multiply-handicapped, civic and church groups, and youth organizations. The innovative camp, opened in April 1974, is reached by road, yet is surrounded by extensive tracts of woodlands and the Bear Creek Waterfowl Management Area at the headwaters of Lake Barkley. It is a place where inner city and disadvantaged children can discover social studies, nature, and history. Brandon Springs is located near the Buffalo Range, ruins of the Great Western Iron Furnace, and the Homeplace 1850. A staff of recreational personnel is on duty year-round to assist in the planning and leading of such activities as swimming (pool on site), fishing, sailing, canoeing, and games in the five playfields.

Camp Energy is specifically designed for organized groups of tent campers from 4 to 400. Because of its location near the Environmental Education Center (EEC), and the fact that it's within easy driving distance of Taylor Bay, Curry Hollow, Boardinghouse Hollow, and the Mulberry Flats area—all deer hunting hotspots—it's not surprising that Camp Energy is extremely popular with bowhunters. Open year-round, the camp overlooks 350-acre Energy Lake, a constant-level subimpoundment of the Crooked Creek embayment of Lake Barkley. There is a canoe livery at the control building of the campground, and paddles, life preservers, and canoes are available to campers without charge. The showers, toilets, and wash basins with mirrors are in four heated, centrally-located buildings. All campsites have graveled tent pads, picnic tables, and grills.

Electrical outlets are scattered throughout the campground, though only about one-fourth of the sites actually have easy access to them. It is suggested that campers who wish to use the electricity bring up to 200 feet of heavy duty extension cord.

The five campsites that are located at the electrical outlets are A-11, B-2,3, C-12, and D-12. The campground is laid out in a series of loops, with sites A-6, 7, and 8, C-5, 6, and 7, and D-4, 5, and 6 overlooking the lake. All sites in complex B are located in the woods between the archery range and the amphitheater. The cost for camping per night, per site is $3.

A series of day-hiking trails circles the lake, the woodlands surrounding the camp, and the waterfowl refuge frequented by Canada geese and ducks in the fall and winter.

Wetlands with interesting aquatic vegetation, beaver dams, foot bridges across the creek, canebrakes, and abandoned homesites are the highlights of the trail system. Camp Energy is on Energy Lake Road, six miles south of its intersection with Mulberry Flat Road, the southern boundary of the Environmental Education center (EEC).

Lake Access Campgrounds and Day-Use Areas

In addition to family and group campgrounds in LBL, there are 21 lake access campgrounds and nine day-use areas. These informal use sites are spread through LBL on both the Kentucky Lake and Lake Barkley shorelines. They are isolated and offer more solitude than the family and group campgrounds at the expense of fewer facilities. Chemical toilets, trash cans, and picnic tables are standard throughout. Boat launching ramps are available at all but the four inland sites, and drinking water is available at all but six sites. All informal use areas are open year-round with a 14-day camping limit.

There are 12 lake access campgrounds north of highway US-68. The campground closest to the northern entrance to LBL is at Nickell Branch on Lake Barkley, one mile east of the Trace across Barkley Canal from Grand Rivers, Kentucky, and the U.S. Army Corps of Engineers-managed Canal Recreation Area. Twin Lakes Lake Access Area, with drinking water, chemical toilets, and overnight camping, is adjacent to the North Information Center one and one-half miles south of Barkley Canal and just seven river miles above Kentucky Dam at one of the lake's widest points. Demumbers Bay Lake Access (five primitive sites), reached via a paved road off the Trace, is approximately three miles southeast of the North Information Center overlooking one of the largest embayments on the lower end of Lake Barkley. The paved access road to the campground crosses Willow Bay.

Upstream from Grand Rivers, Kentucky, Lake Barkley winds in an easterly sweep before heading due south, paralleling Kentucky Lake. The northernmost point of LBL is Kuttawa Landing, once a river port. The Lyon County town had to be relocated north of LBL before the gates could be closed on Barkley Dam. The informal use area with six primitive sites is reached via Old Ferry Road off the Trace and is adjacent to Ramey Overlook, a day-use area with chemical toilets and picnic tables.

The Eddyville Ferry, in operation before the Cumberland River was dammed, once transported farmers with produce raised "'tween the rivers" to market in Eddyville, another riverside community that was relocated to higher ground. Launching ramps are located at the former ferry site.

The Star Camp (Wayside Area) is right off the Trace, approximately three miles south of Barkley Canal in the Willow Creek bottoms, halfway between Pisgah Bay on Kentucky Lake and Demumbers Bay on Lake Barkley. There are 10 unimproved sites on the grounds.

The Cravens embayment of Lake Barkley, a waterfowl refuge closed to hunting, has the largest lake access campground in terms of acreage in LBL. In addition to the 20 designated primitive sites, there is plenty of room for camping along the lake and in the hilly woods overlooking the embayment. Cravens Bay is reached via the eastern or Barkley Lake side of Old Ferry road off the Trace, and a three-mile gravel road marked by signs. Drinking water is available at Cravens Bay Lake Access Area.

There are two lake access campgrounds south of Hillman Ferry Family Campground on the Pisgah embayment of Kentucky Lake. On the northside is Pisgah Point, reached via Lee Cemetery Road, with 10 primitive campsites, picnic tables, launching ramp, grills, and pit toilets. Birmingham Ferry Lake Access Area is across from Pisgah Point and has drinking water in addition to the facilities standard to most other informal use areas. Birmingham Lake Access Area, reached via Old Ferry Road, was the site of a ferry across the Tennessee River before the lake was impounded. The next cove southward is Smith Bay, also off limits to waterfowl hunting. There are 40 unimproved sites in the campground. As in all informal use areas there's a 14-day limit, but no charge for camping. At this writing a major waterfowl management facility is being constructed in Duncan Bay.

The next lake access campground south is on the Barkley Lake side at Taylor Bay, just south of the Environmental Education Center. Taylor Bay has 13 unimproved campsites, boat launching ramp, chemical toilets, picnic tables, and grills. Taylor Bay is west of Empire Farm off Mulberry Flat Road. Large concentrations of fallow deer make the area popular with bowhunters, and during the October season the lake access area is usually full. At Energy Dam, off Mulberry Flat Road, two embayments over from Taylor Bay, there's a day-use area with a launching ramp for easy access to the Crooked Creek embayment of Lake Barkley.

The two remaining informal use areas in northern LBL (north of US-68) are on Kentucky Lake, at Sugar Bay, two miles west of the Trace on Ironton Road, and at Jenny Ridge Wayside at the Sugar Bay Area along the Trace, one mile from its intersection with US-68. There are 16 unimproved sites, mostly in the woods, with drinking water, chemical toilets, boat launching ramp, and picnic tables and grills. The Jenny Ridge site is small and located right beside the busiest road in LBL; nonetheless the area is popular with bowhunters. Drinking water is not available.

There are nine lake access campgrounds and four day-use areas south of US-68. Elbow Bay, Fenton, Bacon Creek, Turkey Bay, and Redd Hollow are all lake access areas in the Kentucky portion of southern LBL; Colson Hollow Overlook is the only day-use area. The Devil's Elbow Lake Access

Area (10 primitive sites) is off US-68, one mile from the Henry R. Lawrence Bridge over Lake Barkley. The campground's complement is Fenton, off US-68 at the Eggner Ferry Bridge on Kentucky Lake. The lake access campground has 10 primitive sites, launching ramp, chemical toilets, and garbage cans.

The Turkey Bay Lake Access Area (10 primitive sites, no drinking water) is the main campground for the 2,500-acre Turkey Creek Off-Road Vehicle (ORV) Area. A series of roads crisscrosses the unit that lies to the north of the campground overlooking Kentucky Lake. Reached via the Trace, one mile south of Golden Pond, then one mile west on Turkey Creek Road, Turkey Bay is open all year.

Bacon Creek Lake Access, reached via the Trace and Lick Creek Road, is just north of Wrangler's Camp on Lake Barkley. The campground, with 15 primitive sites, is a popular boat launching area for waterfowl hunters whose blinds are situated on the main lake adjacent to the levied waterfowl management area at river mile 70 in the Lick and Fords Creek embayments.

The rugged, hilly shoreline of Kentucky Lake and the lake itself are visible from Colson Overlook, three miles south of Golden Pond on the Trace. The day-use area with chemical toilets, picnic tables, and grills, is located on the Trace one and one-half miles east of the Colson Hollow Group Camp, a staging area for special events. One embayment south, Redd Hollow is one of the most popular lake access campgrounds in southern LBL. in the summer of 1977, 25 new campsites were constructed and the 15 original sites were renovated. Drinking water is available at the campground in addition to pit toilets, picnic tables, and boat launching ramp. Because of its relative seclusion and commanding lakefront view, the area is extremely popular with fishermen and bowhunters.

The Tennessee section of LBL has its share of campgrounds. In recent years visitor trends have shifted towards southern LBL, in part because of increased populations of whitetail deer and wild turkey there. Hunters camping during LBL's special hunting seasons make up a large percentage of the fall visitors. In addition to five lake access campgrounds and one day-use area, two of the three family campgrounds in LBL are located in Tennessee.

The newest lake access campground in the Tennessee portion of LBL is on Ginger Bay across from the backcountry camp. A launching ramp, chemical toilets, picnic tables, and grills are located at the lakeside camping area at river mile 53 on Kentucky Lake. To reach both the backcountry camp and lake access area, turn right off the Trace just past the Buffalo Range onto Ginger Creek Road. Turn left before Hendon Cemetery, right as you go into the Clay Creek bottoms, and right again at the sign.

Just across the state line in Tennessee's Neville Bay, adjacent to the Saline Unit of the Lake Barkley Wildlife Management Area (primarily for hunting waterfowl) on Lake Barkley, is another lake access campground. Reached via the Trace and a gravel road, four miles southeast of the ruins of the Great Western Iron Furnace, there are five unimproved sites, a launching ramp, chemical toilets, picnic tables, and grills at the lakeside facility.

Bards Dam and Gatlin Point are the remaining two access points on the Lake Barkley side of the Tennessee section of LBL. Bards Dam is a day-use area with one launching ramp which provides access to the 320-acre subimpoundment adjacent to Brandon Springs Group Camp. Gatlin Point overlooks extensive mudflats of Bear Creek Waterfowl Management Area; the area has 11 unimproved sites, launching ramp, chemical toilets, picnic tables, and grills. Both areas are reached by the Trace, Bards Lake via the turnoff at the former site of Tharpe, Tennessee, and Gatlin Point via the Jackson Cemetery turnoff, one and one-half miles south of Brandon Springs Road.

The remaining two lake access areas on the Kentucky Lake shoreline of the Tennessee portion of LBL are located in the vicinity of the old Fort Henry, a Confederate outpost on the Tennessee River captured by the Union in 1862. Both lake access areas, Blue Springs and Boswell Landing, are reached via Blue Springs Road, off the Trace. There's a launching ramp at Blue Springs near the mouth of the Panther Creek embayment. Boswell Landing, on the opposite point of the embayment, has 23 campsites, drinking water, chemical toilets, launching ramp, picnic tables, and grills. Historical markers, hiking trails, and breastworks from Confederate fortifications highlight the area.

Policy Statements

1. Reservations can be made one year in advance and only through the Golden Pond Headquarters.

2. No confirmation will be made without a deposit of one day's user fee, and commitment must be confirmed 30 days prior to date of reservations.

3. Cancellations must be made by telephone or letter 30 days prior to scheduled time of arrival. Groups not cancelling during the prescribed time will forfeit their deposit.

4. TVA-Land Between the Lakes reserves the right to refuse a reservation to any group that has camped at Camp Energy during prime time for two consecutive years.

5. A group is entitled to exclusive use of a shelter structure if they have rented one-half or more of a section.

6. The use of the campfire theater, assembly building, and shelter buildings can be reserved through permission by the park attendant.

7. The park attendant has the authority to check out special equipment, designate overflow sites, arrange special outings, and levy special charges for property and equipment damage.

8. Only one camper vehicle per site. Motorized and trailer-type camping vehicles will be charged $3 per night for a campsite.

Application for Reservation
Camp Energy
Land Between the Lakes
Group Camp

Name of Group _____

Sponsoring Organization_____

Group Leader_____

Street Number _____

City & State _____ Zip _____

Home Telephone Number _____

Business Telephone Number _____

EACH CAMPSITE SHOULD ACCOMMODATE EIGHT (8) CAMPERS.

Number of tent sites needed_____.

Figure the cost on per night basis. Check brochure for discount on one-half section (six campsites), whole section rental (12 campsites).

DEPOSIT ONE DAY'S USER FEE WITH THIS APPLICATION.

Date Desired: First Choice: _____

                 Second Choice: _____

Section Desired: First Choice: (A)   (B)   (C)   (D)

                 Second Choice: (A)   (B)   (C)   (D)

                             Arrival time: _____

                             Departure time: _____

Backpacking and Day-Hiking Trails

At present, Land Between the Lakes has more miles of backpacking and day-hiking trails than any other public outdoor recreation area in Kentucky. This will be the case until the completion of the Sheltowee Trace in Daniel Boone National Forest which will connect Pickett State Park in Tennessee with Kentucky's northern boundary on the Ohio River (via the Jenny Wiley Trail).

Because of the remote woodland character of the region and the lack of permanent human habitation, Land Between the Lakes is attractive to hikers who enjoy striking out on long, rambling treks, knowing they're not going to walk down a steep draw into someone's back yard. LBL's strong appeal to hikers is its 170,000 acres, a sizeable chunk of land more than twice as large as Kentucky's largest national park.

Since LBL is a multiple use area, however, there's a certain amount of overlap in usage. Because of the hunting season, fall is not a good time to hike in LBL. It just isn't safe, nor is it considerate to hunters, who, like hikers, seek out the most isolated places.

The management concept of LBL is not preservation, but rather revitalization of natural resources for multiple-use outdoor recreation and environmental education. Hiking is just a part of what's going on in LBL. The hard-core preservationists may be turned off by the fact that there's no scenery in LBL equal to our national forests and parks—no raging white water rivers, natural rock arches, or towering waterfalls. The huge tracts of oak-hickory woodlands are interrupted by powerlines, pipelines, gravel roads, campgrounds, and agricultural/timber harvest lands. The hiker interested strictly in "wilderness experiences" in its truest sense would probably not enjoy hiking in LBL; nonetheless, there are numerous reasons that make it a great place to take to the trail.

The incident in the introduction to this chapter about the hikers watching the approach of a thunderhead across Kentucky Lake happened to me when I was hiking the Fort Henry Trail system with outdoor/travel writer Richard Dunlop and a troop of Boy Scouts from Arlington Heights, Illinois. It was a stirring moment, watching the wind whip up whitecaps across Kentucky Lake at sunset, while the sky in the distance was lit up with a spectacular display of lightning. I would rank that evening around the fire with my solo hikes in the Rockies and southern California's High Sierra.

I'm convinced that the LBL hiking experience is one that shouldn't be overlooked by serious trail travelers. There are so many square miles of nothing but woods and lakeshore that it would take a person a lifetime to explore everywhere on foot. Also, with such an abundance of wildlife, the likelihood of sighting waterfowl, eagles, deer, beaver, songbirds, birds of prey, mammals, and reptiles is so high that each hike is a lesson in field biology.

The secret to good hiking in LBL is to be there when you'll have the whole place to yourself—late winter and spring, between the April turkey hunting seasons and the summer tourist season. Another advantage to hiking in the early spring is that the woods will be clear of worrisome vegetation for easier hiking and better visibility. Moreover, spring is the season for wildflowers, and you won't have to worry about insects.

The most pesky insects are, of course, ticks, and LBL has an incredible number of them, partly because of the high population of mammals. TVA personnel have been investigating ways to curtail the tick population so that summer hiking will be less of a hazard. Ticks cause discomfort more than anything else, but in rare cases they can cause serious diseases such as Rocky Mountain Spotted Fever.

The problem with ticks in LBL is the young of the year, or seed ticks, as they are commonly called. Reddish-brown in color, sightly smaller than the head of a straight pin and somewhat larger than a common chigger, the small critters cause intense itching and irritation. They're found in greatest numbers north of US-68, and usually appear in July and persist until the first killing frost. People become infested with these pests by brushing up against leaves of herbaceous ground plants in low, damp stream valleys and at the edges of fields. As many as a hundred bites may be sustained at one time. When the ticks get on your clothing, they may bite right away or crawl upward before attaching themselves, and, because of their small size, go undetected until it's too late.

The best way to prevent infestation is to avoid areas where ticks live. If you're hiking, stay on prepared trails and avoid low, damp areas. Insect repellent and yellow sulfur powder will provide some protection. If you think they're all over you it might not be a bad idea to take off your pack, take your wallet out of your pocket, and jump in the lake! Clothes covered with seed ticks should be handled with care, because carpeting in your car or house, clothing, sleeping bags, and tents can become infested.

All hikers in LBL are requested to check in at any one of the three information centers (two miles south of Barkley Canal on the Trace, at Golden Pond, or on the Trace north of US-79 in Tennessee), and report their itinerary. Likewise, hikers are asked to check out so all groups may be accounted for. Topographic maps of LBL and a trails brochure are available at all three information centers. The basic rules for hiking trails in LBL are:

1. Pack out all garbage.
2. No horses or motor vehicles are allowed on trails.
3. Hunting is allowed during legal seasons with proper state license and LBL permits.

4. No sidearms are permitted at any time.

5. Trailside water should not be consumed without proper treatment.

6. Leave the plants and flowers for others to enjoy.

7. Campfires are permitted any time except during periods of high fire danger.

8. Overnight camping is allowed at informal use areas or at trailside only; no camping at family or group campgrounds during hikes is permitted.

9. Don't cut live trees or bushes for firewood.

10. Camping is limited to one night at any campsite along trail.

The recently completed North-South Trail is the backbone of the 158-mile system in LBL. Beginning immediately south of Barkley Canal, the 60-mile (96.5 km.) trail roughly follows the shoreline of Kentucky Lake until just north of US-68, where it leaves the lake, crosses the Trace, and continues through varied terrain—woodlands and agriculture fields—before ending at the South Information Center. The trail follows the age-old route farmers took when they drove their stock and produce to market. The section north of US-68 is characterized by numerous lake views, rocky lakeshore trails, and hilly woods south of Sugar Bay. It passes four lake access campgrounds and one family campground. Treated drinking water is available only at Twin Lakes Access Area and Hillman Ferry Family campground, both on the first 10-mile leg of the hike.

After crossing the Dodd's creekbottoms and Pisgah Point Lake Access Area, the trail parallels Pisgah Bay and crosses Old Ferry Road. After circling Smith Bay, the hiker climbs to the ridge top where the trail crosses a gravel road. South of that road, the trail passes Michusson and Fulks cemeteries and a small spring, before crossing Duncan Creek at the head of Duncan Bay. Pisgah and Smith bays are waterfowl refuges, so winter and fall hikers should be on the lookout for ducks and geese. Duncan Bay is an eagle refuge and closed to all activity between November 1 and March 31. After crossing powerlines at the head of Duncan Bay, the trail heads due east, parallels Sugar Bay, and crosses the North Fork of Sugar Creek, passing Sugar Bay Lake Access Area on the south end of the embayment. Beyond Sugar Bay, the trail enters a section of narrow ridges, then skirts Rhodes Bay and follows the ridge out to the lake, past numerous springs near Savell's Cemetery.

The trail passes Vickers and Chambers cemeteries, and crosses a pipeline right-of-way after circling Vickers Bay. Then it follows Barnett Creek to its headwaters at Jenny Ridge Wayside Area, just one mile north of US-68 and Golden Pond, Kentucky.

The section of the North-South Trail south of US-68 is neither as strenuous nor as scenic. Beyond Golden Pond, neither treated drinking

water nor camping facilities are available. Never coming close to either
lake, the trail practically follows the ridge top divide between streams
flowing east to Lake Barkley and west to Kentucky Lake. It parallels the
Trace from US-68 to the southern terminus at the Information Center two
miles north of US-79 in Tennessee. One-half mile south of US-68, the trail
passes Ross Cemetery and crosses the Trace west to east at the boundary to
the Turkey Creek ORV area. Then it crosses the west fork of Laura Furnace
Creek, east of Colson Hollow Overlook. A side trail leads to the day-use
area. '

Paralleling the Trace, a mile to its east, the trail crosses numerous
branches of Laura Furnace Creek and, eventually, the creek drainage's
graveled access road. Just south of the Kentucky-Tennessee line, the trail
again crosses the Trace, this time east to west, and plunges into the drainages of Rushing and Ginger creeks, both of which flow into Kentucky Lake.
Ginger Creek Road is the next graveled road to be crossed. After skirting
several wildlife openings, the trail crosses the Clay Creek Road at a cemetery and Lookout Tower, near the head of the Byrd Creek drainage. After
passing the Fuqua cemetery, the trail crosses Tharpe Road and the Morgan
cemetery before entering the final 10-mile stretch between Brandon Creek
and Stilly Hollow on a ridge divide.

Trail signs are strategically located throughout the trail, indicating
mileages, water sources, and points of interest. It is necessary to carry
water through some stretches of the trail, especially south of US-68, as
many of the headwater tributaries to lake embayments are "wet weather"
creeks.

The next longest trail in LBL is actually a system of trails that could be
hiked all at once for a multi-day trip or in short sections for a number of
day-hikes. The Fort Henry Trail System in southwestern LBL (Tennessee) is
26 miles of marked footpath (interconnected loops), retracing the route
Gen. U.S. Grant and his men took when they marched on Fort Donelson
after the victorious shelling and surrender of Fort Henry.

The Fort Henry Trail System is reached from the South Information
Station via Blue Spring-Fort Henry Road, a paved highway heading west
from the Trace. The entrance and parking area to the system are adjacent
to the Boswell Landing Lake Access Area where 23 campsites, drinking
water, chemical toilets, launching ramp, picnic tables, and grills are available. The trails originate from the remaining Fort Henry breastworks; the
original site of the fort is now under the waters of Kentucky Lake.

The Blue-Gray Trail, a one-mile audio-interpretive trail, also originates
from the former gun emplacement sites. The Fort Henry trails parallel
Panther Bay and crisscross Devil's Backbone, Buckingham Hollow, the
North Fork of Piney Creek, and Bear Creek. The network of trails can also
be reached from Piney, a family campground two miles further south on

Fort Henry Road. The Fort Henry Trail System ends at the South Information Center; thus it can be hiked in conjunction with the North-South Trail. Patches are available to persons who complete these trails. TVA would like to see both these trails included in the National Trails System, to tie up with the Natchez Trace to the southeast.

The 5,000-acre Environmental Education Center, the focal point of the environmental awareness program in LBL, has six day-hiking trails which concentrate on the plant and animal communities in the area.

Woodland Walk, a half-mile loop trail beginning and ending at Center Station, provides the visitor with an insight into the iron industry and includes a slave cemetery and a limestone quarry amid dense woodlands. Deer may be seen in the open areas in the early morning and late afternoon, and geese feed in the nearby wheat field in the spring. Rest benches are located near these areas.

Long Creek Trail, a one-fifth-mile flat, paved trail for handicapped persons, wanders through shaded woodlands along a quiet stream. A shelter is provided for wildlife observation. Nine interpretive stations along the trail encourage sensory awareness. The trail begins across from the ruins of Center Furnace.

Center Furnace Trail, a three-tenths-mile trail located just south of Center Station near the former site of Center Furnace, is a short, yet very rewarding, wood chip-surfaced historical trail whose theme is the iron industry of the nineteenth century. Points of interest along the way include charcoal and iron ore pits, a momument to iron magnate Thomas Watson, and the remains of the community of Hematite.

Hematite Trail, a two-and-one-fifth-mile interpretive trail, winds its way around 250-acre Hematite Lake through a wide variety of habitats. Near the trail in the spring, one may see nesting giant Canada geese; in summer, a wide variety of flowering aquatic vascular plants, muskrat, and beaver may often be sighted. Migratory waterfowl flock to the lake during fall and winter. Observation areas are located on the north and west sides of the trail and a photography blind is located on the south side. A wooden boardwalk traverses the wetlands at the lake's headwaters.

Honker Trail, two-and-one-half miles each way, begins at Center Station, circles Honker Lake (a Canada goose breeding area and waterfowl refuge), crosses Honker Dam, and ends on a gravel road off Mulberry Flat Road between Empire Farm and Youth Station. Empire Farm can be reached from Honker Trail via a one-and-six-tenths-mile trail. Large stands of cottonwood trees in the area encourage visits from some species of birds not often seen, especially the pileated and redheaded woodpeckers.

The Trail of These Hills, off Mulberry Flat Road, is a mile-and-a-quarter audio-interpretive trail that explains the resource story of the region, as does the eight-mile Motor Resource Tour Trail which begins at Center

Station and runs southward on Energy Road to the Pond Hollow Bivouac Area. Stops along the way explain habitat manipulation for wildlife management and forestry techniques, integral parts of TVA's land-use plan for LBL.

At extreme northern LBL by Barkley Canal is the trailhead of LBL's longest continuous footpath and a 14-mile complex of loop trails that contour the shorelines of both Kentucky Lake and Lake Barkley. Points of interest include Pilgrims Rest Overlook, a day-use area, and Nickell Branch Lake Access Area, where unimproved campsites, chemical toilets, picnic tables and grills, and a boat launching ramp are available.

Miscellaneous day-hiking trails in LBL include four and one-half miles of paved and graveled paths for bicyclers and hikers at Piney Campground, with one loop trail especially devoted to observing songbirds. The Hillman Heritage Trail is one of 72 designated national recreational trails. This 10-mile series of loops and crossovers at Hillman Ferry Campground was built in conjunction with the Kentucky Lake Chapter of National Campers and Hikers Association. Other day-hiking trails include the Cedar Bluff day-hiking trail at Rushing Creek Campground and the Paw Paw Path, a 1500-foot paved trail for handicapped persons at Brandon Springs Group Camp. In addition, there are nine miles of regular trails at the camp which encircle Bards Lake, a subimpoundment of Lake Barkley.

Resource Management

At LBL's inception in 1964, the isthmus of land between Kentucky Lake and the Cumberland River was dotted with homes, farms, and businesses. The complex ownership situation involved the Bureau of Sport Fisheries and Wildlife, real estate companies, corporations, and individuals. As a result, the condition of the land ranged from badly eroded areas to isolated pockets of harvestable timber, but a majority of it was in various stages of plant succession. Many acres had been cleared for agricultural use; a smaller percentage of the area was taken up by churches, groceries, community buildings, graveyards, and privately-operated recreational facilities on the eastern shore of Kentucky Lake. The 63,000-acre Kentucky Woodland National Wildlife Refuge in the Cumberland bottoms and adjoining ridgetop forests had been under Federal management since the 1930s.

The area was in a state of general economic decline, and man's impact on the land was highly visible. For the nearly 150 years since the first settlers arrived "'tween the rivers," the resources had been utilized with a virtual absence of conservation measures. The philosophy towards resources was clearly exemplified by the iron industry's savage, indiscriminate cutting of the forests.

This is not to say that all the people who lived in the area before TVA began managing it as LBL mistreated the land. Even though the soil was thin and cultivation was restricted to the narrow valleys, there were a few prosperous farmers, responsible people who made a good living off the land without abusing it. It is these people who were perhaps the most unhappy with TVA's takeover; and even today, almost 10 years since land acquisition was completed—either through outright purchases or through land condemnation proceedings—some hard feelings persist. This is to be expected. As project after project proves, land acquisition by Federal or state agencies is a controversial issue, and especially so in the case of LBL, where both the agency and the project are aggressive and innovative. New approaches and ideas always meet with opposition.

It is my contention, however, that as time passes, the critics of LBL— and there are no longer that many—will be silenced. More and more people are coming to understand that the development of the area would not have been possible without moving everybody out and starting from scratch.

From the resource manager's standpoint, LBL is unique, a fishbowl situation of sorts where renewal and utilization of timber and wildlife resources and their by-product, resource-dependent recreational activities, can be closely scrutinized. LBL doesn't lend itself to preservation management. The land simply isn't wilderness in character and doesn't meet the criteria for true wilderness as defined by the Wilderness Act of 1964. Thus, LBL is a unique multiple-use area whose time has come. Unlike the case of our national forests where special interest groups may sooner or later directly oppose the forest's broader management goals, LBL's management plan has been implemented from the start by outside consultation rather than direct management. LBL is successful because TVA has had total control over its operation and owns all the land within LBL's boundary.

The LBL resource management-based land-use plan will someday be fully appreciated, not only in concept but because of the fact that its unique appeal may help relieve the visitor load on our other parks and forestlands. Certainly, our national parks and wilderness areas can't accommodate many more visitors. The necessity of limiting the number of persons that visit these lands is not inconceivable somewhere in the future.

Our national forests are having other troubles, as well. In our own Daniel Boone National Forest, coal mining interests are clamoring for "dual ownership" rights to strip mine land; that is, the coal companies would own the mineral rights while the United States Forest Service (USFS) would retain the surface rights. The ideal solution to the problem would be for the USFS to purchase all private land holdings and compensate coal companies for the mineral rights they own. Since sufficient money simply isn't available, the coal companies are suing for the right to mine.

Perhaps I am prejudiced in my view of LBL and its merit, but I am firmly convinced that the future of our natural resources lies in conserving those which are nonrenewable and identifying those areas with great renewable resource potential that are now held by private interests. The future of our fish, wildlife, and woodland resources and high-quality outdoor recreation is dependent upon the development of more such areas as LBL. TVA has proven that it can be done.

One of the earliest programs TVA initiated in Land Between the Lakes was a detailed resource management plan. The plan was developed by a TVA team of specialists in cooperation with wildlife management experts from Virginia Polytechnic Institute and Louisiana State University. The plan is updated as new resource management techniques develop. Forest fire control is provided under contract with the Kentucky and Tennessee State Divisions of Forestry.

For convenient management of the resources, the peninsula is divided into 65 work areas ranging from 1,060 to 3,800 acres in size, each inventoried, analyzed, and managed in seven-year cycles. The first step in evaluating the units for wildlife and timber potential is aerial photography. A rough estimate of all the timber in each unit is made by reviewing the crown size of the trees and the density of cover from the air. Next, foresters reconnoiter the area and take inventory, noting such things as access, water holes, timber conditions, timber volume of both hardwoods and pulpwood, open land, and extent of browse and cover. It is only after these field findings have been reviewed by both wildlife and game management personnel that the two groups confer to decide what is best for the work area. The findings, including a present condition map and work schedule, are then recorded on McBee cards and fed into a computer for permanent storage and easy recall so that no unit will be neglected because of lost materials.

Since only approximately 15 percent of LBL is open land, the rapidly growing timber must be manipulated in its various stages of succession. The areas to be worked at a given time are widely dispersed so that the impact of timber harvest will not drastically affect wildlife and recreation.

At the present time only 3,000 acres of saw timber are being harvested annually, a volume amounting to some 3.5 million board feet. This represents seven percent of the annual sawtimber growth of 20 million board feet in LBL, and less than one-half of one percent of the total timber volume of over 450 million board feet.

Since one of LBL's resource management goals is to increase and upgrade the quality and appearance of open lands, landscape architects are utilized for some projects. Woods openings of 3 to 10 acres are developed so that the heavily wooded areas will be broken by the "edge effect." Fallow deer and young wild turkeys and rabbits especially need these openings. Approximately 245 such openings have been created by land clearing. In stretches of open woods the availability of water is sometimes a problem for wildlife, so one-quarter-acre potholes are constructed where necessary. When evergreen cover is inadequate, pine cover plantings of 5 to 20 acres are strategically located at half-mile intervals. By the time the pines are 15 years old, they have begun to produce seeds utilized by wildlife. Sometimes autumn olive, a shrub which produces berries preferred by deer and turkey, is planted in with the pines. At maturity the pines are cut for pulpwood.

The foresters and wildlife managers work in close cooperation toward a sustained yield of sawtimber and stabilized populations of wild turkeys, whitetail and fallow deer, rabbits, waterfowl, quails, doves, Wilson snipe, woodcocks, and furbearers. Cooperative programs to benefit nongame species—birds of prey and songbirds, especially—are also implemented.

Hunting is the major outdoor recreation use of the land except in the visitor use areas (about 5,000 acres) which are off limits to hunters. In an era when it's harder and harder to find a place to hunt, the idea of one chunk of 165,000 acres set aside especially for hunting is a paradise indeed. Populations of deer, wild turkeys, and some species of small game are high enough that hunter success is much better than the statewide average. TVA sets special hunting seasons for most of the game species; seasons for migratory birds are set by the U.S. Bureau of Sport Fisheries and Wildlife.

The whitetail deer (*Odocoileus virginianus*) is the game species most sought after in LBL. Because of continuous timber harvesting, there is always an "edge effect," an area where tender shoots and shrub growth provide browse, so essential in a deer's diet. Likewise, stands of mature oaks which produce lots of acorns, a staple food in the winter diet, are essential to healthy deer herds. Biologists at LBL are not managing the area solely for deer; that is, they're not interested in allowing the herd to reach its peak, but rather in producing a stable, healthy herd year after year.

Deer kill data for both bowhunting and gun seasons indicate that 1974 may have been the banner year for deer hunting in LBL. That year, 7,393 gun hunters in the Kentucky portion harvested 1,172 deer, while in Tennessee the total take was 1,237 deer by 5,472 hunters. The success percentages were 15.85 percent and 22.60 percent, respectively, or 19.22 percent overall.

A healthy deer herd is dependent on ideal habitat, a balance of open land, reverting fields, cover, plenty of browse, and large stands of acorn-producing oaks—in effect, all the stages of succession towards a climax oak-hickory forest. Overly mature trees produce fewer acorns (mast) and thus can support fewer deer. Timber volume in LBL is increasing faster than it's being cut, and the continuation of large, healthy herds may depend on increasing the amount of timber being cut.

One rather unique wildlife management aspect of LBL is the presence of a large herd of fallow deer (*Dama dama*), smaller but stockier than whitetails, with distinctive spotted coloration ranging from reddish-brown to pure white, black and white, and jet black. In America, fallow deer are found in only nine states. The herd in LBL (approximately 600 animals) is thought to be the largest herd in the U.S. The fallow buck, with large, palmated antlers, is a prized trophy among sportsmen; it takes fallow deer approximately four and one-half years to develop antlers, considerably longer than whitetails. Whitetail and fallow deer utilize nearly the same habitat—shrubby, thicket-stage growth, woodlands, and pasture land—and exhibit similar behavior in regard to the males' shedding and regrowing antlers. Fallow, however, begin the rut earlier and drop their antlers later. The bucks will often groan and grunt continuously for hours in hopes of attracting does. Fallow are also known for a rather funny-looking, stiff-legged running gait.

LBL's fallow deer herd originated from 20 deer released in 1918 when the Barnes Hollow region (now the Environmental Education Center) was under the ownership of the Hillman Land and Iron Company. The herd has always been especially attractive to bowhunters and has drawn many biologists and outdoor journalists to the region in search of this majestic animal.

Fallow deer have to be managed more closely than whitetails, as their numbers are not as readily renewed year after year. Differences in their reproductive rates make it necessary to close the season on fallows when their numbers decline. Whitetail does usually give birth to twins and occasionally triplets, whereas fallow commonly have only one fawn. Also, fallow does don't breed until they are at least two years of age; whitetail fawns barely nine months old have been known to breed. In order to maintain a stable herd of fallows when they range with whitetails, the numbers of deer harvested by hunters must be closely monitored.

Gun permits for deer hunting are drawn from applicants prior to the season. These quota hunts in both the Kentucky and Tennessee portions of LBL are filled at random by computer. Some 28,000 requests for gun permits were received by TVA in 1976; of those, 12,278 were selected, but not all of those selected chose to hunt.

Bow permits are issued to anyone who has appropriate licenses and deer tags. The trend toward bowhunting, the most popular fall activity in LBL, results from the combination of an excellent deer population, outstanding facilities, and long season. The number of permits issued and the number of deer taken by archers have grown steadily since the early seventies. TVA statistics indicate that 5,083 permits were issued in 1972, and 169 deer were taken for a hunter success rate of 3.32 percent. The 1976 figures show a dramatic increase in the number of bowhunters, and consequently their hunter-hours afield. Some 10,777 permits were issued and archers took 456 deer. The hunter success rate for 1976 was 4.32 percent.

Hunting from tree stands has proven to be one of the most successful ways of bagging a deer with a bow and arrow. Regulations for tree stands and climbing devices were enacted when foresters became concerned that the increasing number of nails being driven into trees was causing harm by inviting insects or disease. Regulations now forbid the nailing of boards to trees or the use of permanent screw-in steps or platforms. Permanent stands and climbing devices that damage trees are strictly prohibited. Stands may be chained, belted, clamped, or tied with rope, and may have stabilization spikes or blades for aid in adhering to trees. Climbing blocks are the preferred method for climbing trees, although ladder stands and the widely-used "climbing stands" that can be purchased in sporting goods stores are acceptable.

All tree stands must be removed after the season ends or after the first portion of a split hunting season. All stands must bear the owner's name, address, telephone number, and Social Security number affixed to the bottom of the platform. As a deterrent to tree stand thefts, persons must prove by permission in writing the right to possess and use tree stands owned by others.

The bow season for deer runs concurrently with the bow season for wild turkey, usually beginning in late October and running for about three weeks. The second half of the split season begins approximately December 15 and continues until the end of the year. Any deer, does, or bucks are legal; however, only gobblers with visible beards may be harvested.

The future of turkey hunting should be a bright spot in the overall game management program, according to biologists at LBL. These majestic birds (*Meleagris gallopavo silvestris*), with eyesight like high-powered binoculars and hearing an audiologist would be envious of, are the upcoming game species. The flock is expected to increase gradually for a number of reasons. Among them is the fact that more and more acres of land are coming into mast production, as the timber volume increases faster than trees are being cut. Also, as more of the resource units are intensely managed, the proportion of open lands, water holes, cover, and mature timber will reach an optimum level for survival of the young, an important factor in the overall population growth.

Adult birds, which may weigh up to 22 pounds, prefer mature forests with little understory growth, the reverse habitat requirements of deer. Open fields, where young turkeys forage for insects on summer nights, and thick edge cover where the nests are built are also needed for turkey survival. The poults are adversely affected by wet weather. In addition, turkeys need tall trees in which to roost and open woods in which to feed. Their diet consists of various seeds, fruits, mast (acorns, beechnuts, gum, blackberry, dogwood, wild cherry, and greenbrier), wild grapes, field crops (wheat and corn), and small invertebrates.

The spring mating season, when the gobblers court hens by strutting their magnificent plumage and gobbling loudly in response to the soft clucks of the female, is the birds' most vulnerable time. Fewer than 50 of these wary birds have ever been taken in one year, and only two with bow and arrow since the annual seasons began at LBL. Curry and Racetrack Hollows on the Lake Barkley side in northern LBL, Jenny Ridge on the Kentucky Lake side off US-68 and the Trace, and the hilly land just south of US-68 on both the east and west sides of LBL are considered the best hunting areas for turkey.

The Lake Barkley, Kentucky Lake, and LBL recreational complex lies in the path of migrating waterfowl on the Mississippi flyway. The birds stop over to rest and feed in the shallow back bays and mudflat islands of the lakes and in the corn, millet, and buckwheat fields in Land Between the Lakes. During statewide seasons, waterfowlers take Canada geese, buffle-heads, American and hooded mergansers, scaup, goldeneye, gadwalls, widgeon, wood ducks, green and blue-winged teal, mallards, and black ducks. Pintail, redhead, and canvasback ducks are also transient visitors, but in smaller numbers. Land Between the Lakes is within a 75-mile radius of four major rest stops on the Mississippi flyway—Reelfoot National Wild-life Refuge; Ballard County Wildlife Management Area, where peak popu-lations at the 8,000 acres of riverbottom fields and sloughs reach from 60,000 to 100,000 geese and 55,000 ducks; Tennessee National Wildlife Refuge on Kentucky Lake at Paris, Tennessee; and Cross Creeks National Wildlife Refuge, which was created when TVA took control of the Ken-tucky Woodlands National Wildlife Refuge. Peak populations of waterfowl at Cross Creeks National Wildlife Refuge average 13,000 to 16,000 geese and 80,000 ducks.

Tennessee Valley Authority's long-range programs devoted to resident and migratory waterfowl management seek to improve the quality and distribution of the entire region's population of ducks and geese; to protect, identify, and/or restore breeding habitat for resident birds; and to increase the numbers of migratory waterfowl through refuge development and im-provement of existing programs. At Land Between the Lakes, TVA's com-mitment to waterfowl management is in part a continuation of the pro-grams initiated during the 1930s, when roughly one-fourth of the land now managed at the recreational area was Kentucky Woodlands National Wild-life Refuge.

Cooperation among the Kentucky Department of Fish and Wildlife

Resources, Tennessee Wildlife Resources Agency, and TVA has established a system of waterfowl refuge and management areas on Lake Barkley and Kentucky Lake to promote the growth of duck and goose populations to stable, huntable numbers. Lake Barkley Wildlife Management Area, operated by the Tennessee Wildlife Resources Agency, encompasses 3,609 acres in the Saline Creek and Dover bottoms on the eastern shore of Lake Barkley. The blind sites are awarded by draw. Hunters must build their own blinds and remove them after the season closes. The management area is planted extensively in waterfowl food and offers consistent hunting throughout most of the season (unless the area freezes up), because of limited hunting pressure and its proximity to Cross Creeks National Waterfowl Wildlife Refuge. Hunting is permitted at Lake Barkley Wildlife Management Area only on Wednesdays, Thursdays, Saturdays, and Sundays, and on the opening and closing days of the statewide duck season.

If a blind is not occupied by the time legal shooting hours begin, it is open to whoever claims it for that day. Thus, it is possible for hunters other than those designated by the draw to hunt on the waterfowl management area. Applications for the drawing of blind sites must be received before August 1, prior to the statewide season. Inquiries for blind site applications and the special regulations for hunting on Tennessee wildlife management areas may be made to "Blind Site Drawing," Tennessee Wildlife Resources Agency, P.O. Box 40747, Nashville, Tennessee, 37204.

Bear Creek Waterfowl Management Area, one of the foremost duck-hunting spots on Lake Barkley, is the single TVA-managed hunting area in the Tennessee section of Land Between the Lakes. One hundred acres of levied fields are planted in waterfowl foods and flooded prior to the season. Blind sites for this public hunting area are also drawn before the season. Forty blinds are authorized; the best ones are on Pintail and Black Duck Slough, and Indian and Mallard ponds. The 1500-acre tract is open to waterfowl hunting on Mondays, Tuesdays, Fridays, and Saturdays. Information on blind regulations is available by writing Waterfowl Management, Land Between the Lakes, TVA, Golden Pond, Kentucky, 42231.

The TVA resident waterfowl development program is concentrated on two species—Canada geese and wood ducks. A small flock of approximately 300 geese has been established at Honker Lake, a subimpoundment of Lake Barkley. Wildlife biologists have solved the problem of flooded nesting sites by building nesting islands and rafts that rise and fall with the water level. Nesting boxes for wood ducks have been erected along the shorelines in hopes of establishing a resident flock of 4000 to 6000 ducks. The resident waterfowl management area, off limits to hunting, is located between mile 51 and mile 57 (Hayes Landing Light and Crooked Creek Light) on the west side of Lake Barkley, and includes Cravens, Fulton, Jake Fork, Taylor, and Honker bays, and Hematite Lake.

As is the case in all duck hunting, weather conditions and the availability of food are perhaps the most important factors. On Lake Barkley and
Kentucky Lake, the wind is equally important. When the main lakes are
rough with whitecaps, as they often are in the winter, a majority of the
ducks will seek out calm water in coves. During periods of prolonged cold
weather and high winds, the ducks become restless and drift out to surrounding embayments in search of food. Hunting pressure is also a factor
in the movement of ducks between coves. It's hard to get ducks to decoy
over open water, but in the coves they will be less hesitant. When picking
a spot to blind up in a cove, remember that ducks have a preference for
points, eddies at creek mouths.

Cove hunting is especially effective on the eastern shore of Kentucky
Lake, north of US-68, in the Sugar, Rhodes, Vickers, and Barnett embayments. Nearby Duncan, Smith, and Pisgah bays are closed to waterfowl
hunting to give the ducks a place to rest, thus encouraging their continued
use of the area. By scouting the bays open to hunting, it is possible to spot
a pattern of use in the embayments; on one hunt a few years back, this
technique worked well and our party of hunters was able to decoy a small
flock of wary black ducks that returned at mid-morning to rest in the
isolated cove.

Large spreads of decoys and goose half-body layouts on mudflat islands are used frequently, although in the case of cove hunting, small
groups of decoys will do fine. Shallow-draft johnboats up to 16 feet long
and 54 inches wide with 22-inch sides, and carrying lots of decoys and
gear and bucking the whitecaps, are a popular choice with lake region
waterfowlers. Olive drab is the all-around best choice of color. Bright-colored gas tanks and outboard motors are often painted flat brown or olive
drab green, or covered with burlap sacks. Outside the main channel of the
Cumberland River, Lake Barkley is shallow, with stump beds and brushy
islands. Carrying extra shear pins for your outboard motors is a good habit.

Floating blinds are popular on Lake Barkley, although there are special
regulations for their use. For information regarding regulations on both
floating and permanent blinds, contact: U.S. Army Corps of Engineers,
Barkley Dam, Gilbertsville, Kentucky, 42044; telephone: (502) 362-4236.
Permanent blinds on both reservoirs must be registered with the appropriate agency. On Kentucky Lake write TVA, Land Between the Lakes,
Golden Pond, Kentucky, 42231; telephone: (502) 924-5602.

The small game species hunted in Land Between the Lakes include
squirrel, quail, rabbit, dove, Wilson snipe, woodcock, raccoon, opossum,
gray fox, and woodchuck. Squirrel is the first species hunted during the
fall. The season usually begins in mid-August and runs until bow season for
deer opens in early October. A late season begins after the end of the gun
season for deer and lasts until the end of December. The squirrel popula-

tion is very high due to the acres and acres of mature oak-hickory forest. Biologists report that the squirrel is a grossly underhunted species.

Quail and rabbit seasons traditionally open Thanksgiving weekend and run until late February. TVA, in cooperation with Murray State University, has planned future studies to determine why rabbit populations aren't as high as biologists think they should be. Quail hunters report that the birds are numerous in LBL, but are exceptionally smart and have a nasty habit of getting up as a covey and flying to the center of fields from cover in the woods, making it extremely difficult for dogs to work them. Populations are scattered throughout LBL but are centralized around agricultural fields in the southern reaches.

Mourning doves, Wilson snipe, and woodcock, all regulated by the Federal fish and wildlife officials, may be hunted in LBL during statewide seasons prior to the beginning of bow season for deer and after the gun quota hunts. The furbearer (opossum and raccoon) seasons occur on selected days in December and January each year. No trapping is allowed and there are special regulations for hunting these animals. A late winter hunt for gray fox and a spring hunt for woodchucks are the only varmint seasons. No electronic equipment may be used for calling foxes, and the March woodchuck hunting is subject to special regulations. This special season on groundhogs was declared after contract farmers complained that the "whistle pigs" were destroying their crops.

Environmental Education and Special Activities and Areas

As our society has become more urbanized and industrialized, prople have drifted farther and farther away from the natural environment—wetlands, roaring white water rivers, snow-capped mountains, sweeping forests and wildlife—a heritage that has been kept from dying out all together by the efforts of a few visionaries and the awakening realization that this planet's resources aren't infinite.

The fact is indisputable that millions of Americans know virtually nothing about the natural system that supports them. It seems almost incomprehensible that there are people who grow to adulthood without ever spending a night in the woods in a sleeping bag, or that millions of Americans have never experienced the whoosh of wings as a flock of wood ducks lights on a slough at sunset, the quiet dampness of a woodlot in the morning after a night of rain, the exquisite patterns of frost on autumn leaves, the delicate fronds of a fern uncurling in the spring woodlands. It is indeed a sad footnote to the American way of life that in a land founded on equality and the pursuit of happiness, there are children who don't know the taste of fresh-brewed sassafras tea or the call of a warbler. What an injustice!

Environmental education nationwide has come a long way since Earth Day, April 22, 1970, the day set aside as a conscious effort to remind Americans of their tie with the natural system. There's more awareness of the need to educate our youngsters about trees, flowers, wildlife, insects, fish, aquatic and terrestrial systems, weather, and Nature's blessing of renewal. Environmental education has become an imperative, for it is the only practical way to reverse the trend which threatens to completely alienate our society from the Earth.

TVA's environmental education efforts in LBL have been met with open arms by educators everywhere. Never before have so many innovative field programs and facilities been offered on such a large scale as a supplement to formal education. The whole-concept approach and its unique "classroom" have made learning about nature easy and enjoyable for children in school, church, civic, and Scout organizations.

The 5,000-acre Environmental Education Center (EEC), bounded on the east by Lake Barkley, on the north by Silver Trail, on the south by Mulberry Flat Road, and on the west by the Trace, is the hub of TVA environmental education in LBL. Center Station is a major interpretive facility, with numerous exhibits dealing with the area's geology, primitive inhabitants, animals, and plant life. Indian artifacts, schematic geological charts, taxidermic mounts of birds and animals, and historic documents relating to local Civil War action are on display. Supplementary reading is available through field guides to the region's wildflowers, archaeological sites, lichens and ferns, mammals, amphibians, and reptiles, on sale for a few dollars each at Center Station. The field guides are interesting and informative, and many feature color photography. Admission to Center Station and the audio-visual presentation is free of charge. The hours are 8:30 a.m. to 4:30 p.m., February 18 through December 15. Center Station's telephone number is (502) 924-5509.

Another point of interest in the EEC is Empire Farm, a 120-acre farm designed to familiarize visitors with farm animals and the role of agriculture in our society. A farmhouse, rough-hewn farm buildings, split-rail fences, goats, sheep, mules, cattle, and work horses create an atmosphere of early rural life. The farmhouse is now a museum that houses displays of farm implements, household goods, and a photographic exhibition.

The educational opportunities and facilities at Youth Station include classrooms, labs, a fishing pier, canoes with paddles and life preservers, day-hiking trails; aquatic, insect, geological, and weather stations for collections and observation; and resource management interpretation.

In addition to educational facilities, there are numerous special-interest recreational activity areas and scenic/historic points of interest in LBL. It is TVA's policy, as interpreted through LBL's multiple-use concept, that diverse recreational life-styles will coexist in the 170,000 acres. Radically opposed groups, such as horseback trail riders and off-road vehicle (ORV) enthusiasts, each have a sizeable area in which to "do their thing." LBL's policy of maintaining separate trails for horses, hikers, and motorized vehicles is the most sensible way I've ever heard to insure that everyone has a place to enjoy without interference.

ORV enthusiasts have 2,500 acres all to themselves in LBL. The Turkey Bay ORV Area just south of US-68 on the Kentucky Lake side is designated especially for motorcycles, four-wheel jeeps and trucks, and modified three-wheel "buggies." There are numerous roads through the unit, all full of ruts and mudholes to delight any four-wheeler. There are camping facilities on Turkey Creek Road, off the Trace (pit toilets, picnic tables, grills, and launching ramp), and two "staging areas" for ORVs. The Turkey Bay ORV Area is utilized extensively; it's the only Federally-owned land in Kentucky open to full off-road vehicle use.

Horseback riding enthusiasts also have 2,500 acres in which to ride to their hearts' content. Wranglers Camp in the Lick Creek Valley of Lake Barkley south of US-68 is laced with daisy-chain trails through wooded hills and open fields. Barn space and primitive camping facilities (chemical toilets only) are available free of charge on a first-come, first-served basis, even during club-sponsored trail rides. There are six trails in the Wranglers Camp, a total of twenty-six miles.

The following rules are in force:

1. Horses must be tethered far enough from trees to prevent damage to bark; use hitching posts.
2. Muck all stalls before leaving.
3. Horses must be under control at all times.
4. Don't litter trails.
5. Racing is prohibited on trails.
6. Riding is prohibited in planted fields, cemeteries, and posted areas.

The development of recreational facilities in LBL has not been limited to major projects. Two small facilities which draw a lot of visitor use are the 14-target field archery range, one mile east of Golden Pond headquarters off US-68, and a floating fishing pier at the Devil's Elbow Lake Access Area. The pier is 100 feet long and 8 feet wide, and is equipped with double railings for safety and ramps for the handicapped.

The return of buffalo (American bison) to the land they once roamed in great numbers is one of the interesting projects undertaken by TVA in LBL. Although the buffalo is usually associated with the western plains, small herds ranged from Georgia to the Hudson Bay and from the Appalachians to the Rockies. There is evidence that Daniel Boone observed buffalo during his early explorations into Kentucky in the 1770s.

The ancestral buffalo migrated to the North American continent from Asia crossing over the land bridge that connected the two continents during several periods of prehistory. At their peak, possibly before the discovery of America, it is thought that they may have numbered 60 to 70 million. The LBL herd that now roams a 200-acre pasture alongside the Trace near the former site of Model, Tennessee, began with 19 animals transplanted in 1969 from the Theodore Roosevelt National Memorial Park near Medora, North Dakota. Calves have increased the herd to its present numbers.

The American bison native to this region are of the woodland variety. Since buffalo in different sections of the country varied in size and color, it was believed there were three types: the larger, darker wood buffalo; the paler, smaller prairie form; and the still smaller mountain buffalo. Experts now generally agree that all American buffalo belong to the same species, *Bison bison*. The variations in appearance probably result from differences in living conditions.

Largest of the land animals in North America, the bison normally lives 15 to 20 years, but may live up to 40 years. Both the cows and the bulls have sharp, curved horns. Full growth, 2,000 pounds or more for a bull and 1,300 pounds for a cow, is usually reached in seven or eight years. A deceptively quick and agile animal, the buffalo can stop instantly, whirl, and gallop up to 35 mph over rough terrain. Buffalo need little care since they are extremely hardy. They can survive extreme weather conditions where other large animals would perish, and are even known to have given birth during blizzards. Buffalo are generally docile, but can be very unpredictable. Sometimes humans can walk within a few feet of the animals before they will bother to move; at another time the same behavior may cause the beast to charge.

Breeding season occurs in July and August. The gestation period for buffalo varies from 270 to 285 days, with most young being born in May. Usually, a cow will give birth to a single calf, occasionally to twins. Newborn calves show no sign of the hump trademark until they reach about two months.

In spring, to hasten the shedding of their heavy winter coats and possibly relieve their itching skin, the buffalo rub against large stones and trees. Travelers in the 1880s wrote of highly polished stones and rubbing trees with the bark stripped six to seven feet above the ground. Without the protection of their coats, the animals are especially vulnerable to the attacks of insects in the summer. To escape their tormentors, the buffalo wallow in dust or sand. Early travelers on the Plains wrote of buffalo wallows a foot or more deep and 15 feet across.

Under the climatic conditions in this part of the country, an adult buffalo requires four acres of land. In order to prevent overgrazing and possible parasite infestation of the pasture, it is necessary to practice population control. Since reproduction capacity of the herd averages 10 to 16 animals per year, the herd must be reduced by this number each winter. Some of the animals are sold to state parks for the purpose of resale to park restaurants. The remaining buffalo are retained for the dining rooms at Brandon Springs Group Camp and the Youth Station in Land Between the Lakes.

The design, development, and construction of an 1850s living history farm across the Trace from the Buffalo Range was completed in 1978, unveiling a new concept in the study of agriculture in the nineteenth century. Typical of the early subsistence family farming operations, the 60-acre rural homestead farm is a regional research and training center for pioneer architecture and agricultural living history programs. It provides educational and recreational opportunities for visitors, organized groups, and higher education classes.

Interpretation of the early settlement period and the sociocultural and economic dynamics of early farming is stressed, along with study of nineteenth century agricultural practices, household crafts, and cottage industries common to the region between the rivers. In the future, the farm will serve as a center for workshop programs for apprentice craftsmen interested in restoration and reconstruction skills, and as a study area for historical architects and cultural interpreters. The 1850s living history farm is located east of the Trace in the Pryor Creek Valley in Stewart County, Tennessee. The complex is a two-generation family farm with two homesteads and 14 "outbuildings" relocated or reconstructed from rough-hewn timbers recovered during TVA's inventory of purchased lands prior to the area's official opening.

The Apollo Project is a youth-oriented program which stresses physical, mental, and educational challenges to help college-age students gain confidence in their abilities. The project is conducted under the auspices of the Upward Bound program at Murray State University in nearby Murray, Kentucky. The imaginative program was designed to increase self-confidence and teach outdoor living and survival skills to prospective teachers. The on-site activities include compass and map reading, spelunking, sailing, canoeing, field and aquatic biology, rappelling and rock climbing, social sciences, and astronomy. The Apollo Project conducts its programs in the backcountry areas of LBL, the Pond Hollow Bivouac Area and the Colson Hollow Group Camp.

Another leadership-inspiring program, the BSA High Adventure Camp for teenagers and young adults, is conducted at the BSA High Adventure Area on the Shaw Branch of Lake Barkley. The water-oriented base camp is equipped to handle a full scope of learning experiences in the outdoors—trips on pontoon boats, sailing, canoeing, backpacking, camping skills, cooking, and rappelling. The High Adventure Camp in LBL is one of seven such Boy Scout bases throughout the United States. The 250-acre base camp is on the Crooked Creek embayment of Lake Barkley.

Educational opportunities at LBL are not limited to the special areas and programs mentioned thus far. Perhaps the greatest potential for learning comes from the many special activities held throughout the year. Some are annual events which grow more popular each year, while others are special one-time programs which draw participants from all parts of the country—lecture and slide presentations, craft exhibitions, recreational management seminars, and resource symposia. The list of special activities is astounding and serves to underline the rich culture of the region which has been revived in part through TVA's eagerness to sponsor and provide facilities for so many groups.

One of the most popular annual events is the Eagle Weekend held each February. The three-day weekend is devoted to study, lectures, and a census count of bald and golden eagles in LBL. Field excursions guided by noted ornithologists, nature photographers, and environmental educators highlight the weekend. The activities are limited to 200 registrants. Co-sponsored by the Kentucky Department of Parks and LBL, the package includes overnight accommodations and meals at either Kentucky Dam Village, Kenlake, or Lake Barkley State Resort Park, all within an easy 10-minute drive of TVA's national demonstration area.

The symbol of America's majesty, the bald eagle (genus *Haliaeetus*) and his cousin the golden eagle (*Aquila chrysaetos canadensis*) range throughout North America. The birds which winter in LBL are from populations centered in the Mississippi Flyway, a waterfowl migratory route. Eagles once nested in Kentucky but are now transient visitors in the winter. Although primarily fish eaters, the eagles also will take waterfowl, and biologists agree that the number of eagles migrating southward from their nesting areas in Wisconsin, Michigan, Minnesota, and Canada is often directly proportionate to weather conditions in the Great Lakes region. When severe cold weather causes the river to freeze over, the eagles, like ducks and geese, are forced southward along open water routes. The isolated back bays and inlets of Kentucky Lake and Lake Barkley are natural hangouts for the giant birds of prey. Although populations of eagles can vary from year to year, winter-time activity on the lakes and weather conditions up north may be critical reasons that fewer birds of the so-called Northern subspecies have been sighted in recent years. Eagles are extremely secretive birds who don't like human activity in their immediate environs. Furthermore, because of the close proximity of several large national waterfowl refuges, many eagles simply never wander into LBL.

The largest number of eagles ever sighted in LBL in the annual census was 43 in 1970.

There have been some encouraging recent developments relating to eagles in LBL, however. A couple of years back a pair of mature bald eagles was spotted building a nest on the Taylor and Jake Fork embayments of Lake Barkley. The last active nesting in Kentucky had occurred more than 20 years ago. Although the birds never successfully hatched young from the nest, it was nonetheless encouraging. Duncan and Smith bays of Kentucky Lake are other embayments set aside for eagles to rest, feed, roost, and escape the disturbances of man. It is hoped that nesting will someday take place in these refuges off limits to winter-time boating, fishing, and waterfowl hunting.

Other special weekends held annually are the Rivers Workshop, where spinning, weaving, stitchery, woodworking, whittling, chair-caning, river dances, and folk ballads are demonstrated; the Archaeology Weekend, when both amateur and professional archaeologists lead field trips to prehistoric Indian sites along flood plains, ridges, and valleys within LBL; National Hunting and Fishing Day Observances (September), when seminars are conducted on bow-hunting, trotlining, turkey calling, and other such outdoor skills; Piney Campers Fair, a regional outdoor arts and crafts show in September which features live music, square dancing, children's puppet shows, and literally hundreds of other goings-on; the Great Escape Weekend in September, with recreational activities to meet every taste— horseback riding, archery, canoeing, backpacking, rappelling, nature photography seminars, and orientation and nature walks; Amateur Bicycling, ABLA-sanctioned 25-mile bicycle races for Olympic-class cyclists in April; Civil War Weekend, the annual Blue-Gray Affair Weekend devoted to retracing the steps of U. S. Grant as he took Confederate-held Ft. Henry and Ft. Donelson in 1862; Statewide Bowfishing Tournament, in May, a shoot for carp, buffalofish, and gar; Wilderness Weekend, in October, a primer on survival in the style of mountain men, with demonstrations of primitive fire-making, the gathering and preparation of wild foods, shelter-building, muzzleloading rifle-shooting, and tanning; "Between the Rivers Homecoming," a "family" reunion held each August for those displaced by the TVA project; and the Rushing Creek Summer Fest in July, a good old-fashioned country get-together with sack races, softball, flea market, and tent dance.

The incredible number of special one-time events held in recent years prohibits listing them all, but many will no doubt be held again. LBL publishes *Preview*, a seasonal calendar of events, to inform prospective visitors of upcoming special activities. As an overview, these events have included such activities as junior fishing rodeos, campfire yarn spinning (telling tall tales), wildflower slide shows and walks, insect collection field trips, birdlife films, iron-era historical profiles, stream ecology field trips, exhibitions on Southern cultural heritage, pioneer crafts workshops, hayride and cookout, nocturnal discovery walk, fallow deer life history seminars, Life Science Career Day, and junior naturalist programs to increase youngsters' awareness of the natural environment. For additional information write TVA, Land Between the Lakes, Golden Pond, Kentucky, 42231, or telephone (502) 924-5602.

Kentucky Streams and Lakes

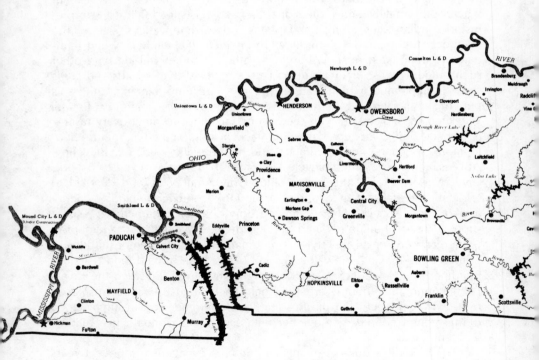

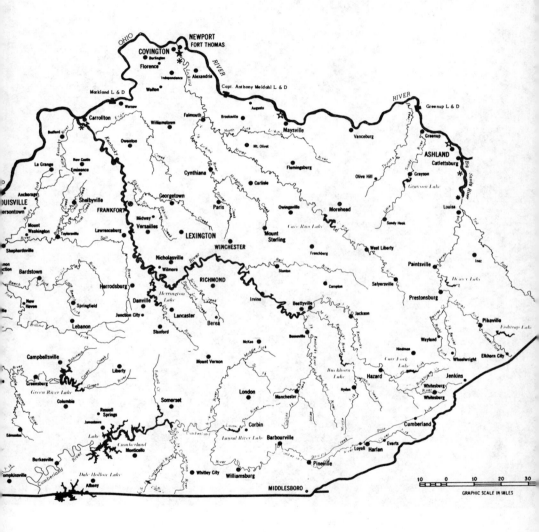

Nolin River Lake. Photograph by U.S. Army Corps of Engineers.

4
Major Lakes
Their Parks, Marinas, and
Campgrounds

Introduction

Open water, miles of secluded shoreline, sun, wind, and the lure of the deep—these are just some of the reasons for the immense popularity of Kentucky's major lakes. Fishing, water skiing, sailing, power-boating, houseboating, scuba diving, and swimming are enjoyed by millions of persons each year, especially during the summer months.

It's only in the last 35 years that these impoundments have entered the recreational scene. Kentucky's first major impoundment, Dale Hollow Lake, was completed in 1943. A year later, the Tennessee Valley Authority (TVA) finished Kentucky Lake. Lake Cumberland was the only major lake built in the 1950s, but the sixties were a decade of unparalleled growth in the number of major impoundments: Rough River Lake, 1961; Nolin River Lake, 1963; Barren River Lake, 1964; Lake Barkley, 1966; and Green River Lake, 1969. Both Laurel River Lake and Cave Run Lake were completed in 1974. Kentucky Lake is generally thought to be the Commonwealth's largest lake (in length and surface acres), although in actuality only 49,511 of its 160,300 acres are in Kentucky. Kentucky's largest impoundement is, therefore, 50,250-acre Lake Cumberland. Lake Barkley is the third largest with 42,020 acres. For reasons of organization, all impoundments of more than 5,000 surface acres are classified as major lakes and discussed in this chapter.

Nine of these major impoundments were built by the U.S. Army Corps of Engineers, one by the Tennessee Valley Authority (TVA). The Flood Control Act of 1938 was the primary piece of legislation giving the U.S. Army Corps of Engineers the jurisdiction to build the impoundments for the purposes of flood control, generation of hydroelectric power, outdoor recreation, and improved inland navigation.

The U.S. Army Corps of Engineers, through its district offices in Louisville, Kentucky, Nashville, Tennessee, and Huntington, West Virginia, oversees the planning, development, and, in most cases, management of recreational facilities on the lakes it builds. Through lease agreements, private concessionaires are permitted to locate facilities on Federally-owned lands. The recreational facilities at two of the Corps-built lakes in Kentucky—Cave Run Lake and Laurel River Lake—are the responsibility of the United States Forest Service, as the lakes are located in Daniel Boone National Forest. The Tennessee Valley Authority issues permits for the development of all recreational facilities on Federally-owned lands on Kentucky Lake.

Kentucky's lakes are patrolled by officers of the Division of Water Enforcement, Kentucky Department of Transportation, Frankfort, Kentucky, 40601. Boaters can receive a copy of the Boating and Safety Guide by writing the agency. Registration requirements (fees and registration numbering), accident reporting, regulations on life preservers, and boat lighting, signaling, and equipment requirements are covered in this free brochure.

The state parks, state-operated and privately-owned campgrounds, and marinas on each lake are listed in an effort to organize the facilities so that visitors have an overall picture of what is available.

Houseboating is a wonderful way to spend time on the lake. The relaxing pace and the inherent freedom of mobility in an atmosphere of self-contained luxury have contributed to an increase in the popularity of houseboating in recent years. In fact, marinas at eight major lakes in Kentucky have at least one rental houseboat. At Lake Cumberland, Lake Barkley, and Kentucky Lake, many docks have small fleets of rental boats for overnight, weekend, "middle of the week," or week-long cruises. Some marinas offer special off-season rates.

Since virtually everything needed is onboard, the houseboat can be more private than traditional lodge accommodations. A houseboat is your own swimming and fishing dock, sun deck, dining room, and motel bed—your "floating home away from home." On the larger lakes there are plenty of secluded coves in which to get away from it all.

Whenever available, the rental costs, lengths of the houseboats, and accommodation capacity will be included in the information for each marina that rents houseboats. Even though the cost for a houseboat seems high (almost always you pay for gas as well, and advance deposits are often required), the actual cost, when broken down on a cost-per-person basis, is usually less that the cost of lodge accommodations, restaurant meals, and ski/fishing boat rentals for a family of four.

For those who think that running a houseboat requires special skill, it may come as a suprise that anyone who can "skipper" an automobile can handle a houseboat. The dock proprietor will show you how to control the throttle and steering and give you a few tips on docking, the most difficult houseboating maneuver.

Most houseboats are not equipped with 110-volt current, so don't plan on bringing electrical appliances. Most, though, have gas stoves and ice boxes or refrigerators. Usually, tableware and linens are provided. Some of the fanciest houseboats even have gas grills for cooking out. The following is a suggested list of additional items you may want to bring along: flashlight, portable radio or tape player, fishing tackle, first aid kit, beer or liquor (all of the major lakes in Kentucky are in dry territory), groceries, garbage bags, cards and games, camera, suntan lotion and ointment for treatment of sunburn, sweaters (nights on the lake get cool even in the summer), life preservers and ski vests, plenty of towels, coolers with block ice, gas lanterns, and charcoal.

Dale Hollow Lake

Completed in 1943 as one of the initial projects undertaken by the U.S. Army Corp of Engineers after passage of the Flood Control Act of 1938, Dale Hollow Lake was impounded from the Obey River, a tributary of the Cumberland. Straddling the Tennessee-Kentucky boundary, the 35,000-acre lake (at seasonal pool) lies in Clinton and Cumberland counties, Kentucky, and Clay and Pickett counties, Tennessee. Sulphur, Illwill, Fanny's, and Wolf River, all to the southeast of Albany, are the major embayments in the Kentucky portion of the lake. The major portion of the lake and its 620 miles of shorelines is in Tennessee. The Kentucky portion of the lake is accessible via highways Ky-738, Ky-485, and Ky-61.

Dale Hollow Lake State Park and marina at Frogue, Kentucky, 12 miles south of Burkesville via Ky-61, Ky-449, and Ky-1206, was scheduled to open April 1, 1978. The 3,497-acre park on the Sulphur Creek embayment has a swimming pool free to campers at the park, with an admission charge for day-use visitors; two large playgrounds; recreational center (gamerooms); and a huge campground. All 144 sites have both water and electrical hookups. Drinking water, two RV dump stations, three bathhouses with showers and flush toilets, and a coin laundry are included in the plans for facilities and services. A state-operated marina will be located at the park. Gas, boat launching ramp, tackle and live bait, fish cleaning facilities, freezer space, and 70 uncovered slips will be available. A restaurant that seats 100 persons and features a fast-food walk-up service will be built on the marina. The park and marina will be open seasonally, from April 1 to October 31. Mailing address: Dale Hollow Lake State Park, Bow, Kentucky, 42714. Telephone: (505) 433-7431.

There are four privately-owned marinas on the Kentucky waters of Dale Hollow Lake. Hendricks Creek Resort is west of the state park on Ky-61, five miles south of Littrell, Kentucky. Eight rental housekeeping cottages which sleep up to six persons each are available. There is no restaurant at the resort, but there is a large grocery store. Sandwiches, soft drinks, and snacks are available at the marina, which has rental aluminum fishing boats, outboard motors, and houseboats. Other facilities include both covered and open rental slips, tackle, live bait, ice, fish cleaning facilities, and boat launching ramp. Mailing address: Hendricks Creek Resort, Box 37, Burkesville, Kentucky, 42717. Telephone: (502) 433-5353.

The other point of recreational interest west of the state park is the Sulphur Creek Marina and Dale Hollow KOA Complex, six and one-half miles south of Burkesville on Ky-61, then two and one-half miles south on Ky-485. The campground, open seasonally from March 1 to November 1, has 44 drive-through sites with electrical and water hookups, drinking water, showers, flush toilets, dumping station, grocery, lounge, ice dumping station, swimming beach, boat tieup, gas, picnic tables, and grills. Mailing address: Dale Hollow KOA, Kettle, Kentucky, 42752. Telephone (502) 433-7200.

The adjacent Sulphur Creek Marina (telephone: (502) 433-7272), has 40- and 57-foot rental houseboats, fishing boats and outboards, 16-foot ski boats, snack bar, 30 covered slips, and fishing guide service available on request. The marina is open daily from 6 a.m. to 8 p.m., year-round. Tackle and live bait (meal worms, crickets, nightcrawlers, and minnows) may be purchased at the marina.

East of the state park on Ky-553 is the Wisdom Creek Resort, a marina and housekeeping cottage complex open year-round, 24 hours a day. There are 28 rental cabins; most sleep 6, but one larger cottage sleeps 10. There's a restaurant on the premises and a campground with 21 sites, most with electrical hookups, and a bathhouse with showers and flush toilets. The bathhouse closes when severe cold sets in. Fishermen have a cleaning area and limited storage in two ice houses. Tackle and bait supplies, ice, and Kentucky and Tennessee licenses are sold. Aluminum boats, outboards, and houseboats are available for rental. Mailing address: Wisdom Creek Resort, Route #2, Albany, Kentucky, 42602. Telephone: (606) 387-5821.

Six miles west of Albany on Ky-738 is the Wolf River Dock, motel, and campground. The campground and restaurant are open March 15 to November 1, weather permitting. There are 15 housekeeping cottages for occupancy by up to eight persons, and an eight-unit motel. Additional facilities include 65 camping sites with varying facilities in the campground, drinking water, flush toilets, grocery, ice, bottled gas, picnic tables and grills, and showers. Open 24 hours a day year-round, the marina has rental 14-foot fishing boats, outboards, and pontoon boats; live bait, artificial lures, and tackle (at grocery); fish cleaning area and freezer space; snack bar; and covered and open slips. Mailing address: Wolf River Dock, Route #2, Albany, Kentucky, 42602. Telephone: (606) 387-5841.

Cave Run Lake

Impounded in 1973, Cave Run Lake promises to be one of the most successful outdoor recreational facilities in Kentucky. Built by the Huntsville (West Virginia) District of the U.S. Army Corps of Engineers, the 8,200-acre lake (at seasonal pool) lies southwest of Morehead, Kentucky, in the northernmost district of Daniel Boone National Forest in Menifee, Morgan, Bath, and Rowan counties at the edge of the Cumberland Plateau.

Cave Run Lake is accessible via highways Interstate-64, Ky-519, Ky-801, US-60, Ky-211, US-460, Ky-36, Ky-1274, and Ky-985, and Forest Service Roads 918, 1017, and 129. Construction, management, and maintenance of the lake's campground, picnic areas, and sanitary facilities are the responsibility of the National Forest Service. The lake's two marinas are operated on Federally-owned land through a lease agreement. Both have boat launching ramps. The larger of the two marinas on Cave Run Lake is at Scott Creek, on the main lake just up from the dam, two miles east of Farmers, Kentucky, off Ky-801. Open year-round, 16 hours a day, the 200-slip marina has a grocery store and restaurant in addition to tackle, water skiing and boating accessories, and live bait sales. The restaurant is open 12 hours a day in the off-season on Saturdays and Sundays only, 16 hours a day every day seasonally. Cushions and life preservers are available for rental, as are 14-foot aluminum boats with 9.9 horsepower outboards and houseboats from 26 to 50 feet. The 50-footers sleep 10 persons and rent for $100 a day plus fuel. Mailing address: Cave Run Marina, Morehead, Kentucky, 40351. Telephone: (606) 784-9666.

A satellite marina operated by the same concessionaire, the Longbow Marina, five miles north of Frenchburg off Ky-1274, has 50 slips, all covered except those for houseboats. These is no restaurant at the Longbow Marina, but hot sandwiches, snacks, and grocery items are available. The Longbow Marina is open at the same times as the Scott Creek facility and has rental fishing boats and live bait and artificial tackle for sale. There's no telephone at the dock.

The only campground on the lake is at the Twin Knobs Recreation Area, five and one-half miles southeast of Farmers, via Ky-801, then one and one-half miles south (turn right) on FS Road 1017. The campground, open from April 1 to October 31, has a picnic grounds, two boat launching ramps (the one outside the campground also closes October 31), drinking water, flush toilets, showers, swimming beach, bathhouses, and 147 campsites. There are 81 single camping units and 33 doubles for tents or RVs under 32 feet.

Six other boat launching ramps, all open year-round, are: Twentysix, east of Ezel, Kentucky, off US-460 in Morgan County on Ky-985, providing good access to the extreme headwaters of the lake; Bangor, off Ky-519, southeast of Morehead; Poppin Rock, north of the Bangor site, also off Ky-519; Claylick, on Ky-1274 off Ky-519, southeast of Morehead; Warix Run, east of Farmers on Ky-801, approximately three miles by road from the dam; and Leatherwood, south of Farmers via US-60 and Ky-211 and east on FS Road 129. Two primitive campgrounds are under development, one at Poppin Rock, the other at Claylick. At this writing there are no facilities, but both are open to boat access camp. Future development is also planned at Zilpo, off Ky-211 on FS Road 918 (construction beginning 1979), and at Caney, off Ky-211. Picnic facilities are now available at the dam on Ky-826 off US-60 adjacent to the Kentucky Department of Fish and Wildlife Resources Minor Clark Fish Hatchery.

Nolin River Lake

Because of its proximity to Mammoth Cave National Park and the scenic, woodland character of the region, Nolin River Lake is a favorite with Louisvillians. The 5,800-acre lake (at seasonal pool) was built in south central Kentucky where Edmonson, Grayson, and Hart counties meet, an hour and a half south of Louisville. This area of the state has a surprisingly small population, beautiful countryside, interesting old-fashioned country stores on many of the county backroads, and great fishing, hunting, and camping.

Accessible via Interstate-65 and Ky-88 from Munfordville, and Ky-259, Ky-728, and Ky-88 from Leitchfield, the 39-mile-long lake was impounded from the Nolin River, a tributary to the Green River. Construction on the project began in 1959 and was completed in March of 1963. The U.S. Army Corps of Engineers owns all the land around the reservoir and private businesses lease the right to build facilities. There are two public marinas on the lake, four Corps-operated campgrounds, two Corps-operated day-use areas, and two privately-owned campgrounds. The address for the U.S. Army Corps of Engineers office at Nolin River Lake is Brownsville, Kentucky, 42210; telephone: (502) 286-4813.

Iberia Site, 11 miles south of Clarkson on Ky-88 on the Rock Creek embayment, and the Dam Site, two miles southeast of Bee Springs on Ky-728, are day-use areas with rest rooms, boat ramps, and parking. Picnic grounds and drinking water are also available at the Dam Site. The four Corps-operated campgrounds are Brier Creek, Dog Creek, Moutadier, and Wax. The Brier Creek Site is eight miles east of Bee Springs, Kentucky, and is reached via Ky-259, Ky-728, and Ky-1827. Open free of charge year-round, the campground has 100 sites for tents and RVs, with pit toilets, drinking water, and picnic tables. The Dog Creek Site, up the lake and reached by automobile via Ky-728 and Ky-1015 from the dam, is also a limited facility, open year-round free to the public. There are 25 sites for tents or RVs, drinking water, pit toilets, and picnic tables.

The two largest and most complete facilities on the lake are at Wax and Moutadier. At the Wax site, 15 miles south of Clarkson on Ky-88, the Corps-operated campground is open year-round, as are the privately-owned marina and motel. The recreational complex includes a restaurant open seasonally, 44 sites for tents or RVs, drinking water, flush toilets, showers, picnic tables, and boat launching ramp. The Wax Marina, open 24 hours a day, has 96 rental slips, including 52 covered, 30 uncovered, and 14 especially for houseboats. Fourteen-foot aluminum fishing boats and 7½-horsepower outboard motors, gas, ice, bait (crickets, red worms, and minnows), and artificial tackle are available. In addition to the campground, there is a 12-unit motel with both single and double occupancy rooms. Mailing address: Wax Boat Dock, Wax, Kentucky, 42787. Telephone: (502) 242-7205.

Moutadier is four miles north of Bee Springs, Kentucky, off Ky-259, and it too has a Corps-operated campground within walking distance of the marina. Open 24 hours a day during the summer and 6:00 a.m. to 10:00 p.m. the rest of the year, the marina has a whopping 300 slips for overnight as well as monthly and yearly rental. Bait—red worms, minnows, and nightcrawlers—and tackle, 14-foot fishing boats, 7½-horsepower motors, pontoon boats, lockers, a place to clean fish, and freezer space are available. The 30-acre recreational complex includes five one-bedroom and four two-bedroom redwood cottages (complete housekeeping units with pots, pans, and linens) and a grocery store that sells delicatessen sandwiches. Mailing address: Moutadier Boat Dock, Bee Springs, Kentucky, 42207. Telephone: (502) 286-4069.

The two privately-owned campgrounds on Nolin River Lake are Greensward, six and one-half miles south of Leitchfield on Ky-259, then one and one-half miles east on Ky-226 and three miles on Ky-88; and Ponderosa Fishing Camp, 12 miles south of Clarkson via Ky-88 and Ky-889. Greensward is open April 1 to November 30 and has 15 sites for tents only, with drinking water, grocery, ice, playground, picnic tables and shelters, and beach nearby. Lean-tos and tree houses can also be rented as overnight accommodations. Mailing address: Greensward, Route #2, Clarkson, Kentucky, 42726. Telephone: (502) 242-7771.

Ponderosa Fishing Camp, six miles south of Peonia, Kentucky, via Ky-88 and Ky-889, is open April 1 to October 31 and has 62 sites for tents and RVs, some with water, electrical, and sewer hookups. The grocery, restaurant, and six-unit motel are also open seasonally. Drinking water, playground, pit toilets, and ice are also available. Aluminum fishing boats can be rented at the fishing camp and nearby at Conolway Bait House. A petition for the construction of a marina has been submitted to the Corps of Engineers. Mailing address: Ponderosa Fishing Camp, Route #2, Box 117, Clarkson, Kentucky, 42726. Telephone: (502) 242-7215.

Barren River Lake

In the late eighteenth century, "longhunters" hacked out the Cumberland Trace through a region of south central Kentucky called "The Barrens," a hunting ground of the Cherokee Indians. Tradition says the area got its name because of the periodic burning over of the vegetation to attract deer, elk, and buffalo, which came to graze on the fresh, new shoots the practice encouraged.

Today the rolling countryside is patchworked with farms and small towns and is the site of Kentucky's newest state-operated vacation resort— Barren River Lake State Resort Park, 13 miles south of Glasgow on US-31E, at Lucas, Kentucky. A sprawling expanse of wood, glass, and sandstone molded into sharp contemporary lines, the lodge has 50 guest rooms on three levels that command lake views. The lounge, dominated by a great stone fireplace, has an upstairs loft designed for reading or quiet conversation. The main dining room, which seats 250, overlooks the lake. Other facilities at the lodge include an arts and crafts gift shop, a coffee shop, recreation room, two private dining rooms, and a convention and meeting room.

Each guest room is furnished with extra-long double beds, wall-to-wall carpeting, television, telephone, and all-season climate control. In addition to lodge accommodations, there are 12 two-bedroom executive cottages in the woods on nearby Lewis Hill. Accomodations are open year-round.

The 1,799-acre park, completed in 1969, is on the southern shore of 10,000-acre Barren River Lake. A beach area with beach house and snack bar is located north of the lodge. Picnic grounds, riding stables, a nine-hole golf course and pro shop, cottages, and marina are within walking distance.

The park's campground has 101 sites for either tents or RVs, all equipped with electrical hookups. The facilities and services include: drinking water, showers, flush toilets, dumping station, ice, coin laundry, picnic tables, and nearby shelter. Mailing address: Barren River Lake State Resort Park, Lucas, Kentucky, 42156. Telephone: (502) 646-2151.

Barren River Lake is in Barren, Monroe, and Allen counties of south central Kentucky, about 20 miles north of the Kentucky-Tennessee border. It was impounded from the Barren River, a tributary of the Green River, and is the southernmost lake in the Louisville District of the U.S. Army Corps of Engineers. Completed in 1964, the lake offers excellent opportunities for boating, fishing, and other water-related recreation. The lake is accessible via highways US-31E, Ky-87, Ky-100, Ky-252, and numerous county roads.

The Corps manages six recreation/access points on the lake, four of which have campgrounds. The other two are primarily day-use areas. The largest of the Corps-operated sites is Bailey's Point on Ky-517, approximately three miles upstream from the dam off Ky-252, the main road between Scottsville and Haywood. The facility is open all year, and includes 98 sites for tents or RVs, flush toilets, dumping station, drinking water, and boat launching ramp. The Beaver Creek site, five miles south of Glasgow, Kentucky, then three miles west on Ky-252 to signs, is open all year and has 50 sites for tents or RVs. Drinking water, pit toilets, picnic tables, and boat launching ramp are available. The campground is located on a point separating the Skaggs Creek and Beaver Creek embayments.

The Narrows, a peninsula separating the main channel of the Barren River from the lower end of Beaver Creek, offers a commanding view of the widest parts of the lake and numerous islands, and is adjacent to the recreational facilities at Bailey's Point and Peninsula Marina. The Narrows is easily reached by boat from Bailey's Point or by car from Lucas, Kentucky, off US-31E, 15 miles south of Glasgow. Open all year, the campground has 56 sites for either tents or RVs; drinking water, boat launching ramp, pit toilets, and picnic tables are available at the site.

The Dam site campground, 10 miles north of Scottsville, then 7 miles west on Ky-252, overlooks the lake just above the dam. The 48 campsites for tents or RVs are located just below the dam beside the tailwaters, which offer excellent fishing opportunities. Drinking water, pit toilets, and picnic tables are available at the site. The campground is open year-round.

Brown's Ford site, a day-use area which provides access to the extreme headwaters of the lake, is 10 miles east of Scottsville on Ky-98. The facilities are limited to pit toilets, picnic tables, parking lot, and boat launching ramp. The other Corps-managed day-use area on the lake is the Austin site, 13 miles south of Glasgow, then 7 miles southeast on Ky-87 to Austin, Kentucky, and southward. Facilities include drinking water, boat launching ramp, parking lot, picnic area, and pit toilets. Overnight primitive camping is allowed although there are no developed campsites. The campgrounds are fee areas. Mailing address: U. S. Army Corps of Engineers, Route #2, Glasgow, Kentucky, 42141. Telephone: (502) 646-2055.

In addition to the Corps-managed recreation areas, there are two privately-owned campgrounds on Barren River Lake. Carver's Point, 12 miles south of Glasgow on US-31E, is open year-round with 22 sites for RVs (electrical hookups) and 10 sites without electricity for tents. Other facilities include showers, flush toilets, grocery, drinking water, ice, playground for kids, and dump station. Telephone: (502) 622-5100. Nearby is the Walnut Creek Marina and Campground, eight miles north of Scottsville, then two miles east on Ky-1855. The full-service facility is among the largest on the lake with 50 sites for tents or RVs, electricity, pit toilets, grocery, picnic tables and shelter, boat launching ramp, and marina which rents 14-foot aluminum boats with up to 10-horsepower outboards. The marina has a snack bar, complete artificial tackle sales, live bait (shiner minnows and nightcrawlers), and carp dough. There are 100 slips at the dock with rental plans for overnight, monthly, or yearly rates. The Walnut Creek Marina is run by the Allen County Fish and Wildlife Club. Telephone: (502) 622-5858.

The other two marinas on the lake, Adam's Boat Dock and Peninsula Marina, are state-operated through concessionaires. Adam's Boat Dock, located within walking distance of the lodge at Barren River Lake State Resort Park, is equipped for fuel sales; 20-foot pontoon boat rentals; ski-boat rentals, complete with skis and life vests; boat slip rentals (50 open and 40 covered); houseboat rentals; and boat and motor rentals for fishing (14-foot aluminum boats with 7½-horsepower motors). A launching ramp is nearby. Services for fishermen include bait and tackle sales and a fish-cleaning house with free freezer space. Telephone: (502) 646-2357.

The Peninsula Boat Dock, on Ky-252 two miles north of the dam, is open 24 hours a day every day during the summer and all night on Thursdays, Fridays, and Saturdays the rest of the year. The 100 slips are available for rental on a monthly or yearly basis only. A snack bar and live bait sales—minnows and red worms—are available. Boat rentals include 14-foot johnboats with 15-horsepower outboards and 35-foot pontoon boats. Telephone: (502) 646-2223.

Laurel River Lake

In the spring of 1974 Laurel River Lake reached its seasonal pool of 5,660 acres for the first time. The newest major reservoir in Kentucky, Laurel

River Lake was built in the 39,706-acre Laurel River Unit of Daniel Boone National Forest, an area that has had relatively little recreational use in the past compared with other units under U.S. Forest Service management.

Built by the Nashville District of the U. S. Army Corps of Engineers, the lake has 192 miles of shoreline, much of it rugged cliffs and plateauland clothed in mature pine and hardwood forests. Visitor use, formerly limited because of poor access to Laurel River, has increased with the new lake, which has opened up the region to a wider variety of recreational pastimes. Laurel River Lake is in the London District of Daniel Boone National Forest and is the boundary between Laurel and Whitley counties in the southeastern part of the state, accessible via Ky-192, Ky-312, US-25W, Ky-1277, and numerous Forest Service Roads, including 132, 62, 774, 758, and 558. The lake lies west of Corbin, Kentucky.

Administration, operation, and maintenance of recreational facilities at the lake are the responsibility of the Forest Service. Privately-owned campgrounds and marinas on Federally-owned lands are operated under lease agreements. Development of recreational facilities is still under way.

At present, there are two primitive campgrounds on the lake. The White Oak Campground, reached by boat or footpath, is open year-round. There are 36 primitive sites, drinking water, and pit toilets. The campground, on the northern end of the lake, is reached by a two-mile trail beginning at the parking lot of the Marsh Branch Boat Ramp off Ky-192 and FS Road 774, or by boating to the main lake from Marsh Branch. The campground is on the point. The Craigs Creek Campground is just two embayments down the lake from White Oak, accessible by automobile by continuing west on Ky-192 and turning left onto FS Road 62. There are 28 primitive campsites, drinking water, pit toilets, and a boat launching ramp. The Craigs Creek Campground is open seasonally; the ramp is open year-round.

Other lake access sites and their locations are: Marsh Branch boat ramp on FS Road 774 off Ky-192 north of Corbin; Laurel Bridge, at the extreme headwaters of the lake on Ky-312 one mile west of Corbin; Hightop, southwest of Corbin off US-25W; Flatwoods, west of Corbin on FS road 758; and Holly Bay, off Ky-1193 north of Laurel River Dam. A marina is currently under construction at the Holly Bay site and the ramp is closed. The marina is scheduled for completion in 1978 and will have covered slips, restaurant, live bait and tackle supplies, rental fishing boats and houseboats, and outboard motor repair service. All the boat launching ramp sites are normally open year-round. Mailing address: London Ranger District, Daniel Boone National Forest, Box G, London, Kentucky, 40741. Telephone: (606) 864-4163.

Rough River Lake

A favorite trading spot of the Shawnee in the 1700s, the Falls of the Rough was later the hub of a vast farm whose timberlands, water-powered mill, and large tracts of tillable soil required numerous hired hands. Eventually a small town—cabins, post office, general store—sprang up around the founding family's homeplace. Not surprisingly, the community was called Falls of Rough. Today, although the once-thriving settlement has disappeared, the charming countryside still beckons travelers. The Falls of the Rough is just a "Sunday drive" over shady backroads from Rough River Dam State Resort Park, the center of interest on 35-mile-long Rough River Lake, completed in 1961.

Rough River Lake is another of the impoundments built by the U. S. Army Corps of Engineers. The 5,100-acre lake (at seasonal pool) is 67 miles southwest of Louisville in Breckinridge, Hardin, and Grayson counties, and is accessible via highways Ky-79, Ky-259, Ky-110, and Ky-737. The Western Kentucky Parkway is 24 miles to the south of the dam-site at Leitchfield, reached via Ky-79 and Ky-54. There are five major developments on the lake managed by the Corps, and one parking/boat launching site at Everleigh, four miles north of Leitchfield off Ky-259.

Rough River Dam State Resort Park, open all year, is a 377-acre lakeside park with complete facilities: a 40-room lodge, 15 housekeeping cottages, dining room (200 seating capacity), swimming pool, beach with bathhouse complex, campgrounds, horseback riding stables, golf driving range and nine-hole par-3 course, archery range, boat dock, and playground. Open seasonally from April 1 to October 31, the campground has 50 sites with electrical hookups for either tents or RVs, showers, flush toilets, dumping station, grocery, picnic tables and shelter, coin laundry, and firewood. Recreation specialists conduct daily programs year-round. A cruise boat, *The Lady of the Lake,* makes daily excursions on the lake in season. A 2,500-foot paved air strip on the grounds qualifies Rough River Dam State Resort Park as one of Kentucky's so-called "fly-in" parks.

At the eastern end of the park in an embayment off the main channel is the boat dock, where aluminum fishing boats, outboard motors, pontoon boats, houseboats, fuel, sandwiches, soft drinks, bait, fishing licenses, tackle, boat cushions, and life preservers are available. There are 170 open slips at the Rough River Dam Site Resort Park Dock, some of which are reserved for visitors at the park who bring their own boats. A launching ramp is adjacent to the dock. Mailing address: Rough River Dam State Resort Park, Falls of Rough, Kentucky, 40119. Telephone: (502) 257-2311.

The five Corps-managed campgrounds on the lake are Axtel, Cave Creek, Laurel Branch, North Fork, and Peter Cave. The Axtel site near the junction of Ky-79 and Ky-259 has a parking area, boat launching ramp, picnic shelter, drinking water, showers, flush toilets, and 123 sites for either tents or RVs (no water or electrical hookups). Open year-round, the Axtel site campground is a fee area seasonally. Bronger's Boat Dock, the only boat dock on the lake besides the one at the state resort park, is located at Axtel, adjacent to the campground. There are 300 boat slips, and 28-foot pontoon boats and aluminum fishing boats and outboard motors are available for rental. Sandwiches and soft drinks, picnic supplies, boating accessories, gas, tackle, and bait may also be purchased. Mailing address: Bronger's Boat Dock, McDaniels, Kentucky, 40152. Telephone: (502) 257-9234.

The Cave Creek access site, two miles south of the state resort park off Ky-79, is open all year with no fee for camping. There are 100 unimproved sites at the lakeside campground, as well as drinking water, pit toilets, launching ramp, and picnic tables. The Laurel Branch site on Old Ky-110, which now dead ends in the lake, is a couple of miles south of Axtel (the junction of Ky-79 and Ky-259). Open year-round, the fee area has 72 sites for tents or RVs, all unimproved with no hookups. Facilities include pit toilets, drinking water, and boat launch.

The North Fork site is north of Axtel on highway Ky-259/79. Open year-round, this seasonal fee area has 69 sites for tents or RVs, showers, flush toilets, picnic tables and shelters, and boat launch. The last of the Corps-managed access points is Peter Cave on highway Ky-737, five miles north of Leitchfield. Although Peter Cave was designed primarily as a day-use area for boat launching, primitive camping is allowed when the other campgrounds are full. There are no specific campsites and no fee for overnight stays. Drinking water and pit toilets are available. Peter Cave is open all year. Mailing address: Rough River Lake, Resource Manager's Office, U. S. Army Corps of Engineers, Falls of Rough, Kentucky, 40119. Telephone: (502) 257-2061.

Green River Lake

Completed in 1969, 8,200-acre Green River Lake is located in south central Kentucky's Taylor, Adair, and Casey counties 55 miles downstream from the river's headwaters north of Liberty, Kentucky. The 25-mile-long lake has 147 miles of shoreline, 32,000 acres of which are undeveloped woodlands. Green River Lake was built and is managed by the Louisville District of the U. S. Army Corps of Engineers.

Green River Lake lies to the east of highway Ky-55 between the cities of Campbellsville and Columbia. The 141-foot dirt and rock-fill dam is approximately five miles north of the junction of highways Ky-565 and Ky-55. An interpretive center which outlines the area's natural history, Indian cultures, settlement, geology, and the mission and scope of the U. S. Army Corps is located at the dam site, as are restrooms, drinking water, picnic grounds, and a boat launching ramp, the closest access point to the main lake.

The Corps manages two other lakeside access points, Holmes Bend and Pike Ridge. The Corps has also secured sites at Butler and White Oak creeks for future development as visitor use dictates. No timetable has been set for construction of these facilities.

The Holmes Bend site is best reached via Ky-551 on Holmes Bend Road north of Columbia. Open from April 1 to October 31, with charges for camping between May 24 and September 2, the site features 225 sites for tents or RVs, 100 of which are unimproved. Electrical hookups, showers, drinking water, flush toilets, picnic area, grills, dumping station, swimming beach on lake (no lifeguard), and general store are located at the site. Houseboat and pontoon boat rentals, launching ramp, aluminum boat and outboard motor rentals, tackle, bait, ice, snack bar, and fuel are available at the dock near the campground. Mailing address: Holmes Bend Dock, Route #1, Columbia, Kentucky, 42728. Telephone: (502) 384-4425.

The Pike Ridge site is three miles east of Campbellsville on Ky-70, then three miles southeast on Ky-76. Open all year, the campground has pit toilets, launching ramp, drinking water, and 50 unimproved sites for either RVs or tents. Mailing address: U. S. Army Corps of Engineers, Route #5. Campbellsville, Kentucky, 42718. Telephone (502) 465-4463.

Green River Lake State Park, under development, is located at the Lone Valley access site, six miles south of Campbellsville, right off Ky-55. The 1,400-acre park, whose master plan calls for the construction of an 18-hole golf course, hiking trails, horseback riding stables, and possible lodge accommodations if funds are available, has limited facilities at present. The 20-acre campground is open all year and has 94 campsites for either tents or RVs. The park's services and facilities include electrical and water hookups, drinking water, showers, flush toilets, 250 picnic tables, grills, firewood, and two beaches (open seasonally)—one for the park's campers, the other for the general public (both complete with lifeguards and buoy lines). Mailing address: Green River Lake State Park, Campbellsville, Kentucky, 42718. Telephone: (502) 465-8255.

State-owned and privately managed, the Green River Marina near the state park is a fully-equipped marina open 24 hours a day, year-round. Live bait (minnows, crickets, and red worms) and cut bait are available, as well as rental aluminum boats and outboard motors, pontoon boats, and fishing guides. The marina restaurant specializes in breakfast and short orders.

The Green River KOA campground is less than two miles away, south of the dock overlooking the lake off Ky-55. The facilities and services include 100 sites with water and electrical hookups, rental trailers, showers, flush toilets, dumping station, coin laundry, ice, grocery, picnic tables, grills, firewood, playgrounds, and swimming pool. Reservations are accepted. Mailing address: Green River KOA, Route #5, Campbellsville, Kentucky, 42718. Telephone: (502) 465-3916.

The Smith River access site has a dock and campground, both operated by Taylor County. The adjacent facilities are fully equipped. Reached via highway Ky-70 from Campbellsville, then three miles on Ky-372, the recreational complex is the largest on the lake. Open March 1 to December 1, the campground has 100 sites with electrical hookups for tents or RVs. The services and facilities of the campground include showers, flush toilets, dumping station, grocery, ice, bottle gas, coin laundry, picnic tables, grills, and firewood. Reservations are accepted. Mailing address: Taylor County Campground, Box 131, Campbellsville, Kentucky, 42718. Telephone: (502) 465-7710. The Taylor County Boat Dock, destroyed by the 1974 tornado which ravished central Kentucky, has been rebuilt to its original size, with 50 covered and open slips, tackle shop (the largest on the lake), restaurant, boating and water skiing supplies, boat cushion and life preserver rental, and ski boat, pontoon boat, and fishing boat rentals, as well as live bait and fuel. The dock, open 24 hours a day year-round, is three miles east of Campbellsville on Ky-382. Mailing address: Taylor County Boat Dock, Box 282, Campbellsville, Kentucky, 42718. Telephone: (502) 465-3412.

Lake Cumberland

Lake Cumberland extends westward from Daniel Boone National Forest across Whitley, Laurel, Pulaski, Wayne, Russell, and Clinton counties in south central Kentucky. Steep rock cliffs border the headwaters in fjord-like grandeur. West of Mill Springs the lake widens; its serpentine path contours the forested hills of the Cumberland Plateau. At sunset, the azure waters glisten, highlighting rocky islands, once mountaintops, which jut up from the cool depths.

Lake Cumberland, the largest of Kentucky's 10 major impoundments (50,250 acres), is fed by mountain rivers and creeks and hundreds of springs which help keep the lake cool and clear. Dense woodlands are the backdrop for the 1,255 miles of rocky shoreline.

One of Kentucky's foremost recreational areas, Lake Cumberland is a prime area for water skiing, sailing, houseboating, fishing, lakefront camping, powerboating, and swimming. And there's plenty of room for everybody to find an embayment all to himself.

Lake Cumberland has been tremendously popular since its impoundment in 1952. Though extensively developed, the lake has lost none of its rugged character, because the marinas, fishing camps, and campgrounds are well spaced throughout the 101-mile-long lake.

Lake Cumberland is accessible from the north by the Cumberland Parkway via a number of two-lane roads, mainly Ky-92, US-127, Ky-196, Ky-76, Ky-761, Ky-80, and US-27. The southern shore of the lake is best reached via Ky-90 from Burnside, near the headwaters, and Monticello on Ky-1275, Ky-789, Ky-9, Ky-1546, and Ky-734. Lake Cumberland was built by the Nashville District of the U. S. Army Corps of Engineers. All Corps-managed campgrounds on Lake Cumberland are open seasonally from April 1 to November 1, although they may open or close earlier without notice, depending on the weather. The address of the lake's management office is Route 8, Box 173T, Somerset, Kentucky, 42501. Telephone: (606) 679-6337.

There are two state-operated parks on Lake Cumberland. The larger of the two, Lake Cumberland State Resort Park, is one of the showplaces of the Kentucky State Park System. The 3,000-acre peninsular park overlooking Pumpkin Creek and the main lake is approximately 14 miles southwest of Jamestown off Highway US-127 on Ky-1370. Open all year, the full-facilities park has two lodges—Lure Lodge with 48 rooms, each with two double beds, and Pumpkin Creek Lodge with 15 rooms, each with one double bed. All rooms have telephone, television, climate control, and tile bath with tub and shower. Both one-bedroom and two-bedroom rental housekeeping cottages are available. Ten of the larger ones are special "wildwood cottages" with living/dining room, kitchen, bath, fireplace, porch deck, telephone, color television, electric heat, and air conditioning. Tableware, cooking utensils, and linens are furnished in all cottages. The dining room in Lure Lodge seats 160 and is open for breakfast from 7:00 to 10:30 a.m., lunch from 11:30 a.m. to 2:30 p.m., and dinner from 5:30 to 9:00 p.m.

A gift shop, meeting room, hospitality hall (for groups up to 500 persons), recreation room (with billiards, cards, checkers, chess, table tennis, and foosball), and special accommodations for handicapped persons are included in the park's services and facilities. The Nature Center is complete with interpretive displays on area history and wildlife. Whitetail deer, raccoons, and foxes are often seen on the grounds. The par-3, nine-hole golf course, Olympic-size swimming pool, tennis courts, horseback riding stables, and shuffleboard are open Memorial Day to Labor Day, the campgrounds April 1 to October 31. There are 150 paved sites with electrical hookups. Drinking water, showers, flush toilets, dumping station, picnic tables and shelters, grills, and firewood are available. Mailing address: Lake Cumberland State Resort Park, Jamestown, Kentucky, 42629. Telephone: (502) 343-3111.

The Lake Cumberland State Resort Park marina has the largest fleet of rental houseboats on the lake. Houseboat reservations may be made either by mail or by phoning (502) 343-3236. A $100 deposit is required for confirmation 10 days after the reservation is made. Forty-six-foot houseboats rent for $85 a day or $500 weekly; 49-footers for $95 a day or $600 a week, and 53-footers for $110 a day or $660 a week. These prices are effective on weekends between May 1 and Labor Day. Off-season, weekend rates are reduced up to 30 percent. In addition, a four-day "middle of the week special" (Monday through Thursday) features houseboat rentals at reduced prices—30 percent off the weekend prices, even after Labor Day. This means that during the middle of the week in off-season, the rate is a full 60 percent off the seasonal price for weekends. All rental houseboats are fully carpeted and come with grills, flush toilet, lavatory, deck chairs, dishes and linens, 3-burner gas range, icebox, and cooler. The boats sleep eight; renters should bring their own blankets and pillows.

The State Dock also has rental fishing boats, pontoon boats, and runabouts for skiing. Complete live bait, tackle, snack bar, boating supplies, and open slips for overnight boaters are available. A launching ramp is adjacent to the marina. Mailing address: Lake Cumberland State Dock, Jamestown, Kentucky, 42629. Telephone: (502) 343-3236.

Burnside Island State Park was named in honor of Civil War Union General Ambrose E. Burnside (1824–81), a field commander in the bloody September 1862 Antietam campaign, who in March of 1863 assumed responsibility for holding eastern Kentucky for the Union and routing the Confederates from Knoxville, Tennessee. When Lake Cumberland was impounded, a 400-acre island was formed where the South Fork of the Cumberland River flows into the main river. One mile south of Burnside, Kentucky, off US-27, the "island" park is reached by a leveed highway. Open seasonally from April 1 to October 31, the park has an 18-hole golf course, beach, and bathhouses. The campground has 129 sites with electricity for tents or RVs, drinking water, showers, flush toilets, dumping station, ice, picnic tables and shelter, firewood, and beach. Mailing address: General Burnside State Park, Burnside, Kentucky, 42519. Telephone: (606) 561-4104.

Near the state park, and accessible via Lakeshore Drive from Burnside, is Burnside Marina, open 24 hours a day in the summer and 8 hours a day the rest of the time. There are 82 covered slips, tackle, live bait, snacks, launching ramp, fish cleaning table, and freezer space available at the dock. Rental boats include: 14-foot aluminum fishing boats with 6- to

25-horsepower outboards, 22-foot pontoon boats with 50-horsepower outboards, and 50-foot houseboats. The houseboats are fully equipped except for towels and rent for $90 a day or $560 a week year-round. Mailing address: Burnside Marina, Box 67, Burnside, Kentucky, 42519. Telephone: (606) 561-4223.

Farther south on US-27 is Cumberland Cove, a privately-owned campground overlooking the South Fork of the Cumberland River. Open April 15 to November 1, Cumberland Cove Campground has 30 sites, 15 of which have water and electrical hookups. Showers, drinking water, flush toilets, dumping station, picnic tables and grills, and housekeeping cottages are available. The one-bedroom cottages rent for $11 a day or $60 a week, the two-bedroom ones for $15 a day or $80 a week, and the three-bedroom cottages for $18 a day or $100 a week. Reservations are accepted. Mailing address: Cumberland Cove, Burnside, Kentucky, 42519. Telephone: (606) 561-4215.

Buck Creek Dock and Campground are the farthest upstream of all facilities on Lake Cumberland. Eight miles south of Somerset on Ky-769 at Haynes, Kentucky, the dock (open year-round) and campground (open April 1 to November 15) are located on Buck Creek a mile from its confluence with the Cumberland River, just north of the Daniel Boone National Forest boundary. In addition to a small campground (six sites with water and electrical hookups, six full-service hookups), two rental trailers are available by the day or week. The dock has 35 covered slips, launching ramp, snacks, fish cleaning table, fuel, live bait (minnows and nightcrawlers), tackle, 24-foot pontoon boats with 35-horsepower outboards, 14-foot aluminum fishing boats with 6-horsepower outboards, 42-foot houseboats ($55 a day plus gas), and 46-foot houseboats ($75 a day plus gas). Mailing address: Buck Creek Dock and Campground, Somerset, Kentucky, 42501. Telephone: (606) 382-5542.

The campgrounds closest to Wolf Creek Dam are Cumberland Campground and Foley's Camper Court, both privately owned, and a Corps-managed site, Kendall Recreation Area, immediately below the dam alongside the tailwaters. Cumberland Campground, open year-round, is nine miles south of Jamestown on US-127. Drinking water, 30 campsites with complete hookups, a trailer court for long-term visitors, showers, flush toilets, dumping station, ice, coin laundry, playground, and picnic tables and shelter are available. In addition to the campground, a rafting and canoeing rental and shuttle service is being operated on the Cumberland River below Lake Cumberland. Boats include life preservers and paddles. Auto shuttle to put-in and from take-out point is included in the cost. Four-mile, two-hour or seven-hour, and 13-mile trips are scheduled in the summer. Mailing address: Cumberland Campgrounds, Route #2, Jamestown, Kentucky, 42629. Telephone: (502) 343-3721.

Nearby Foley's Camper Court is also off US-127. Open year-round, the court has 60 campsites (48 with electrical hookups, 12 with water hookups), drinking water, showers, flush toilets, grocery, ice, playground, picnic tables, and firewood. Rental trailers are available, ranging in cost from $15 to $20 a day, $95 to $110 a week. Reservations are accepted. Mailing address: Foley's Campers Court, Route #2, Box 109, Jamestown, Kentucky, 42629. Telephone: (502) 343-4616.

The Corps-managed Kendall Recreation Area, 12 miles south of Jamestown on US-127, is very popular and often full during the summer. The reason is that the Lake Cumberland tailwaters are highly productive fishing waters for white bass and rainbow trout. If you're interested in river fishing rather than lake activities, this is your best bet. A launching ramp, free to the public, is conveniently located for access to the river. Recently expanded, the area now features 39 sites with electrical hookups for tents or RVs, showers, flush toilets, dump station, picnic tables and grills, playground, and one-mile nature trail. The fee area is open April 1 to November 15. Mailing address: Kendall Recreation Area, U. S. Army Corps of Engineers, Route #8, Box 173 T, Somerset, Kentucky, 42501. Telephone: (606) 679-6337.

The U. S. Army Corps of Engineers operates eight campgrounds on Lake Cumberland and one launching ramp on the South Fork of the Cumberland River, which is within easy boating distance of the headwaters of the lake at Burnside. Cave Creek and Omega campgrounds are both approximately 10 miles upstream from Burnside. Cave Creek is in Daniel Boone National Forest and is accessible via Highway US-27 and Blue John Road (FS Road 50). There are 10 sites for tents or RVs, with drinking water, flush toilets, picnic tables and grills, and a boat launching ramp. The Omega Campground on the northern bank of the Cumberland River is reached via Ky-769, eight miles southeast of Somerset, then five miles west on a county road (follow the signs). The facilities at Omega include 12 sites, drinking water, flush toilets, picnic tables and grills, and boat launching ramp. The Echo Point launching ramp on the South Fork of the Cumberland River is approximately eight miles south of Burnside off Ky-776.

Continuing down the lake, the next Corps-managed campsite is Waitsboro Ferry, which is reached by automobile via US-27. Waitsboro Ferry is near the Corps Resource Manager's Office on the northern shore of the lake, approximately eight miles south of Somerset. The facilities include 20 campsites, drinking water, flush toilets, picnic tables and grills, beach, and boat launching ramp.

Five miles down the lake from Waitsboro Ferry is the mouth of Fishing Creek. Approximately five miles up Fishing Creek is another Corps camping area, the Fishing Creek Campground, reached via Ky-80 four miles west of Somerset, then three miles on Ky-1248. The Fishing Creek campground has 45 sites, showers, flush toilets, dumping station, picnic tables and grills, nature trail, and boat launch. The Cumberland Point Campground, at mile 34 of the lake, is reached by automobile via Ky-80 eight miles southwest of Somerset, then one mile south on Ky-235 and 10 miles east on Ky-761. There are 10 sites for tents or RVs, with drinking water, showers, flush toilets, dumping station, picnic tables and grills, and boat launching ramp.

The Fall Creek Campground, on the southern shore of the lake at mile 27, is reached via Ky-90 and Ky-1275 approximately eight miles north of Monticello, Kentucky. There are 10 sites for tents or RVs, drinking water, flush toilets, picnic tables and grills, and a boat launching ramp at the campground.

Down the lake at mile 13 is the mouth of Wolf Creek. Near its headwaters is the newest of the Corps-managed campsites, the Wolf Creek Recreation Area. Reached from Russell Springs via Ky-80 and Ky-910, then south from Salem, Kentucky, on Ky-76 and Ky-1383, the Wolf Creek Recreation Area adjoins Alligator Dock #2. There are 13 picnic tables and grills, 15 campsites, flush toilets, and drinking water at the campground.

The only campground with good access to the lower end of Lake Cumberland is Grider Hill Recreation Area, eight miles north of Albany via US-127 and Ky-734. The campground, adjacent to Grider Hill Marina, overlooks the middle fork of Indian Creek, five miles by boat from Wolf Creek Dam, which impounds the lake. There are 10 sites for tents or RVs, showers, flush toilets, drinking water, and picnic facilities. Grider Hill Dock (telephone (606) 387-5501) and Indian Creek Lodge are adjacent to the Corps-managed campground. The overnight accommodations at Grider Hill include an 18-unit lodge, eight one-bedroom housekeeping cottages, and a restaurant open from mid-April to mid-October. The 130 covered-slip dock is open 24 hours a day year-round and has facilities for cleaning fish, freezer space, and live bait sales—worms, nightcrawlers, and minnows. A boat launching ramp is on the premises. Rental 14-foot fishing boats with 6- to 20-horsepower outboards, 16-foot fiberglass ski boats with 85-horsepower outboards, and 34- to 50-foot houseboats at daily rates ranging from $55 to $100 are also available. Weekly reduced rates are available.

Driving to the Grider Hill Dock you pass the Ridgemont Trailer Park, open April 1 to November 1. There are only seven campsites open for short-term visitors (complete hookups for sewage, water, and electricity), as most of the space is reserved for trailers. Grocery, ice, bottle gas, showers, playground, picnic tables, and grills are on the premises. Air conditioner hookups are available at extra cost; campsite reservations are accepted. One- and two-bedroom cottages rent for $10 to $18 a night, sixth night free. Two-bedroom cabins sleep six. Mailing address: Ridgemont Trailer Park, Route #4, Albany, Kentucky, 42602. Telephone: (606) 387-6273.

Beaver Creek Marina is reached by driving nine miles southwest on Ky-92, then one mile on Ky-674 from Monticello. The restaurant, eight sleeping rooms, and two housekeeping cottages are open from March 1 to November 1. The marina, open year-round, has 30 slips and rents out pontoon boats and 14-foot fishing boats (with 10-horsepower outboards). Live bait—minnows and nightcrawlers—snacks, and boating supplies are sold at the dock. Freezer space and a fish cleaning area are available. Mailing address: Beaver Creek Marina, Route #3, Monticello, Kentucky, 42633. Telephone: (606) 348-3386.

Across from the mouth of Beaver Creek, Lake Cumberland twists around a rocky peninsula and the adjacent Lowgap Island, a favorite lake-front camping spot. There are no established campsites, but plenty of room in the woods. Rather than circling the island, many boaters take the "cut-off," the most direct route to the state park marina and Jamestown Dock across from the park. This area of the lake is often very crowded with water skiers and boats.

Jamestown Dock, one of the most popular marinas on the lake, is just three miles south of Jamestown, Kentucky, on Ky-92. The recreational complex includes a 100-slip marina, housekeeping cottages, restaurant, and swimming pool for guests only. The cottages (six one-bedroom, five two-bedroom, three three-bedroom, and three four-bedroom) are open between late March and early November, as is the restaurant. The marina is open 24 hours year-round. Live bait, a complete line of tackle, rental 14-foot fishing boats with 15-horsepower motors, pontoon boats, and 50- and 54-foot house-boats ($480 a week plus gas) are available. There's a fish cleaning area and freezer space at the dock. Mailing address: Jamestown Dock, Route #2, Jamestown, Kentucky, 42629. Telephone: (502) 343-3535.

On the upriver side of this rocky peninsula at mile 13 is the mouth of Wolf Creek. One of the major tributary embayments of Lake Cumberland, Wolf Creek has two marinas and two private campgrounds, in addition to the Corps-managed campground discussed earlier. To get to these facilities go three miles east on Ky-80 from Russell Springs, Kentucky, then eight miles southeast on Ky-910, Ky-76, and Ky-1383.

Alligator Dock #1 is a full-facilities marina, restaurant, and housekeeping-cottage complex. The 45-slip marina is open 24 hours year-round. The rest of the complex—four mobile homes rented on a short-term basis, trailer court, restaurant, 10 housekeeping cottages (one-, two-, and three-bedrooms), and one motel unit—is open seasonally, April 1 through November 1. Alligator Dock #1 has 21 rental houseboats, 40-, 45-, 50-, and 55-footers. The range in rental fees is from $60 per day ($375 per week) for the 40-footers to $95 per day ($600 per week) for the 55-footers. There is a two-day minimum for weekday houseboat rentals. Twenty-six and 32-foot pontoon boats, 14-foot aluminum fishing boats with 5½-horsepower outboards, gasoline, snacks, live bait, tackle, and artificial lures are also available at the dock. Mailing address: Alligator Dock #1, Route #5, Russell Springs, Kentucky, 42629. Telephone (502) 866-3634.

About halfway between the two marinas is Pine Crest Park, open seasonally April 1 to October 1. There are 124 campsites at the park, 49 with complete water, electricity, and sewage hookups for mobile homes, another 35 with full hookups for RVs, and 40 with water only. Other facilities include sites for tents, drinking water, showers, flush toilets, grocery, ice, playground, picnic tables and grills, and swimming pool for guests. Mailing address: Pine Crest Park, Route #5, Box 279-A, Russell Springs, Kentucky, 42642. Telephone (502) 866-5615.

Alligator Dock #2, open year-round, 24 hours a day seasonally, has a whopping 146 slips, 108 of which are covered. Nine rental houseboats, all 58-footers with gas grills and showers, and renting for $100 a day ($600 a week) during the season and $85 a day ($510 a week) off-season, are available. A 32-foot pontoon boat and 14-foot aluminum fishing boats with 5½- to 9½-horsepower outboards are rented out of the dock. Facilities include a fish cleaning area with water source, freezer space, snack bar, grocery, and boating and fishing supplies. Mailing address: Alligator Dock #2, Route #5, Russell Springs, Kentucky, 42629. Telephone: (502) 866-6616.

Adjacent to the marina is the Indian Hills Lake Cumberland KOA campground with a total of 240 campsites, 40 of which have complete hookups; 200 have water and electrical hookups only. The campground, open year-round, also has drinking water, showers, flush toilets, RV dump station, ice, bottle gas, coin laundry, playground, picnic tables and grills, tennis, large and kiddie swimming pools, horseback riding stables, and pony ring. The seven housekeeping cottages are open from April 1 to November 1. One-bedroom cottages rent for $14 a night, three-bedroom ones for $22 a night. Mailing address: Indian Hills Lake Cumberland KOA, Route #5, Box 285, Russell Springs, Kentucky, 42642. Telephone: (502) 866-5615.

The next recreational complex up the lake is Conley Bottom Resort, eight miles north of Monticello on Ky-1275. The campground, housekeeping cottages, efficiencies, and marina are open year-round, the restaurant from March 1 to November 1. Off-season (September 5 to May 25) rates are available for the accommodations. The 120-site campground with water and electrical hookups, showers, flush toilets, dumping station, grocery, ice, bottle gas, picnic tables, shelters and grills, and boat launching ramp, is connected to the marina by a floating walkway. Water is not available at the campground from November through March. Hiking and motor bike trails circle the lakeside woodlands in the vicinity of the campground.

The resort's marina is open 24 hours a day in the summer, and from

6:00 a.m. to 8:00 p.m. weekdays and 6:00 a.m. to 10:00 p.m. on week-ends during the off-season. There are more than 50 covered slips at the marina; camping costs include free docking. Pontoon boats (24- and 34-footers), 14-foot fishing boats with 6-, 10- and 18-horsepower out-boards, 16-foot ski boats with 40- and 85-horsepower outboards (includes skis, ropes, and life preservers), and houseboats are available. The 46-foot "superwide" houseboats complete with linens, tableware, and cookware, and comparably equipped 38-footers, can be rented in season at daily, "mid-week special," and weekly rates. Fuel, tackle and live bait, boating supplies, and a fish cleaning area and freezer space are available at the dock. Mailing address: Conley Bottom Resort, Monticello, Kentucky, 42633. Telephone: (606) 348-6351.

Forty-three miles up the lake from Wolf Creek Dam is Fishing Creek, the site of a privately-owned campground and marina, in addition to a Corps-managed lakeside facility. Lee's Ford Dock, six miles west of Somerset off Ky-80, has a 100-slip marina, restaurant, six housekeeping cottages, a 10-unit motel, small grocery store, and buoy lines for overnight or long-term moorings. The dock, which is open 24 hours a day in the summer, has rental 14-foot aluminum fishing boats with 9.9-horsepower outboards, pontoon boats, 48-foot houseboats ($75 a day or $450 a week), 50-footers ($90 a day or $540 a week), tackle, snack bar, fuel, live bait—minnows and nightcrawlers—, and boating supplies. The restaurant is open seasonally, March to November. Mailing address: Lee's Ford Dock, Box 753, Somerset, Kentucky, 42501. Telephone: (606) 636-6426.

Two miles west of Lee's Ford Dock on Ky-80 and one mile north on Ky-1248 is the municipally-owned Pulaski County Campground, open April 15 to November 15. There are 24 sites with electrical hookups, flush toilets, drinking water, dumping station, playground, picnic tables and shelters, boat launch, and firewood. Mailing address: Pulaski County Park, Route #1, Box 164, Nancy, Kentucky, 42544. Telephone: (606) 636-6450.

Lake Barkley

Lake Barkley, named in honor of the late Senator and Vice-President from Kentucky, Alben Barkley, is a 118-mile-long impoundment of the Cumber-land River which stretches from Dickson County, Tennessee, to Grand Rivers, Kentucky, in Lyon County. Barkley Dam is at mile 30.6 of the lower Cumberland River. Completed in 1966, the 7,985-foot-long dam, designed by personnel of the Nashville District, U.S. Army Corps of Engineers, and constructed under their supervision, is an earth and concrete structure with navigation lock, canal, and hydropower generating plant. The 115-foot-high dam, built at a cost of $145,000,000, forms a shallow, winding 57,920-acre lake (42,020 acres in Kentucky), whose main body is in Livingston, Lyon, Caldwell, and Trigg counties, Kentucky.

Lake Barkley is more like a river at floodstage than a lake, with swift current in its channel and miles of mudflats, once ridgetops, which border the deep water. Its shallow embayments are filled with stump beds, brush, and submerged creek channels, all excellent structure for bass and crappie. In fall and winter these same shallows are rest stops for migrating waterfowl. Lake Barkley, more so than its "twin," Kentucky Lake, has excellent year-round recreational potential.

The U.S. Army Corps of Engineers operates and maintains 21 lake access/recreation areas on the east bank of Lake Barkley in Kentucky. The resource manager's office may be reached by mail at this address: U.S. Army Corps of Engineers, P.O. Box 218, Grand Rivers, Kentucky, 42045; telephone: (502) 362-4236.

The farthest south (upstream) of the Corps-managed recreation areas in Kentucky is the Linton site, 12 miles south of Canton, Kentucky, on Ky-164. The 56-acre day-use site has picnic tables and grills, a boat launching ramp, and paved parking lot. There's a lake access point at Donaldson Creek, four miles downstream. The 50-acre Donaldson Creek site, reached via Ky-164, has a launching ramp and paved parking lot. Across the embayment is the Calhoun Hill site, also equipped with launching ramp and paved parking lot. Devil's Elbow Recreation Area, one mile south of Canton, Kentucky, on Ky-164, is open year-round. The 30-acre site on the Lick Creek embayment of Lake Barkley has 21 campsites for tents or RVs, picnic tables, grills, pit toilets, launching ramp, and paved parking area.

Kentucky's grandest vacation resort, Lake Barkley State Resort Park, is located on the Little River embayment, seven miles west of Cadiz off US-68. The park entrance road winds through wooded hills, and at night the approach is lit with rows of lights which encircle the sprawling redwood lodge overlooking the lake. Open year-round, the lodge and the 3,600-acre park (the largest in the Kentucky State Park System) offer some of the finest accommodations and recreational opportunities in the mid-South. Nationally acclaimed in travel magazines, Lake Barkley State Resort Park has an 80-site campground, 200-capacity dining room, coffee shop (open from 7:00 a.m., Memorial Day to Labor Day), an indoor recreation room (billiards, table tennis, card tables, and video games) in the lodge, an 18-hole golf course, horseback riding stables (open seasonally), marina, heated swimming pool and sand beach with bathhouse (open seasonally), lighted tennis courts, and basketball courts. There are 120 lodge rooms and four lodge suites. The rooms are well appointed with tasteful furnishings, wall-to-wall carpeting, indirect lighting, individually controlled air conditioning, split-area dressing room/bath with shower, and private balcony. The lodge suites are equipped with kitchenettes. The nine executive cottages have custom kitchens, two studio couches which convert to double beds, two bedrooms with two double beds in each, bath, air conditioning, and electric heat. Tableware, cooking utensils, and linens are furnished. Off-season rates are available for all accommodations. Specially-equipped rooms for the handicapped are available.

During the season, entertainment and planned recreation programs are held daily. The golf course and trap range are open from April 1 to November 15, weather permitting. Rental clubs, riding and pull carts, a "Golfer's Groove" machine, and golfing supplies are available at the pro shop. Guns may be rented and shells bought at the trap range, which has a recreation director on duty at all times for supervision and optional instruction. Fees are charged for each round. There are three short day-hiking trails on the park grounds, all open year-round. Interpretive information is available from the park naturalist.

The park's campground, also open year-round, has 80 campsites, all with water and electrical hookups. Services and facilities include central service buildings with showers, flush toilets, and drinking water; ice, launching ramp, picnic tables, grills, shelters, and playground.

The park's marina, one-half mile west of the lodge, open year-round, has 152 slips, 112 of which are covered. Rental boats include 14-foot aluminum fishing boats with 7½-horsepower outboards ($5 an hour, $18 a day), 24-foot pontoon boats (four with 35-horsepower outboards that rent for $10 an hour or $50 a day, one with a 70-horsepower outboard motor that rents for $12 an hour or $65 a day), two runabouts with 70-horsepower outboards ($10 an hour or $50 a day), and two jet boats (rental costs not available). Fuel, grocery staples, fishing equipment, live bait (minnows, red worms, and night crawlers), and limited freezer space for cleaned fish are available. A boat launching ramp is nearby. Mailing address: Lake Barkley State Resort Park, Route #2, Cadiz, Kentucky, 42211. Telephones: marina, (502) 924-9954; lodge, (502) 924-1171.

The Cadiz Recreation Area, in Cadiz, Kentucky, on US-68, is a 75-acre day-use area on the Little River, a tributary to Lake Barkley. Picnic tables, grills, a shelter with flush toilet restrooms, drinking water, playground, launching ramp, and paved parking area are available at the site, which is a good put-in place for a float trip to the lake. Approximately 15 miles downstream is the 31-acre Little River Recreation Area (five miles northwest of Cadiz on Ky-274 by automobile), and a day-use area with picnic tables and grills, pit toilets, and launching and paved parking areas. The recreation area is a good take-out point for float trips on the Little River because it is located at the headwaters of the embayment; beyond that point, there's not much current.

Near the mouth of the Little River embayment is another Corps-managed lake access point. The Rivers End site, reached via Ky-274 from Cadiz, has a launching ramp and paved parking lot, and is open year-round.

Lake View Hills Camping Resort, nine miles north of Cadiz, Kentucky, on Ky-274, is near the Corps-managed Rockcastle lake access area south of the Hurricane Creek embayment. Open April 1 to November 1, the campground has 89 campsites (32 with complete hookups, 32 with water and electricity, and 25 primitive sites). Services and facilities include showers, flush toilets, picnic tables and shelter, grocery, coin laundry, playground, and private boat dock with launching ramp for guests. Rental camping trailers are available. Mailing address: Lake View Hills Camping Resort, Route #4, Cadiz, Kentucky, 42211. Telephone: (502) 522-6848.

Port Prizer Point Recreation Area, 12 miles northwest of Cadiz on Ky-274, is open year-round. The 95-acre site is equipped for 16 tents or trailers. Picnic tables, grills, shelter, flush toilets, drinking water, launching ramp, and paved parking lot are available. Nearby is the Rockcastle lake access area with launching ramp and paved parking area.

Port Prizer Point Marina, next to the Corps-managed lake access area, is open March 1 to December 1. There are 81 boat slips (46 covered, 35 open) and four housekeeping cottages that sleep six adults. The rental fee is $21 a day. Fourteen-foot aluminum fishing boats with 9½-horsepower outboards rent for $15 per day. A rental fleet of 41- and 45-foot houseboats is also moored at the marina. Powered by inboard 155- to 225-horsepower engines, they rent for $500 a week. Fuel, live bait (minnows, red worms, and crickets), a fish cleaning station, freezer space, boat launching ramp, and fishing tackle are available. Mailing address: Port Prizer Point, Route #4, Cadiz, Kentucky, 42211. Telephone: (502) 522-3762.

The Hurricane Creek Recreation Area is located at the headwaters of the embayment, a mile northward off Ky-274. There are 51 sites for tents or RVs, some with electrical hookups. Facilities and services include an RV dumping station, picnic tables, grills, flush toilets, showers, drinking water, playground, boat launching ramp, and paved parking lot. A fee of $3.50 is charged per campsite per night, $4 with use of electricity. The area is open year-round.

Cannon Spring Recreation Area, 16 miles northwest of Cadiz via Ky-274 and Ky-1285, is a 219-acre day-use area on the north fork of Drydens Creek. A boat launching ramp, picnic tables, and grills are open year-round. North of the Cannon Spring Recreation Area is the Drydens Creek lake access site, with boat launching ramp and paved parking area.

Dryden Bay Resort, adjoining the Corps-managed Drydens Creek Recreation Area, is nine miles south of Eddyville, Kentucky, via Ky-93, then two miles south on Ky-274. Open April 1 to October 31, the campground and cottage complex has five campsites with water, electrical, and sewer hookups, and seven two-bedroom cottages that sleep four and rent for $21 a day. Showers, drinking water, and flush toilets are located in the bathhouse. Picnic tables, grills, shelter, snack bar, and ice are available. Mailing address: Dryden Bay Resort, Route #1, Eddyville, Kentucky, 42038. Telephone: (502) 388-9459.

Ramey Campground, nine miles south of Eddyville on Ky-93, then two miles east on Ky-274, has 62 campsites (28 with water and electrical hookups, 2 with water, electrical, and sewer hookups, and 30 primitive sites). Open April 1 to November 1, the campground is equipped with a bathhouse (showers and flush toilets), a grocery (ice and camping and picnic supplies), playground, recreation room, RV dump station, picnic tables, grills, and boat launching ramp. Mailing address: Ramey Campground, Route #1, Eddyville, Kentucky, 42038. Telephone: (502) 388-9260.

One of the most popular Corps-managed recreation areas is at Eddy Creek. The 102-acre site, open April 1 to November 15, is eight miles south of Eddyville, Kentucky, on Ky-93. There are 24 campsites, showers, beach, picnic tables, grills, drinking water, flush toilets, boat launching ramp, and paved parking lot. Between the Eddy Creek and the Eddyville recreation areas are two Corps-managed lake access points—the Coleman Bridge site on the south side of Eddy Creek and the Holloway Hill site on the north side. Both sites have launching ramps and paved parking areas.

Adjacent to the Eddy Creek Recreation Area is Eddy Creek Port Marina, open April 1 to November 1. There is a total of 135 slips, 68 covered and 67 open. Sit-down meals or carry-out box lunches are available from the marina's restaurant. Accommodations at the recreational complex include motel rooms ($16 a day, $96 a week), efficiencies ($20 a day, $120 a week), and cottages ($25 a day, $150 a week). Fishing boats without outboards may be rented from the marina, as well as 14-footers with 6- or 10-horsepower motors for $15 per day, 26-foot pontoon boats for $40 per day (three-day minimum), and 36-foot houseboats, $300 for three-day minimum or $500 a week. The carpeted houseboats sleep eight and are equipped with air conditioning, water heaters, showers, galley, charcoal grills, and linens. The marina has a souvenir ship featuring nautical gifts. Fishing supplies, licenses, ice, fuel, oil and LP gas, fish cleaning station, freezer space, live bait (red worms, minnows, and crickets), an outboard motor repair service, and fishing guide on call, are also available. There's a launching ramp next to the marina. Mailing address: Eddy Creek Port Marina, Route #1, Eddyville, Kentucky, 42038. Telephone: (502) 388-7743.

Holiday Hills Camping Resort, five miles south of Eddyville, Kentucky, off Ky-93, is open March 21 to November 1. The campground and marina complex on the Eddy Creek embayment of Lake Barkley has a 116-site campground and 19-slip marina. Half the campsites are equipped with water, electrical, and sewer hookups; the remaining 58 sites are primitive. Flush toilets, RV dump station, showers, grocery, ice, coin laundry, recreation room, and sun deck are located at the central service building. A heated pool, sand beach, playground (basketball and badminton courts and bicycle rentals), day-hiking trail, group campfire, picnic tables, and charcoal grills are within easy walking distance of the campground. The resort's marina rents 14- and 16-foot fishing boats ($13 per day, seventh day free). Other services and facilities include fuel, bait (minnows, red worms, night crawlers, crickets, and cut bait for catfish), a fish cleaning station, freezer space, and launching ramp. Mailing address: Holiday Hills Camping Resort and Marina, Eddyville, Kentucky, 42038. Telephone: (502) 388-7236.

Datona Shores Campground, among the largest on Lake Barkley, may be reached by driving two miles south of Eddyville on Ky-93, then left on Ky-293, following the signs. The campground complex is open April 15 to October 31. There are a whopping 300 campsites, 125 with water, sewer, and electrical hookups, 75 with water and electricity, and 100 primitive sites. The bathhouse has flush toilets, showers, and a grocery. There's a pavilion for square dancing, a playground for children, adults' club, laundromat, picnic tables and grills, and volleyball courts; a water slide and miniature golf course are under construction. Mailing address: Datona Shores Campground, P.O. Box 437, Eddyville, Kentucky, 42038. Telephone: (502) 388-7709.

The Eddyville Recreational Area, at the former site of Eddyville, Kentucky, is two miles southwest of new Eddyville, off Ky-93. The 15-acre day-use area has picnic tables, grills, flush toilets, drinking water, boat launching ramp, and paved parking lot. Five miles down the lake near Kuttawa, Kentucky, another town relocated when the Cumberland River was impounded, is the Kuttawa Recreation Area, a 60-acre day-use area off US-641/62 with tables, grills, flush toilets, beach, drinking water, playground for youngsters, boat launching ramp, day-hiking trails, and paved parking lot.

Tarryon Camping Resort, open year-round, is one mile southwest of Kuttawa on US-641, then south on Ky-810. There are 100 campsites with water and electrical hookups, 39 with complete hookups (water, electrical, and sewer), and 30 primitive sites. Tarryon Camping Resort is one mile south of Leisure Cruise Marina and three-quarters of a mile upstream from Boyd's Landing Recreation Area. The campground's facilities and services include drinking water, showers, flush toilets, grocery, ice, picnic tables, beach, tennis and basketball courts, and a gift shop featuring hand-painted china. Mailing address: Tarryon Camping Resort, P.O. Box 305, Kuttawa, Kentucky, 42055. Telephone: (502) 388-7389.

Iron Hill Campground, two miles southwest of Kuttawa on US-62, then one mile south on Ky-810, is open April 1 to November 1. There are 110 complete hookups for mobile homes, 30 RV sites with complete hookups, and 24 primitive tent sites. The campground's services and facilities include drinking water, showers, flush toilets, dumping station, grocery (canned goods, camping supplies), ice, bottled gas, gravel boat launching ramp, boat dry dock service, and mobile home rental (three 12- by 50-foot two-bedroom mobile homes, $15 a day), picnic tables, and grills. Mailing address: Iron Hill Campground, P.O. Box 273, Kuttawa, Kentucky, 42055. Telephone: (502) 388-7002.

Kuttawa Harbor Marina, three miles east of Kuttawa, Kentucky, off US-641/62, is open year-round. The 122-slip marina is at the mouth of the Knob Creek embayment. A restaurant is under construction. Rental fishing boats, 14- and 16-footers equipped with 9- and 18-horsepower outboards, rent for $14 and $19, respectively, with the seventh day free. Twenty-four-foot pontoon boats with 25-horsepower outboards can be rented for $35 per day. Fuel, boating accessories, live bait (crickets, minnows, and red worms), a fish cleaning station, freezer space, gift shop, a complete line of artificial lures, and launching ramp are available at the dock. A hull-scrubbing service is available, and there's a sundeck atop the marina. Mailing address: Kuttawa Harbor Marina, Route #2, Kuttawa, Kentucky, 42055. Telephone: (502) 388-9563.

There are two lake access areas off US-641 on Poplar Creek, the Poplar Creek and Buzzard Rock sites. Both have launching ramps and paved parking areas.

Leisure Cruise Marina adjoins the Corps-managed Buzzard Rock Recreation Area off US-641/62 one mile west of Kuttawa, Kentucky. Open year-round, the 120-slip marina (100 of which are covered), has one of the largest fleets of rental houseboats on Lake Barkley. A restaurant on the dock is open April 1 to October 31. Fourteen-foot fishing boats with 7½-horsepower outboards rent for $15 per day, seventh day free. Twenty-four-foot pontoon boats with 40-horsepower outboards rent for $40 a day, also with the seventh day free.

The rental houseboats are available in three sizes. The 45- by 12-foot Sumerset Cruisers sleep 10 and are equipped with stacked bunks and double beds, head with shower, galley with stove, sink, and refrigerator, and a hide-a-bed couch. Rental fees are $475 for three days, $525 for four days, $575 for five days, and $625 for a week.

The 44- by 11-foot Captains Craft houseboats sleep eight. Stacked double beds, shower, dinette which folds down to a bed at night, galley with ice box, sink, and stove, vanity, and hide-a-bed are the features of this boat, which rents for $375 for three days, $425 for four days, $475 for five days, and $525 for a week.

The smaller 38- by 12-foot Sumerset Cruisers sleep up to seven but are perfect for two couples. They are equipped with stacked double bunks, head with shower, dinette, galley with stove, sink, and ice box, and hide-a-bed couch. Rental cost is $275 for three days, $325 for four days, $375 for five days, and $425 for a week. Fuel and food are extra. All houseboats are powered by 130-horsepower Volvo inboards. Boarding time is 3:00 p.m., checkout time is 10:00 a.m. A $100 deposit, required with reservations, will be refunded under terms of rental contract agreement. Operating lessons are given free of charge before departure. The marina has two launching ramps, a fish cleaning station, freezer space, and live bait—minnows, crickets, and red worms. Mailing address: Leisure Cruise Marina, Box 266, Kuttawa, Kentucky, 42055. Telephone: (502) 388-7925.

The Boyd's Landing Recreation Area, off Ky-810 seven miles south of Suwannee, Kentucky, is open year-round and has 20 campsites, all with water and electrical hookups for tents or RVs. Facilities at the 50-acre site include pit toilets, picnic tables, grills, boat launching ramp, and paved parking lot. Nearby is the Eureka Recreation Area, reached via US-641/62 and Eureka Ferry Road (Ky-1271). The 120-acre site, which adjoins Barkley Dam, is open year-round and has 35 campsites, picnic tables, grills, a picnic shelter, boat launching ramp, and paved parking lot.

The largest of the Corps-managed lake access campgrounds is the Canal Recreation Area, overlooking the two-and-one-half-mile canal connecting Kentucky Lake and Lake Barkley at Land Between the Lake's northern boundary. The 140-acre site, open April 1 to November 15, has 90 campsites, 46 with electrical hookups and 44 primitive sites. The fee per night, per campsite is $3 without electricity, $3.50 for hooking up. Facilities include a trailer dumping station, flush toilets, showers, playground, a day-hiking trail, paved roads and parking lot, a boat launching ramp, and ORV area. Canal Recreation Area is reached via Ky-453 (the Trace), one mile south of Grand Rivers, Kentucky.

The only other Corps-managed campground on the west bank of Lake Barkley is located at Grand Rivers on a 90-acre site adjoining the town of 600. There are 44 sites for tents or RVs, all with electricity and water. Picnic tables, grills, and a shelter are located in the picnic areas beside the campground. Facilities include flush toilets, showers, playground, launching ramp, paved roads, and parking lot. The campground is open April 1 to November 15.

Arant Houseboat Rentals operates the Port Ken Bar Marina adjacent to the Corps-managed Canal and Grand Rivers recreation areas at Grand Rivers, Kentucky. The marina is one-half mile north of Barkley Canal via Ky-453. The marina is open year-round, but boat rentals are offered only from April 1 through Thanksgiving. There are 237 boat slips, 75 of which are covered. The Flying Bridge Restaurant, built on pilings over the lake, offers plate lunches and carryout box lunches, and breakfast and coffee are available. Houseboat rentals include 34-footers, 42-footers ($300 for three-day weekend, $325 four days mid-week, and $450 for a week), and 50-footers ($375 for a three-day weekend, $375 for four days mid-week, and $600 for a week). Twenty-four foot pontoon boats are available at $50 a day. Deposits are required on all houseboat and pontoon boat rentals. Fourteen-foot fishing boats rent for $6 a day without motor, $12 with motor included. Live bait (minnows, crickets, and night crawlers), fuel (regular, mixed, and diesel, available at five-pump fuel dock), a fish cleaning station, freezer space, boat launching ramp, marine store, artificial bait, and tackle are available at the marina. Mailing address: Arant Houseboat Rentals/Port Ken Bar Marina, Route #9, Paducah, Kentucky, 42001. Telephone: (502) 898-3188 or 362-8239.

Kentucky Lake

Kentucky's second largest lake, 184-mile-long Kentucky Lake, was impounded from the Tennessee River in 1944 by the Tennessee Valley Authority. An astonishing engineering feat, and today one of the major recreational drawing cards in the mid-South, Kentucky Lake has more than 160,300 total surface acres of water, 49,511 of which are in western Kentucky, the rest in Tennessee.

The first-built of the so-called "sister lakes," Kentucky Lake is joined to Lake Barkley by a mile-and-a-half canal at Grand Rivers, Kentucky. The parallel lakes virtually surround TVA's 170,000-acre national recreational area, the 45 mile-long wooded isthmus known as Land Between the Lakes. Both lakes have immense recreational potential, be it fishing, water skiing, houseboating, waterfowl hunting, sailing, or nature study.

Kentucky Dam was six years in the construction (July 1, 1938, to August 30, 1944), with as many as 5,000 men working on the project at one time. Located just 25 miles upstream from the Tennessee's confluence with the Ohio River northeast of Paducah, Kentucky Dam is a 20-story, 8,422-foot-long structure that impounds the nation's fifth largest river. The Kentucky counties which border the lake are Trigg, Lyon, Marshall, and Calloway. The entire east bank of Kentucky Lake is within the boundaries of Land Between the Lakes (LBL), so commercial development is limited to the west bank in Marshall and Calloway counties from New Concord, Kentucky, north to Kentucky Dam at Gilbertsville, with a large concentration of facilities on the Jonathan Creek embayment north of Aurora, Kentucky. The west bank of the lake is accessible via the Western Kentucky

Parkway and highways US-62, US-641, Interstate-24, US-68, Ky-1422, Ky-936, Ky-58, Ky-962, Ky-94, Ky-80, Ky-732, Ky-280, Ky-444, and Ky-121. There are two Kentucky state resort parks on Kentucky Lake, one at Kentucky Dam in Gilbertsville and the other at Aurora, near the junction of highways US-68, Ky-80, and Ky-94.

In 1948 the TVA construction camp for Kentucky Dam was purchased by the state for $84,000. From this facility evolved Kentucky Dam Village State Resort Park, the first complete, large-scale state park facility on the lake and one of the largest such recreational complexes in Kentucky. Kentucky Dam Village State Resort Park, open year-round, is one mile west of Kentucky Dam in Gilbertsville off US-641. For "fly-in" guests there's a 4,000-foot paved, lighted air strip with jet fuel, tie-downs, and rental car service. Upon request, transportation to and from the park to the nearby airfield is provided. The park sits in a small embayment guarded by riprap barriers overlooking the main lake immediately above the dam. The "village" concept of the park derives from the fact that the lodge, housekeeping cottages, marina, coffee shop, golf course, and swimming pool are centrally located within walking distance of one another. The 1,200-acre park officially went into operation in July, 1958.

Across from the 72-room lodge with 300-capacity restaurant and swimming pool is a village complex of tennis courts, golf pro shop, auditorium, post office, coffee shop (open seasonally), and 18-hole golf course. The 69 housekeeping cottages, located either on the lake front or in the woods, offer a wide variety of accommodations: small efficiency cottages with combination bedroom and kitchen; two-bedroom village cottages with living room, dinette, kitchenette, and bath; two-bedroom deluxe cottages with living room, dining room, kitchen, half-bath, full bath, and garage; and three-bedroom executive cottages with custom baths and kitchens, color television, and living room. All cottages are equipped with telephone, television, electric heat, linens, and tableware.

The beach-bathhouse complex and snack bar at lakeside are open seasonally from Memorial Day to Labor Day. Other seasonal recreational programs include such activities as bicycling rides, nature walks in LBL, square dancing, singing groups, craft festivals, and rappelling. The park's campground, one mile east on Ky-282, has a total of 225 sites, all with electrical outlets; 150 are also equipped with water hookups. Drinking water, flush toilets, showers, dumping station, bottled gas, laundry, picnic tables and grills, and grocery and ice are either on the grounds or nearby. Mailing address: Kentucky Dam Village State Resort Park, Gilbertsville, Kentucky, 42044. Telephone: (502) 362-4271.

The largest state-owned boat dock complex in the Kentucky State Park System is at Kentucky Dam, adjacent to the park. There are actually two marinas, one above the dam in the lake, the other below the dam in the

Tennessee River. The docks have a total of 277 boat slips, 176 of which are covered. Fourteen-foot fishing boats with 9½-horsepower outboards rent for $20 per day plus fuel; 24-foot pontoon boats with 40-horsepower outboards rent for $8 an hour or $50 a day (8-hour days).

The dock above the dam is open year-round, the dock in the river seasonally from Memorial Day to Labor Day. Taylor Creek Boats, Inc., operates a rental houseboat business out of the Kentucky Dam Marina. Fully-equipped 42-foot houseboats with 120-horsepower engines (40 gallons of fuel included) rent for $450 a week. The houseboats are equipped with three-burner ranges, icebox, sink, lavatory, linens, blankets, dishes, life jackets, cooking utensils, pots and pans, glassware, wall-to-wall carpeting, and sun deck. Comparably equipped 50-footers rent for $400 Monday through Thursday, $400 Friday through Monday, or $650 a week.

Ski and sailboat rentals are also available. For $15 an hour plus fuel, a 16-foot ski boat with 85-horsepower outboard (includes skis and life preservers) can be rented. A 16-foot Catyak catamaran rents for $3.50 an hour. A full line of boating and fishing supplies, tackle, live bait (minnows, worms, and crickets), cut bait, and snacks are available at the docks. A launching ramp, fish cleaning area, and freezer space are provided for guests. Mailing address: Kentucky Dam Marina, Route #1, Gilbertsville, Kentucky, 42048. Telephone: (502) 362-8500.

West of the Purchase Parkway on US-62 is the KOA Kentucky Lake Dam/Paducah Kamping Resort, a 30-acre campground with 75 sites, all with electrical hookups; 21 are also equipped with water and sewer hookups. Open March 1 to November 30, the campground offers flush toilets, showers, drinking water, grocery, ice, bottled gas, picnic tables, and swimming pool. There are eight sites for tent campers with water and electricity at each site; all sites are pull-throughs which will accommodate large RVs. Services and facilities include air-conditioned gameroom, laundry, playground, free movies on weekends, gift shop, horseshoe pits, volleyball courts, snack bar, and pond stocked for fishing by children only. Mailing address: KOA Kentucky Lake Dam/Paducah Kamping Resort, Route #3, Box 192, Calvert City, Kentucky, 42029. Telephone: (502) 395-5841.

Grand Rivers Campground, open March 1 to November 1, has 50 campsites (45 with water and electrical hookups). The campground is located on Ky-453 at Grand Rivers. Rental campers (18- to 25-foot) that sleep five are $20 to $25 a day, $110 to $140 a week. The campground's bathhouse is equipped with flush toilets and showers. Drinking water, RV dump station, sand beach, picnic tables, swimming pool, and gameroom (pool and pinball) are available. Mailing address: Grand River Campground, P.O. Box 128, Grand Rivers, Kentucky, 42045. Telephone: (502) 362-9911 or 362-8353.

The Moors Resort and Marina, open year-round, is eight and one-half miles south of Kentucky Dam on Ky-963 off US-68. The 40-acre resort has a 150-site campground, including six sites with water, electric, and sewer hookups, 40 with water and electricity, and 104 primitive sites. Facilities include drinking water, flush toilets, showers, RV dump station, picnic tables, and grocery with meat counter and camping supplies. There are 26 lakefront housekeeping cottages with either one, four, or six bedrooms, each complete with kitchen, TV, and air conditioning. Rents range from $20 to $90 a night, seventh night free. Adjacent to the cottages are a sand beach, horseshoe pits, and basketball and volleyball courts. The marina has 116 slips, 90 covered and 26 open. Rental boats include 14-foot fishing boats with 6-horsepower outboards that rent for $11 a day, seventh day free, and a 26-foot pontoon boat with 40-horsepower outboards for $40 per day, seventh day free. Other facilities and services include regular, mixed, and diesel fuel; live bait (minnows, worms, and crickets); launching ramp, fish cleaning station, limited freezer space, dry dock service, and full-time outboard mechanic. Mailing address: The Moors Resort and Marina, Route #2, Gilbertsville, Kentucky, 42044. Telephone: (502) 362-4356.

Big Bear Resort, a motel, cottage, campground, and marina complex open April 1 to November 1, is located where Ky-58 deadends at the Bear Creek embayment eight miles northeast of Fairdealing, Kentucky, off US-68. The lake-view campground has 100 sites, 19 of which are equipped with electrical hookups. The remaining 81 sites are primitive. Flush toilets, showers, drinking water, picnic tables, sand beach, RV dump station, grocery, snack bar, and game room are on the grounds. No reservations are required for campsites. The 12 motel units have electric kitchens, air conditioning, and private bath. Both one-bedroom sleeping rooms and two-bedroom apartments are available. The 38 housekeeping cottages are furnished with dishes, silverware, cooking utensils, bedding, and towels. Comparably equipped three-bedroom cottages (air-conditioned, with living room, TV, and front porch), two-bedroom duplex cottages, two-bedroom single cottages, and a log cabin which sleeps up to 14 persons are also available. A $20 deposit is required on all reservations for housekeeping cottages. Deposits will be refunded only if a written cancellation is received 30 days prior to date of reservation.

The Big Bear Resort Marina, open from 6:00 a.m. until dark April 1 to November 1, has both covered and open slips which may be rented on a daily, weekly, monthly, or yearly basis. Both 16-foot bass boats ($20 to $25 a day) and 14-foot aluminum fishing boats equipped with 6- and 9½-horsepower outboards are available. Rental rates for the aluminum fishing boats and outboards are $10.50 and $15 per day, respectively. Twenty-two foot pontoon boats ($45 per day) and day-use sailboats ($20 per day) may also be acquired from the marina. Fuel, tackle, outboard service, live bait (minnow, crickets, and red worms), a fish cleaning station, and freezer space are also available for use by guests. A launching ramp adjoins the marina. Mailing address: Big Bear Resort, Route #4, Benton, Kentucky, 42025. Telephone: (502) 354-6414.

The Bee Springs Lodge is a campground, housekeeping cottage, and restaurant complex at mile 32.8 of Kentucky Lake on Ky-962 east of Fairdealing, Kentucky. The 60 campsites have electrical hookups, and there are six rental cottages (one-, two-, and three-bedroom), all completely furnished with kitchen utensils, linens, and double beds. The campground's services and facilities include flush toilets, showers, drinking water, launching ramp, picnic tables, and restaurant (breakfast and lunch only, carryout sandwiches and salads). The entire complex is open March 15 to November 15. Mailing address: Bee Springs Lodge, Route #4, Benton, Kentucky, 42025. Telephone: (502) 354-6515.

Hester's Spot in the Sun is a campground, housekeeping cottage, and marina complex three miles east of Fairdealing, Kentucky, off Ky-962 overlooking the lake. Open from the last week in March to Thanksgiving, the resort operates 20 campsites which are rented by the season only. All sites have complete hookups. The four two-bedroom cottages sleep up to 10 persons and rent for $25 to $30 a day. The two one-bedroom housekeeping cottages sleep up to seven persons and are comparably priced. The adjacent marina, open 24 hours a day during the season, rents 14-foot aluminum fishing boats that range in price from $10 to $15 a day depending on the size of the outboard (6- to 18-horsepower outboards available). Twenty-five-foot pontoon boats with 65-horsepower outboards rent for $35 a day. On all rental boats, the seventh day is free. Fuel, live bait (minnows, crickets, and red worms), a fish cleaning station, freezer space, and launching ramp are available for use by guests. Other facilities at Hester's Spot in the Sun include a tennis court, horseshoe pits, shuffleboard courts, and an indoor recreation room. Mailing address: Hester's Spot in the Sun, Route #4, Benton, Kentucky, 42025. Telephone: (502) 354-8280.

Just up the lake from Hester's Spot in the Sun is the Will-Vera Village, a lakeside complex of campsites, motel rooms, housekeeping cottages, and marina reached via highways US-68 and Ky-963, three miles east of Fairdealing, Kentucky. The complex is open April 1 to November 1. The Will-Vera Campground has 400 campsites, 350 of which have both water and electrical hookups. Mobile-home owners may rent space on a yearly basis only. Flush toilets, showers, drinking water, a grocery, grills, picnic tables, gift shop, and swimming pool are available to guests. Pets are welcome. There are 18 one- and two-bedroom housekeeping cottages and six motel units for rent. The 80-slip (40 covered, 40 open) marina is open from March 1 to November 1. Rental fishing and pontoon boats are available at the dock, as are fuel, live bait (minnows, crickets, and redworms), a fish cleaning station, and freezer space. A launching ramp is next to the marina. Mailing address: Will-Vera Village, Route #4, Benton, Kentucky, 42025. Telephone: (502) 354-6422.

The Jonathan Creek embayment has the largest concentration of campgrounds, marinas, and motel/housekeeping cottages anywhere north of the Tennessee line on Kentucky Lake. Four major resorts are located within a three-mile radius of the US-68 bridge over Jonathan Creek—Lakeside Camping Resort and Marina; Sportsman's Campground, Lodge, and Marina; Town and Country Resort; and Lakewood Camping Resort and Marina.

Lakeside Camping Resort and Marina has an 88-site campground, including 68 sites for RVs and 20 sites for tents, all with water and electricity. Flush toilets, showers, drinking water, swimming pool (for guests only), grocery, ice, camping supplies, picnic tables, grills, and playground are located on the grounds. The marina has 10 covered and 10 open slips. Guide service for fishermen is available. Both 14- and 16-foot aluminum fishing boats with 9½-horsepower outboards are available. Pontoon rental boats are equipped with 40-horsepower outboards. Live bait (crickets, minnows, and worms) and cut bait, as well as a fish cleaning station and freezer space, are available. There's a launching ramp at the dock. Both the campground and the marina are open 24 hours a day March 1 through October 31. Mailing address: Lakeside Camping Resort and Marina, Route #5, Benton, Kentucky, 42025. Telephone: (502) 354-8157.

The largest of the four resorts on Jonathan Creek and one of the most popular vacation spots on Kentucky Lake is the Sportsman's Campground, Lodge, and Marina. The 65-site campground is open from March 15 through October 31. There are 43 campsites with water and electrical hookups, 22 with water, electrical, and sewer hookups. The campground's facilities and services include a sanitary dump station for RVs, flush toilets, showers, drinking water, grocery, ice, picnic tables, grills, swimming pool, laundromat, indoor recreation room, and playground with volleyball and shuffleboard courts. An 18-unit motel offers both single sleeping rooms and rooms equipped with two double beds and a kitchenette. There are 34 housekeeping cottages (one-, two-, or three-bedroom), all with tile baths, air conditioning, electric heat, and television.

The Sportsman's Marina, open April 1 to November 1, has 245 slips, 185 of which are covered. Fourteen-foot aluminum fishing boats with 9½-horsepower outboards and 24- and 28-foot pontoon boats with 25- and 40-horsepower outboards are available. The fishing boats rent for $16 per day, the pontoon boats for $45 per day plus gas. A launching ramp is adjacent to the marina. Live bait (minnows, crickets, redworms) and cut bait, fuel, tackle, a fish cleaning station, freezer space, paddleboats ($5 per hour), and a boat wash are available at the marina. Mailing address: Sportsman's Campground, Lodge, and Marina, Route #5, Benton, Kentucky, 42025. Telephone: (502) 354-6568.

The 33-acre Town and Country Resort overlooking the lake has a 56-site campground, 13 motel room efficiencies, rental two-bedroom mobile homes, rental mobile home lots, and a marina. The recreational complex is open all year and off-season rates for all accommodations are in effect from November 1 through February 28. All campsites (open April 1 to November 1) are equipped with electrical, water, and sewer hookups. Drinking water, flush toilets, showers, laundry, grocery, picnic tables, grills, game room, and gift shop are all conveniently located for campers. The adjacent marina has 80 boat slips, 50 of which are covered. Fourteen- and 16-foot aluminum fishing boats, equipped with 9½- or 15-horsepower outboards rent for $15 per day and $17 per day, respectively. The boats alone rent for $5 and $7 a day. Pontoon boats, 24-footers with 40-horsepower outboards, rent for $10 an hour, $30 per half-day, or $45 per day. Other services include fuel sales, fish cleaning (with freezer space available), live bait (minnows, crickets, and worms) and cut bait, and an adjoining launching ramp. Each boat slip is equipped with water and electrical hookups and has its own individual locker. A floating patio is anchored at the dock for parties and cookouts; guide services for fishermen are available through the marina. Mailing address: Town and Country Resort, Route #5, Benton, Kentucky, 42025. Telephone: (502) 354-6587.

The Lakewood Camping Resort, one-quarter mile east of US-68 at the Jonathan Creek Bridge, is open March 1 to November 1. There are 70 campsites, 40 with water and electrical hookups, 30 with water, electrical, and sewer hookups. The campground's bathhouse is equipped with showers, flush toilets, and drinking water. Additional facilities include a playground, RV dump station, grocery (camping needs and ice), picnic tables, grills, picnic shelters, laundry, indoor recreation room, and swimming pool at the lakeside campground. Rental 14-foot fishing boats ($10 per day for boat and 6-horsepower motor; $4 per day for boat only) and live bait (redworms, crickets, and nightcrawlers) are available. Mailing address: Lakewood Camping Resort, Route #5, Benton, Kentucky, 42025. Telephone: (502) 354-8619.

Kenlake KOA Kampground, open year-round, has 75 sites (50 sites with water and electricity, 25 primitive sites). Located in Aurora off US-68, the campground's services and facilities include an RV dump station, flush toilets, showers, drinking water, grocery, laundry, adult lounge, playground, recreation room, ice, picnic tables, swimming pool, and barbecue grills. Mailing address: Kenlake KOA Kampground, Route #1, Aurora, Kentucky, 42048. Telephone: (502) 474-2778.

Aurora-Ken Oak Resort, across from the campground of Kenlake State Resort Park, is a motel, housekeeping cottage, and campground complex. There are 20 campsites, all with water and electrical hookups, an RV dump station, flush toilets, showers, drinking water, ice, picnic tables, two swimming pools, an indoor game room, and outdoor courts for shuffleboard and basketball. There are also 13 completely furnished housekeeping cottages (silverware, linens, etc.). The campground and cottages are open year-round; the 23 motel units are open April 1 to September 30. Mailing address: Aurora-Ken Oak Resort, Route #1, Box 514, Aurora, Kentucky, 42028. Telephone: (502) 474-2288.

Shortly after Kentucky Lake was built at the end of World War II, TVA transferred to the state 1,400 acres that eventually became Kenlake State Resort Park. The lodge was recently renovated and the park acreage expanded to 1,800 acres. Kenlake, open year-round, is one of the all-time favorites in the Kentucky Park System. This is partly because of its central location in Aurora, just across Eggners Ferry Bridge (US-68) from Land Between the Lakes.

Future plans call for the establishment of a major tennis facility on the park grounds. Completion of the project is slated for August 1979. The six tennis courts now in use will be expanded to 10, all outdoor hard-surface lighted courts. An indoor facility with four courts, pro shop, lockers, lounge, and vending machines is also planned. An outdoor amphitheater will be renovated into an outdoor championship arena which will seat 1,200 persons. Because of the park's proximity to Murray, Kentucky, a hotbed of collegiate tennis, it's the hope of Kentucky state park officials that small pro tournaments and exhibitions, college matches, and local amateur tournaments and the hiring of a teaching pro will make the "tennis park" concept successful, and lead to further expansion.

Kenlake State Resort Park is one of Kentucky's "fly-in parks." Murray Airport, 10 miles southwest of the park, has a 4,000-foot paved, lighted airstrip. Hangar space, tie-downs, fuel, and transportation to and from the park (by prior special arrangement) are available.

The park's facilities include the 44-room Kenlake Hotel (four rooms with one queen-size bed, 40 with two double beds, each with lake view, wall-to-wall carpeting, television, telephone, and private bath). There are 36 efficiency cottages, one-, two-, and three-bedroom units with studio couches that convert into beds for large families, combined kitchen and living room, fireplaces, balconies, telephone, television, and air conditioning. Complete linens, tableware, and silverware are included.

Maid service is available to lodge guests as is an auto shuttle service. Breakfast (7:00 to 10:30 a.m.), lunch (11:30 a.m. to 2:00 p.m.), and dinner (5:30 to 9:30 p.m.) are served daily in the 160-seating capacity dining room. Other features include meeting room, gift shop, handicap accommodations, recreation game room (air hockey and bumper pool), and year-round planned recreation program.

The recreational facilities at the park include a 9-hole golf course (rental clubs, pull carts, and gas riding carts are available), horseback riding stable, beach and bathhouse, picnic grounds with tables and shelter, playground, lodge pool for guests at the park (open Memorial Day to Labor Day), shuffleboard courts, and 92-site campground off US-68 overlooking the lake and Eggners Ferry Bridge. All sites have electrical and water hookups. Showers, flush toilets, coin laundry, and dump station are available. A grocery is located in nearby Aurora, as are restaurants and gift shops. The campground is open seasonally, April 1 to October 31. Mailing address: Kenlake State Resort Park, Hardin, Kentucky, 42048. Telephone: (502) 474-2211.

Adjacent to the park is Kenlake Marina, with 210 slips (160 covered, 50 open). Open 24 hours a day year-round, the marina has a snack bar and boating/fishing supplies, live bait (minnows, crickets, and worms) and cut bait, launching ramp, fish cleaning area, and freezer space, and mechanic on duty 24 hours a day. Fourteen-foot fishing boats with 9½-horsepower motors rent for $16 a day, seventh day free, and 24-foot pontoon boats with 35-horsepower outboards rent for $40 a day plus gas. In addition, the marina has 16-foot ski boats with 70-horsepower outboards for $18 an hour and sunfish day-sailboats for $20 a day. Mailing address: Kenlake Marina, Route #1, Aurora, Kentucky, 42028. Telephone: (502) 474-2211, ext. 171.

The Irvin Cobb Resort is located five miles northeast of Murray, Kentucky, off Ky-94 on Ky-732 overlooking the Blood River embayment. There are 35 campsites with electrical hookups and 10 primitive sites. Open April 1 to October 1, the campground, housekeeping cottage, and private dock complex is equipped with a bathhouse (showers, flush toilets, and drinking water for campers), 13 fully-furnished cottages (one- to four-bedrooms, $23 to $44 a day, seventh day free), launching ramp, and picnic area. Mailing address: Irvin Cobb Resort, Route #6, Murray, Kentucky, 42071. Telephone: (502) 436-5811.

The Blood River Dock and Campground, open April 1 to November 15, is nine miles north of Murray, Kentucky, via Ky-94 and Ky-280. Of the 27 campsites, 15 are equipped with water and electrical hookups and 12 are primitive sites. Mobile home sites with water, electrical, and sewer hookups are availabe on an annual basis only. Flush toilets, showers, drinking water, ice, picnic tables, and launching ramp are available at the campground which overlooks the lake. The marina has 40 open slips, and rents 14-foot fishing boats for $3 a day. Fuel, fishing supplies, live bait (minnows and crickets), and cut bait are available. Mailing address: Blood River Dock and Campground, Route #5, Murray, Kentucky, 42071. Telephone: (502) 436-5321.

Some Other Place, a complex of housekeeping cottages, campground, and marina, is the farthest south of the facilities on Kentucky Lake in Kentucky. Some Other Place is 15 miles southeast of Murray, Kentucky, off

Ky-121 on Fort Heiman Trail on the Cypress embayment of Kentucky Lake at the Tennessee-Kentucky line. There are 12 campsites, 8 with water and electrical hookups, 4 primitive. The air-conditioned housekeeping cottages include four two-bedroom units and one four-bedroom unit (rental rates range from $20 to $35 a day) and are completely furnished. A bathhouse at the campground is equipped with showers, flush toilets, and drinking water. Other facilities include a grocery (ice, milk, bread and butter, and canned staples), picnic tables, grills, and sand beach. The marina has 20 boat slips, 15 covered and 5 open. Fourteen-foot fishing boats with 9½-horsepower outboards rent for $12 a day with motor (plus gas), $5 a day without motor. Pontoon boats, 16-footers with 9½-horsepower outboards and 25-footers with 40-horsepower outboards, rent for $16 and $25 a day, respectively. Regular gas, live bait (minnows, crickets, and red worms), a fish cleaning station and freezer space, and launching ramp are available. The complex is open, weather permitting, from April 1 to October 31. Mailing address: Some Other Place, Route #1, New Concord, Kentucky, 42076. Telephone: (502) 436-5519.

Kenlake State Resort Park. Photograph by Kentucky Department of Public Information.

5
Selected Small Lakes Their Parks, Marinas, and Campgrounds

Herrington Lake

Built in 1925 by the Kentucky Utilities Company primarily for the generation of hydroelectric power, Herrington Lake was the first large-scale impoundment built in Kentucky. The 35-mile-long lake is the boundary between Mercer, Garrard, and Boyle counties in central Kentucky. The 1,860-acre lake is east of Harrodsburg, Kentucky, and is reached via Ky-33, Ky-152, Ky-34, US-27, and US-127.

There are nine marinas and four campgrounds on the lake; all are privately-owned. The facilities which follow are listed from the lake headwaters downstream to Dix Dam. Cane Run and Tanyard Branch are both no-wake areas.

Key Landing Campground, three miles east of Danville on Ky-34, is open year-round. There's a total of 21 campsites, 12 with water hookups, 6 with electrical hookups, and 3 primitive sites. The campground's bathhouse has showers, flush toilets, sinks, and drinking water. Ice, canned goods, snacks, and camping supplies are available at the grocery. Other facilities include an RV dump station, boat launching ramp, private boat dock for guests only, and picnic grounds. Mailing address: Key Landing Campground, Route #1, Taylor Road, Danville, Kentucky, 40422. Telephone: (606) 236-4713.

Bryant's Camp and Marina is three miles east of Danville on Ky-34. The housekeeping cottage, restaurant, and marina complex is open April 1 to November 1. There are 10 completely furnished housekeeping cottages with one to four bedrooms. All have lake views and rent for $14 to $40 per night. The marina has 30 open boat slips. Fourteen-foot fishing boats with 6- or 10-horsepower outboards rent for $8 and $11, respectively, gas included. Boats only rent for $4 for a 12-hour day. Regular and mixed gas, ice, launching ramp, tackle, live bait (redworms, minnows, crickets, night-crawlers, and meal worms), fish cleaning station, and freezer space are available. The restaurant, also open from April 1 to November 1, serves breakfast, coffee, and sandwiches from daylight to 9:00 p.m. daily. Mailing address: Bryant's Camp and Marina, P.O. Box 397, Danville, Kentucky, 40422. Telephone: (606) 236-5601.

King's Mill Marina is six miles south of Danville on Ky-34. Open year-round, the marina has 40 open slips and a snack bar on the dock (hot sandwiches, candy, and soft drinks). Fourteen-foot fishing boats rent for $4 a day, $12 a day with a 6½-horsepower outboard. Regular gas, live bait (minnows, worms, and crickets), ice, tackle, artificial bait, and boat launching ramp are available. Mailing address: King's Mill Marina, Route #2, Lancaster, Kentucky, 40444. Telephone: (606) 548-2091.

Gwinn Island Fishing Camp is three miles northeast of Danville, off Ky-33. Open February 28 to November 30, the marina has 10 covered and 30 open slips. There's a restaurant on the grounds (open Memorial Day to Labor Day, 6:30 a.m. to 9:00 p.m daily), as well as 38 housekeeping cottages (fully-equipped except for towels and soap) that rent for $15 to $37 a night, $65 to $125 a week. Rental fishing boats, 14-footers, are $4 a day ($2 a day for cabin guests) or $15 a day with 6-horsepower outboards ($12 a day for cabin guests). Twenty-foot pontoon boats with 35-horse-power outboards rent for $60 a day. Fuel (regular and mixed), live bait (minnows, crickets, and nightcrawlers), tackle, artificial bait, a fish cleaning station, and launching ramp are available. Mailing address: Gwinn Island Fishing Camp, Route #2, Danville, Kentucky, 40422. Telephone: (606) 236-9825.

Paradise Fishing Camp, three miles southeast of Burgin on Paradise Camp Road off Ky-33, is open year-round. There are 10 campsites, 4 of which are rented on an annual basis to mobile home owners. Electrical outlets, drinking water, flush toilets, and picnic grills are available. Additionally, there are four rental cottages, all with two bedrooms and kitchen. Guests should bring their own linens. The cottages rent for $20 per night per couple or $90 a week. The marina has 15 open slips, rental fishing boats ($4 a day boat only, $9 to $15 a day with outboard motor), regular and mixed gas, tackle, live bait (redworms, minnows, and crickets), boat launching ramp, fish cleaning station, freezer space, and part-time me-chanic on duty. Mailing address: Paradise Fishing Camp, Box 356, Burgin, Kentucky, 40310. Telephone: (606) 748-5504.

Red Gate Camp, 11 miles north of Lancaster, Kentucky, is reached via US-27, Ky-753, and Tanyard Road. The marina is on Tanyard Branch, west of Bryantsville, Kentucky. Open 24 hours a day from March 1 to December 15, the marina has 25 open slips and a snack bar (hot sandwiches, soft drinks, and candy). Overnight accommodations are available on a house-boat, which sleeps four persons and is completely furnished, for $10 a day or $50 a week. Fourteen-foot fiberglass boats rent for $4 for a 12-hour day; boats with 7½-horsepower outboard rent for $12 (plus gas). Rental lockers, regular gas, live bait (minnows, crickets, redworms, and nightcrawlers), a fish cleaning station, freezer space, boat launching ramp, and covered 30- by 15-foot fishing dock are available. Mailing address: Red Gate Camp, Route #4, Lancaster, Kentucky, 40444. Telephone: (606) 548-3461.

Old Orchard Inn is four miles east of Burgin, Kentucky, on Ky-152. Open April 1 to October 1, the recreational complex includes a campground, motel units, and housekeeping cottages. There are 10 campsites with water and electrical hookups; two motel rooms which rent for $16 a night; two efficiency apartments, $16 a night (sleep four); one-bedroom cottages with no kitchen, $10 a night; and one large housekeeping cottage, fully equipped, that will sleep up to 10 persons (rates start at $20 a night for four persons, $2 per night per extra person). A bathhouse for campers is equipped with flush toilets, showers, and drinking water. A grocery store (canned foods and camping supplies), picnic tables and grills, RV dump station, laundry, playground, and swimming pool are on the grounds. Mailing address: Old Orchard Inn, Route #1, Burgin, Kentucky, 40310. Telephone: (606) 748-5155.

Camp Kennedy Dock and Restaurant is four miles east of Burgin on Ky-152 at Kennedy Bridge. The marina is open year-round; the restaurant which serves a full menu of foods, is open March 1 to November 30. The 49 covered slips are available for yearly rental only; the 50 open slips and buoy lines can be rented by the month or yearly. There are three fully-furnished bedroom cabins (open year-round) that sleep eight each. The rent is $20 a day (minimum of two days on weekends) or $85 a week. Fourteen-foot fishing boats with 6- or 9-horsepower outboards are available for rental, as well as one 20-foot pontoon boat with 40-horsepower outboard ($35 a day). Other facilities include regular and mixed gas, tackle, live bait (minnows, redworms, and crickets), fish cleaning station, boat launching ramp, and three RV sites, all with water and electrical hookups. Mailing address: Camp Kennedy Dock and Restaurant, Box H, Burgin, Kentucky, 40310. Telephones: dock, (606) 548-2101; restaurant, (606) 548-3341.

Chimney Rock Resort, eight miles east of Burgin on Ky-152, is open April 1 to November 1, weather permitting. The campground (with swimming pool for guests only) has 75 sites: 10 with water and electrical hookups; 40 with water, electrical, and sewer hookups; and 35 primitive sites. Picnic tables, RV dump station, laundry, showers, flush toilets, and drinking water are available. There are six two-bedroom rental A-frames completely furnished (dishes, linens, cable color TV, tableware, and living room) that sleep up to nine persons and rent for $20 per day for two people, $5 per night per additional person. The marina has 24 covered and 200 open slips, all rented by the week, month, or year. Fourteen-foot fishing boats with 7-horsepower outboards, rent for $15 a day or $4 a day for the boat only. Ice, mixed and regular gas, live bait (worms, crickets, and minnows), tackle and artificial baits, fish cleaning station, candy and soft drinks, and boat launching ramp are available. Mailing address: Chimney Rock Resort, Route #1, Harrodsburg, Kentucky, 40330. Telephone: (606) 748-5252.

Freeman's Fishing Camp, open year-round, is three miles east of Burgin on Ky-152. The marina has 60 covered slips and 20 open slips. Fourteen-foot fiberglass fishing boats with 6-horsepower outboards rent for $12 a day, $4 a day for the boat only. Sandwiches, soft drinks, and snacks, tackle, handmade rods, regular and mixed gas, live bait (minnows, worms, and crickets), fish cleaning station, and freezer space are available at the dock. There's an outboard motor sales and service and boat and trailer sales office at the marina. A 30-site trailer park is also on the grounds. Three of the sites are equipped with trailers for daily and weekly rental, $17.50 per night per couple; the remainder are rented year-round only. Mailing address: Freeman's Fishing Camp, Route #1, Harrodsburg, Kentucky, 40330. Telephone: (606) 748-5487.

Royalty's Fishing Camp is on the Curdsville Road, off Ky-33 east of Burgin. Open year-round, there are 105 boat slips at the marina, 40 covered and 65 open. Soft drinks, candy, hot sandwiches, tackle, and boating supplies are available at the dock. The motel has 10 one- and two-bedrooms units, some with kitchens, that rent for $12 to $16 a night, and two fully-equipped housekeeping cottages that rent for $20 a night. Fourteen-foot fishing boats are available for a day, $14 a day with 6-horsepower outboards. Other facilities include mixed and regular gas, live bait (minnows, crickets, and worms), boat launching ramp, fish cleaning station, and freezer space. Mailing address: Royalty's Fishing Camp, Route #4, Harrodsburg, Kentucky, 40330. Telephone: (606) 748-5459.

Williamstown Lake

Williamstown Lake is two miles east of Williamstown, Kentucky, in Grant County between Ky-489 and Ky-467. The 318-acre lake was opened to fishing in 1957. There are two marinas on the lake.

The Williamstown Boat Dock, two miles east of Williamstown on Fairview Road off Ky-489, is open year-round and has 36 boat slips, 16 covered and 20 open. Fourteen-foot fishing boats rent for $8 a day, $16 a day with 6-horsepower outboards. Mixed and regular gas, live bait (minnows, meal worms, crickets, and nightcrawlers), tackle, artificial bait, boating accessories, fish cleaning station and freezer space, boat launching ramp, and factorized service for boats and motors are available. Mailing address: Williamstown Boat Dock, Inc., Route #2, Williamstown, Kentucky, 41097. Telephone: (606) 823-0501.

Young's Boat Dock, five miles east of Dry Ridge, Kentucky, on Ky-467 (Knoxville Road), is open March 1 to November 30. The marina has 15 open slips, snack bar (hot sandwiches, candy, and soft drinks), a six-site campground (pit toilets, drinking water, and picnic tables), and rental fishing boats. The 14-foot boats are $4 a day, $8 a day with 10-horsepower outboards. Regular gas, live bait (minnows, nightcrawlers, and redworms), freezer space, and boat launching ramp are available. Mailing address: Young's Boat Dock, Route #2, Dry Ridge, Kentucky, 41035. Telephone: (606) 823-9031.

Grayson Lake

Grayson Lake, completed in April of 1969, is a 1,510-acre lake built under the supervision of the U.S. Army Corps of Engineers, Huntington, West Virginia. Grayson Lake is seven miles south of Grayson, Kentucky, off Ky-7 in Carter and Elliot counties. The 20-mile-long lake was impounded from the Little Sandy River.

The major recreational development on Grayson Lake is Grayson Lake State Park, opened in 1970. The 2,700-acre park has a campground and marina on the grounds. The campground at Rolling Hills, open April 1 to October 31, has 271 campsites, 71 with electrical hookups and 200 primitive. Flush toilets, showers, and drinking water are available at two bathhouses. The campground's facilities also include RV dump station, beach, laundry, playground, picnic tables, and grills. At the adjoining Bruin Site, there's a three-lane boat launching ramp, pit toilets, and paved parking area. Mailing address: Grayson Lake State Park, Route #3, Box 415, Olive Hill, Kentucky, 41164. Telephone: (606) 474-9727.

The marina, open April 1 to October 31, weather permitting, has 132 boat slips, 48 covered and 84 open, equipped with buoy lines and bank tie-ups. There's a snack bar on the marina, and camping, houseboat, and marine supplies are available. Fifteen-foot fishing boats with and without outboards and 25-foot pontoon boats with 35-horsepower outboards are available. Regular gas, outboard repair, live bait (minnows, worms, crickets, nightcrawlers, and catalpa and horseweed worms in season), boat sales, ski supplies, and boat launching ramp are available. Mailing address: Grayson Marina Recreation, Inc., Route #7, Grayson, Kentucky, 41143. Telephone: (606) 474-6277.

Mailing address for the U. S. Army Corps of Engineers at Grayson Lake: Route #2, Box 73A, Grayson, Kentucky, 41143. Telephone: (606) 474-5107 or (606) 474-5815.

Bullock Pen Lake

Bullock Pen Lake is in Grant County, approximately two miles west of Crittenden, Kentucky, off Ky-491. The 142-acre lake was opened to public fishing in 1953. The only marina on the lake is Lucille's Boat Dock, open February 15 to December 15, weather permitting. The marina has 40 open boat slips, snack bar (candy, soft drinks, and hot sandwiches), and fishing boats, both 14- and 16-footers. The rental cost for a boat only is $4 for five hours, $8 all day; with 5-horsepower outboard, it's $8 for five hours, $16 all day. Mixed gas, live bait (minnows, nightcrawlers, wax worms, meal worms, and redworms), tackle and artificial bait, and boat launching ramp are available. Mailing address: Lucille's Boat Dock, Box 51, Crittenden, Kentucky, 41030. Telephone: (606) 428-1644.

Guist Creek Lake

Guist Creek Lake is approximately two miles east of Shelbyville, Kentucky, off US-60 in Shelby County. The 304-acre lake was opened to public fishing in 1963. The only commercial marina and campground complex on Guist Creek Lake is on Ky-1779 (Benson Road) northeast of Shelbyville. Open March 1 to November 1, the campground has 75 campsites with water and electrical hookups and 20 primitive sites. There are two bathhouses with flush toilets, showers, and drinking water. Picnic tables, grills, and RV dump station are available at the lakeside campground. The marina, also open March 1 to November 1, has 50 open boat slips, a snack bar (soft drinks, candy, and hot sandwiches), and rental 14-foot fishing boats, $5 a day boat only, $13.50 a day with 6-horsepower outboards. Mixed gas, live bait (minnows, nightcrawlers, crickets, meal worms, redworms, and wax worms), and boat launching ramp ($2 launch fee) are available. Mailing address: Guist Creek Dock and Campground, Route #7, Box F25, Shelbyville, Kentucky, 40065. Telephone: (502) 633-1934.

Dewey Lake

Dewey Lake, an 1150-acre impoundment on John's Creek, a tributary to the Levisa Fork of the Big Sandy, was built by the Huntington, West Virginia, office of the U. S. Army Corps of Engineers. Construction on the seven-mile-long lake was completed in 1962. Dewey Lake is in Floyd County, Kentucky, east of Prestonsburg. The main access roads to the lake are Ky-3 and US-460.

The lake's major recreational facility is Jenny Wiley State Resort Park. The 1,700-acre park was named in honor of Jenny Wiley, who lived in the Big Sandy country with her pioneer husband Thomas, her three children, and her younger brother. Their nearest neighbor was a man named Mathias Harmon, a professional hunter whose frequent clashes with the Indians had earned him their undying enmity.

In the early fall of 1789 a small Cherokee war party teamed up with the Shawnee and ambushed Harmon and his fellow hunters on the Tug Fork of the Big Sandy River. Harmon escaped in the darkness but the Indians believed they had killed him. And since they knew where his homestead was, they determined to make their triumph complete by wiping out his entire family.

So it was that on October 1, 1789, the Wiley family's sleep was shattered by the savage screeching and whooping of Indian marauders. They had attacked the wrong cabin but didn't realize it until they examined the corpse of Tom Wiley. By then Jenny's brother and her older children had also been killed. Jenny was dragged off clutching her baby.

The girl's living nightmare was made even more grisly by the fact that she was in late pregnancy. She was forced to keep up with the marauders, who knew they were being hunted. When the baby became a hindrance one of the warriors tore it from Jenny's arms and bashed its head against a tree.

Mathias Harmon and a party of avengers searched frantically for the war party, but the Indians proved elusive. After nine days, they paused on the Cherokee Fork of Big Blain Creek and it was there in a cave that Jenny Wiley bore her fourth child.

The savages had a simple test for babies on the march. If a child cried at the touch of cold water it was a weakling and not worthy of living. So Jenny's new-born infant was thrust into the icy creek, and when it whimpered in protest it was tossed pitilessly out into the swiftly running water.

Although almost mad with grief and pain the bereaved young mother was then loaded like a pack animal and goaded into motion as the agonizing journey resumed. Eventually the war party arrived at the main Shawnee encampment on Little Mud Creek in Johnson County. A wild celebration ensued and Jenny saw another white captive, a young man, being tied to a stake. He was fiendishly tortured by the squaws and the children for hours before being burned alive.

Jenny knew then that she had been spared only to provide gruesome entertainment for the tribe, but life had become such a routine of misery that she no longer cared. Then she began to realize that her hour had been postponed. The Cherokee chief who had joined the Shawnee had been studying Jenny on the journey and had decided to add her to his band of Indian wives. Now he was bargaining with the Shawnee chief. The price settled, the Cherokee strode across to Jenny and examined her as he would a horse, twisting her head roughly by the hair, looking into her mouth, and prodding her muscles.

Finally he grunted approval and the deal was closed. Jenny was pulled roughly to another part of the encampment and tied to a tree. In the chill rain that began to fall Jenny gave way to despair. And then a thrill of excitement brought her head up sharply. The drenching rain had softened and loosened the rawhide thongs that bound her. She worked feverishly until she was free, and then ran blindly into the forest. When she could run no further she crawled into a huge hollow log and collapsed from exhaustion.

Many hours later, somewhat rested but still terrified of being recaptured, she pushed on through the heavy woods until she encountered Little Paint Creek. Normally a peaceful stream, the creek was now swollen to a raging torrent by heavy rains. Jenny saw a white man moving on the far side and when she shouted above the roaring water he turned and she recognized him as an old friend, Henry Skaggs.

Henry managed to launch an old mulberry log and steer it across to Jenny. They clung to it until they had kicked their way back across the roaring creek. Even as they staggered up the bank to safety, wet and numb with cold, they heard angry yelling and saw the pursuing Cherokee chief and his braves across the water. They could distinguish one word clearly in the garbled shouting that was part Cherokee and a little English.

"Honor," the Cherokee kept saying. "Honor, white squaw!" He was obviously trying to impress upon her that he had purchased her in the proper manner and that she had no right to run from him.

Skaggs fired a shot in the general direction of the enraged savages, then he and Jenny lit out through the forest toward family, friends, food, and shelter.

Jenny Wiley died in 1831 at the age of 71. The legend of her ordeal spread throughout the frontier and took its place firmly in the folklore of the Big Sandy country.

Jenny Wiley State Resort Park is open year-round. The lodge has 48 rooms, each with two double beds, bath, TV, telephone, and air conditioning. There are 6 one-bedroom duplex cottages and 10 two-bedroom cottages, each with living room, kitchen, and bath. All cottages have television, telephone, air conditioning, and electric heat. Tableware, cooking utensils, and linens are furnished.

A dining room, gift shop featuring wildlife prints and Kentucky handcrafts, meeting rooms, and recreation room (billiards, checkers, video games, and table tennis) are housed in the lodge. The recreational facilities include a nine-hole golf course, 18-hole miniature golf course, day-hiking trails, horseback riding stables (open Memorial Day to Labor Day), picnic grounds, playgrounds, shuffleboard, swimming pool (for lodge and cottage guests only), community pool (also seasonal), and skylift, which operates daily during the season and on weekends the rest of the year, weather permitting.

The park's campground at Gobel's Branch is open April 1 to October 31. There are 128 campsites, all with electrical hookups, 42 with water hookups. The two bathhouses have flush toilets, showers, and drinking water. Canned goods, camping supplies, soft drinks, and ice are available at the grocery. Picnic tables, grills, and shelters are provided for picnickers. The adjacent Jenny Wiley Marina (Brandy Keg), open year-round, has 199 boat slips, 126 covered and 73 open. A snack bar on the dock, open seasonally, has sandwiches, breakfast, and coffee. A second dock is under construction. Fifteen-foot fishing boats rent for $4 a day; with a 9-horsepower outboard, they're $15 a day, plus gas. Live bait, tackle, and artificial bait, boat launching ramp, and regular gas are available. Mailing address: Jenny Wiley State Resort Park, Prestonsburg, Kentucky, 41653. Telephone: (606) 886-2711.

The U. S. Army Corps of Engineers operates one campground and two day-use areas on Dewey Lake. The German Campground, six miles south of Prestonsburg on Ky-1428, then seven miles east on Ky-194, is the largest Corps-managed site. Open May 15 (earlier if weather is good) to September 5, the campground has 55 primitive campsites, and an additional 65 primitive sites are under construction. The bathhouses are equipped with showers, flush toilets, and drinking water. The facilities include RV dump station, boat launching ramp, picnic tables, grills, playground, and laundry.

The Corps-managed day-use areas are located at the damsite and at Hagar Gap. The facilities at the dam include a playground, picnic tables, flush toilets, drinking water, basketball and tennis courts, and softball diamond. The Hagar Gap site, reached via Ky-304, is a picnic area with picnic tables, grills, shelter, drinking water, and pit toilets. During periods of high visitor use the Hagar Gap site also serves as a primitive campground. Mailing address: U. S. Army Corps of Engineers, Dewey Lake, Prestonsburg, Kentucky, 41653. Telephone: (606) 886-6709.

Adjacent to Jenny Wiley State Resort Park is the only other marina on Dewey Lake, Terry's Boat Dock, open April 15 to November 1. The marina has 175 open slips. Fourteen-foot fishing boats rent for $5 a day, $15 a day with 10-horsepower outboards. Regular gas, live bait (minnows and nightcrawlers), boating supplies, artificial baits and dough balls, tackle, and boat launching ramp are available. Mailing address: Terry's Boat Dock, Route #2, Box 320, Prestonsburg, Kentucky, 41653. Telephone: (606) 886-9727.

Beaver Lake

Beaver Lake is in Anderson County in central Kentucky, approximately 10 miles southwest of Lawrenceburg off US-62. The 170-acre lake was built in 1963 and opened to the public in 1964. The only facilities on the lake are at Beaver Lake Boat Dock, off US-62, open March 1 to November 1, weather permitting. There are 40 open boat slips, a snack bar (sandwiches, soft drinks, and candy), and 14-foot fishing boats available for rental at the dock. Boats are $4 per day, $10.50 per day with 6-horsepower outboards, gas included. Mixed gas, live bait (minnows, crickets, meal worms, and wax worms) and chicken livers, artificial bait, cane poles, reels, boat launching ramp, fish cleaning station, and limited freezer space are available. An adjacent campground, also open March 1 to November 1, has 30 campsites (24 with electrical hookups, 6 primitive), pit toilets, drinking water, and ice. Mailing address: Beaver Lake Boat Dock, Route #3, Lawrenceburg, Kentucky, 40342. Telephone: (502) 839-4402.

Carr Fork Lake

Construction on Carr Fork Lake began in 1962; the 710-acre, five-and-one-half-mile-long impoundment was completed in 1976. The damsite is 8.8 miles above the mouth of Carr Fork Creek, a tributary to the North Fork of the Kentucky River. Carr Fork Lake is approximately 23 miles southeast of Hazard, Kentucky, in Knott County, and can be reached via Ky-15, Ky-1231, Ky-160, and Ky-1410.

Carr Fork Lake was built by the Louisville District, U. S. Army Corps of

Engineers. There are three lake access areas (two with campgrounds and one marina), a day-use recreation area at the damsite, and an overlook/picnic area operated and maintained by the Corps.

The Dam and Tailwater Recreation Area on Ky-1089, one mile north of Ky-15, 14 miles east of Hazard, is open year-round. There are flush toilets, drinking water, boat launching ramp, picnic tables, grills, a shelter, and a nature interpretive trail below the dam on Carr Fork Creek. Nearby is another day-use area, an overlook site on Ky-15 one mile east of its junction with Ky-1089. Picnic tables and grills, pit toilets, and paved parking lot are located at the overlook.

The largest Corps-managed recreation area on Carr Fork Lake is the Irishman Recreation Area on Ky-15, 15 miles east of Hazard. Open May 15 to Labor Day, the campground has 38 campsites, 10 with water hookups. The bathhouse at the campground is equipped with showers, flush toilets, and drinking water. Other services and facilities include RV dump station, picnic tables, picnicking shelter, and sand beach with bathhouse (opens on Memorial Day). Adjacent to the recreation area are a restaurant and marina.

The Irishman Creek Marina has 36 open slips and 20 buoy markers. Open March 15 to November 15, the marina has 14-foot rental fishing boats (boat only, $7 a day; with 10-horsepower outboard, $15 a day); 24-foot pontoon boats with 55-horsepower outboards and 28-foot pontoon boats with 60-horsepower outboards ($45 to $50 a day); and 14-foot runabouts with either 40- or 50-horsepower outboards ($10 an hour). Regular gas, live bait (minnows and nightcrawlers), tackle, a fish cleaning station, freezer space, and launching ramp are available at the marina. A restaurant on the grounds is open year-round. Mailing address: Irishman Creek Marina, Inc., Box 5, Route #15, Red Fox, Kentucky, 41847. Telephones: marina, (606) 642-3280; restaurant, (606) 642-3441.

The other Corps-managed recreation area is the Littcarr Recreation Area, six miles up the lake on Ky-160 off Ky-15 at the confluence of Shingle Branch. There are 28 campsites, about half with water hookups. Flush toilets, showers, and drinking water are available. Open May 15 to Labor Day, the lake-view campground has three picnicking shelters, picnic tables, a boat launching ramp, and RV dump station. Mailing address: U.S. Army Corps of Engineers, Carr Fork Lake, General Delivery, Sassafras, Kentucky, 41759. Telephone: (606) 642-3951.

Buckhorn Lake

Construction on 21-mile-long Buckhorn Lake began in 1956, and the project was completed four years later. The 1,200-acre reservoir, built by the

U.S. Army Corps of Engineers, Louisville District, lies in Leslie and Perry counties of eastern Kentucky, west of Hazard. Buckhorn Dam is located on the middle fork of the Kentucky River, 43 miles upstream from Beattyville, where the three forks of the Kentucky River converge.

The lake's primary recreation development is Buckhorn Lake State Resort Park, 15 miles west of Hazard off Ky-28 on Ky-1833. The 856-acre park is open May 1 to October 31. Construction of the lodge, campgrounds, and recreational facilities was completed in 1962. The 36 lodge rooms are equipped with two double beds, ceramic tile bath with tub and shower, color television, telephone, air conditioning, and a private patio or balcony with lake-view. The 200-capacity dining room in the lodge is open for breakfast from 7:00 to 10:30 a.m., lunch from 11:30 a.m. to 2:30 p.m., and dinner from 5:30 to 9:00 p.m. A gift shop featuring a large assortment of Kentucky-made dolls and a recreation room with air hockey, foosball, table tennis, and video games are also located in the lodge. Other facilities include naturalist-led programs on Leatherwood and Moonshiner day-hiking trails, bicycle rentals, miniature golf, two tennis courts and swimming pool (open seasonally, Memorial Day to Labor Day, for lodge guests only), and seasonal beach and bathhouse complex.

The park's campground, located at the Gays Creek site three miles west of the lodge, is open May 1 to Labor Day, and has 112 sites (72 with electrical hookups, 40 primitive). Flush toilets, showers, drinking water, RV dump station, ice, picnic tables, and grills are available. The Buckhorn Lake State Resort Park Marina, adjacent to the lodge, is open May 1 to October 31, and has 100 open slips. A restaurant on the marina is open May 1 to Labor Day. Fourteen-foot fishing boats with 9-horsepower outboards rent for $3.50 an hour or $15 for 12 hours. Thirty-foot pontoon boats with 20-horsepower outboards rent for $7.50 an hour or $35 for 12 hours. Fuel, both mixed and regular, live bait (minnows, crickets, and worms), tackle, a fish cleaning station, freezer space, and boat launching ramp are available. Mailing address: Buckhorn Lake State Resort Park, Buckhorn, Kentucky, 41721. Telephone: (606) 398-7510; marina extension, 120.

The U.S. Army Corps of Engineers operates four lake access sites, three with campgrounds. The dam-site recreation area on Ky-28, 28 miles west of Hazard, is located below Buckhorn Dam along the tailwaters. Open year-round, the campground has 29 primitive campsites, drinking water, pit toilets, a boat launching ramp on the river, playground, picnic tables, and grills. The Leatherwood Site on Ky-484 at Saul, Kentucky, off Ky-1482 east of Oneida, has 30 primitive campsites, drinking water, pit toilets, picnic grills, and tables. The Leatherwood Site is open year-round and functions basically as a visitor overflow camping area.

The Confluence Site, on Ky-257 west of the Dry Hill Bridge at Confluence, Kentucky, is a day-use area with pit toilets, drinking water, picnic tables, paved parking lot, and boat launching ramp. The Trace Branch Site, east of Krypton, Kentucky, off Ky-451, is open year-round. Facilities include 31 primitive campsites, pit toilets, drinking water, picnic tables, grills, paved parking lot, and boat launching ramp. Mailing address: U. S. Army Corps of Engineers, Buckhorn Lake Resource Manager's Office, Buckhorn, Kentucky, 41721. Telephone: (606) 398-7251.

Kincaid Lake

Kincaid Lake, opened to the public in 1963, was impounded from Kincaid Creek, a tributary of the Licking River. The 196-acre lake is in Pendleton County, three miles northeast of Falmouth, Kentucky, on Ky-159.

The lake was built shortly after Kincaid Lake State Park opened in 1960. The 448-acre park and many of its facilities are open year-round except for a holiday break for the employees, December 18 to January 4. The seasonal facilities (open Memorial Day to Labor Day) include swimming beach and bathhouse complex, miniature golf, tennis courts, and an amphitheater featuring summer children's programs and puppet shows.

The park's campground has 100 primitive sites and 80 sites with water and electrical hookups. Drinking water, showers, and flush toilets are available at the four bathhouses in the campground. The grocery stocks canned goods, meats, milk, and other staples. Picnic tables, grills, ice, RV dump station, laundry, recreation room, playground, horseshoe pits, and volleyball, basketball, and shuffleboard courts are located in the campground.

The Kincaid Lake State Park Marina has 22 open slips, 14 of which are available for rental on a daily, weekly, or annual basis. The fleet of 32 rental boats includes 14-foot fishing boats with 10-horsepower outboards ($4 for boat only or $10 for boat and motor per day) and a 20-foot pontoon boat with 15-horsepower outboard ($30 a day); hourly rates are available. Mixed gas, minnows, worms, crickets, and boat launching ramp are available. Mailing address: Kincaid Lake State Park, Falmouth, Kentucky, 41040. Telephone: (606) 654-3531.

Lake Malone

Lake Malone was built in 1961 and opened to the public in 1963. The 692-acre lake in Muhlenberg, Todd, and Logan counties is 18 miles south of Central City, Kentucky, off US-431 on Ky-973 one mile west of Dunmor, Kentucky.

Virtually the only recreational facilities on the lake are at Lake Malone State Park. Open April 1 to October 31, the 338-acre park has a campground with 60 primitive sites and 20 sites with electrical hookups. Flush toilets, showers, and drinking water are available at the campground's bathhouse. Picnic tables, grills, RV dump station, laundry, and game courts (basketball, horseshoes, volleyball, and badminton) are on the grounds. The beach and bathhouse complex on the lake is open seasonally, Memorial Day to Labor Day.

The park's marina, open April 1 to October 31, has 60 open slips. Fourteen-foot fishing boats with 5½-horsepower outboards may be rented for $3.50 an hour (two hour minimum) or $14 from sunrise to sunset. Mixed gas, live bait (minnows, worms, and crickets), artificial lures and tackle, and boat launching ramp are available at the dock. Mailing address: Lake Malone State Park, Dunmor, Kentucky, 42339. Telephone: (502) 657-2111.

The other marina on Lake Malone is Cherokee Beach and Boat Dock on Ky-1293, off US-431, just southwest of the city limits of Dunmor. Open March 15 to November 1, the marina has 28 slips. Regular gas, live bait (minnows, crickets, and nightcrawlers), and hot sandwiches, soft drinks, and candy are available at the dock. One-bedroom cottages, fully-furnished (linens, TV, air conditioning), are rented for weekends or by the week only. Rental cost for a weekend is $40 to $45, by the week $70 to $80. Fourteen-foot fishing boats rent for $4 a day; with 6- and 18-horsepower outboards, they rent for $10 and $18, respectively. A fish cleaning station, freezer space, swimming beach, and boat launching ramp are available. Mailing address: Cherokee Beach and Boat Dock, Route #1, Dunmor, Kentucky, 42339. Telephone: (502) 657-2595.

Greenbo Lake

Greenbo Lake is in the extreme northeastern corner of Kentucky where Ohio, West Virginia, and Kentucky meet. The 192-acre lake is 15 miles west of Ashland, Kentucky, in Greenup County, and can be reached via Ky-23 and Ky-1. Greenbo Lake was built in 1955 and opened to the public in 1958.

Greenbo Lake State Park was opened two years later. In the late 1960s the 3,300-acre park gained "resort park" status. The lodge and campground facilities are open year-round, the marina from April 1 to October

31. The 36-room lodge is named in honor of the author Jesse Stuart, who grew up in Greenup County. All furnishings in the three-story lodge were made in Kentucky. Each lodge room is equipped with two double beds, television, telephone, tile bath with shower, and private patio or balcony overlooking the lake.

A 225-capacity dining room is open for breakfast from 7:00 to 10:30 a.m., luncheon from 11:30 a.m. to 2:30 p.m., and dinner from 5:30 to 9:00 p.m. The lodge has a gift shop; a meeting room seating 150; a recreation room with billiards, cards, checkers, chess, and table tennis; a playground for children, and a swimming pool, for lodge guests only, open from Memorial Day to Labor Day. The park's other recreational facilities include tennis courts, bicycle rentals, sand beach and bathhouse complex (open from Memorial Day to Labor Day), miniature golf, seasonal horseback riding, day-hiking trails in the vicinity of a nineteenth-century blast furnace, and shuffleboard, basketball, and volleyball courts.

The park's campground, located on Claylick Creek at the head of Greenbo Lake, is open year-round with 106 sites (76 with electrical hook-ups, 30 primitive). There are two central service buildings with showers, drinking water, and flush toilets. The services and facilities also include two RV dump stations, picnic tables, grills, shelters, ice, and playgrounds.

The 10-slip marina is open April 1 to October 31. Fourteen-foot fishing boats with 6-horsepower outboards rent for $3.50 an hour or $14 a day; the boats alone rent for $1 an hour or $5 a day. Pontoon boats, 18-footers with 6-horsepower outboards, rent for $7 an hour, $30 all day. Regular and mixed gas, a boat launching ramp, canoe rentals ($2 an hour), live bait (minnows, crickets, and worms), fishing tackle, and artificial bait are also available. Mailing address: Greenbo Lake State Resort Park, Greenup, Kentucky, 41144. Telephone: (606) 473-7324; marina extension, 322.

Fishtrap Lake

Construction began on Fishtrap Lake in February, 1962, and the dam was dedicated by President Lyndon B. Johnson on October 26, 1968. The 195-foot-high and 1,100-foot-long dam, built by the Huntington (West Virginia) District of the U. S. Army Corps of Engineers, impounds a 16.5-mile lake from the Levisa Fork of the Big Sandy River in Pike County. The 1,331-acre lake is 14 miles southeast of Pikeville, Kentucky, on Ky-1789, off Ky-80. Recreational facilities include one marina, one Corps-managed day-use area, and one Corps-managed campground.

Fishtrap Marina is on Ky-1789 at the Upper Pompey Public Use Area, a day-use area at the dam. Open March 31 to November 31, weather permitting, the marina has 130 boat slips (100 open and 30 covered), a snack bar with soft drinks, hot sandwiches, and candy, rental 14-foot fishing boats with 8-horsepower outboards, regular and mixed gas, tackle, live bait (minnows, crickets, and worms), launching ramp, pit toilets, and picnic grounds. Mailing address: Fishtrap Marina, Inc., Route #1, Box 740, Shelbiana, Kentucky, 41562. Telephone: (606) 437-7456.

The only campground on the lake is nine and one-half miles east of Pikeville on US-119 to Meta, Kentucky, then 16 miles south on Ky-194. Open May 1 to October 31, weather permitting, the Corps-managed Grapevine Campground has 28 primitive campsites, flush toilets, showers, drinking water, laundry room, boat launching ramp, picnic tables and grills, and children's playground. Mailing address: Grapevine Campground, U. S. Army Corps of Engineers, Route #1, Box 501, Shelbiana, Kentucky, 41562. Telephone: (606) 437-7496.

Mauzy Lake

Mauzy Lake is located in the Higginson-Henry Wildlife Management Area, a state-owned and operated public hunting area six miles east of Morganfield, Kentucky, on Ky-56 in Union County. The U. S. Army built Mauzy Lake in 1943; 25 years later the Kentucky Department of Fish and Wildlife Resources purchased 5,420 acres of rolling hills, woodlands, and agricultural land, including the 84-acre lake, for public use.

Primitive camping is allowed year-round at 100 free sites overlooking the lake. Picnic tables, grills, shelter, pit toilets, and three boat launching ramps are available on Lake Mauzy. There are also two small fishing ponds on the grounds. No outboard motors may be used on Lake Mauzy. Mailing address: Higginson-Henry Wildlife Management Area, Lake Mauzy, Route #5, Morganfield, Kentucky, 42437. Telephone: (502) 389-3580.

Oxbow Lakes-
Ballard County Wildlife Management Area

In the 1940s the Kentucky Department of Fish and Wildlife Resources purchased vast tracts of riverbottom wetlands off Ky-1105, north of La Center in Ballard County, just upstream from where the Ohio empties into the Mississippi River. The acreage included several cypress-lined oxbow lakes. Today, the Ballard County Wildlife Management Area is the state's largest public hunting area, encompassing more than 8,000 acres of river-bottom fields, woods, and sloughs. Roughly one-fourth of the management area is a migratory waterfowl refuge, where hunting is not allowed during duck and goose seasons. As many as 80,000 ducks and upwards of 100,000 geese use the refuge as a rest stop each fall and winter.

The 2,000-acre refuge is bounded by the Ohio River on the north and Mitchell Lake on the south. There are seven lakes in the refuge area: Butler, Turner, Little Turner, Shelby, Castor, Turkey, and Goose Ponds. All are open to fishing March 15 to October 14; outboards are not permitted. Some of these lakes are manmade, and have dead standing timber in them which provides excellent fishing for chain pickerel, largemouth bass, and catfish.

Primitive camping is available free of charge for about 125 tent campers, no RVs. There are a few picnic tables and grills for use by campers, and pit toilets are available. Mailing address: Ballard County Wildlife Management Area, Route #1, La Center, Kentucky, 42056. Telephone: (502) 224-2244.

Kentucky Horse Park. Photograph by Kentucky Department of Public Information.

6
State and National Forests

Introduction

Next to soil, clean air, and water, forests are man's most valuable natural resource. Forests produce lumber for building, protect watersheds from soil erosion, and provide a major source of recreation—hunting, camping, hiking, and nature study.

Approximately 46 percent of Kentucky's 26 million acres are covered with forests. In the 1700s, before the pioneers cut the forests for farmlands, some of the finest stands of hardwoods in America grew in Kentucky. It has been said that when the pioneers came to Kentucky, the forests were so vast that a squirrel could have traveled the width of the state without ever touching the ground.

The forest community is a complex ecosystem of plants and animals which exist in an interdependent relationship. Forests provide food and shelter and protect water sources for wildlife. By managing forestlands wisely, man is able to harvest trees for lumber, while still protecting and promoting healthy populations of both game and non-game animals.

Probably the most vital function of a forest in regard to all animal life, including man, is its part in the carbon dioxide-oxygen cycle. The green leaves of plants absorb carbon dioxide from the air, water from the soil, and light from the sun, and through the process of photosynthesis make sugars and starches. A by-product of this process is oxygen, which is released into the air. The importance of this to man is enormous: botanists estimate that one acre of young trees can generate enough oxygen each year to keep 18 people alive for a year. A large tree transpires 100 gallons of water daily. This process increases relative humidity and cools the surrounding air temperature.

Kentucky's state and national forests are managed under a multiple-use concept, encompassing timber, wildlife, and recreation. Kentucky's state forests are managed by the Division of Forestry of the Department of Natural Resources and Environmental Protection; Daniel Boone National Forest is managed by the United States Forest Service. In this chapter the points of recreational interest in Kentucky's state and national forests will be identified and briefly discussed. Some of Kentucky's finest outdoor recreation areas are found in these forests, remote and unspoiled lands where sportsmen can find peace and quiet and escape from the rigors of modern day life.

Kentucky's State Forests

The Kentucky State Forest program began in 1919, when a gift of 3,738 acres of forest land (six tracts in Harlan County) was given to the Commonwealth by the Kentenia-Catron Corporation. This contribution laid the foundation for a state forest system that today has grown to 43,393 acres.

The state forest system of managed timber lands, under the administration of the Division of Forestry, Department of Natural Resources and Environmental Protection, now consists of eight units: Tygarts, Olympia, Knobs, Pennyrile, Kentucky Ridge, Dewey, Kentenia, and Six Mile Island state forests. Most of this acreage was deeded to Kentucky by the United States government; more than 37,247 acres were secured in the three years from 1954 to 1956. Additional acreage was acquired through purchases from private citizens, lease agreements with U. S. government agencies, and gifts from individuals and private foundations.

The forests are managed for timber sales and recreation, including primitive camping, hunting, horseback riding, and day-hiking. All of Kentucky's state forests are open year-round. Access is limited to gravel and unimproved dirt roads (fire lanes) which are often impassable to all but four-wheel drive vehicles during the wet months of the year. Overnight camping is allowed in all of Kentucky's state forests, although there's only one developed camping facility in the system. Mailing address: Kentucky Department of Natural Resources and Environmental Protection, Division of Forestry, 618 Teton Trail, Frankfort, Kentucky, 40601. Telephone: (502) 564-4496.

Tygarts and Olympia State Forests
Mailing address: District Forester, Kentucky Division of
    Forestry, Box 357, Morehead, Kentucky, 40351
Telephone: (606) 784-7504

Tygart's State Forest is adjacent to Carter Caves State Resort Park, north of Olive Hill, Kentucky, off Ky-182 in Carter County. The 800-acre tract of woodlands was added to the state forest system in April of 1957 through a purchase.

Olympia State Forest is south of Olympia Springs, Kentucky, off Ky-36 in Bath County. The state forest, comprising 780 acres, is within the demarcation boundary of Daniel Boone National Forest. There are 12 miles of access roads in Olympia State Forest.

Knobs State Forest
Mailing address: District Forester, Kentucky Division of
    Forestry, Box 663, Elizabethtown, Kentucky, 42701
Telephone: (502) 769-1361

Knobs State Forest is west of Bardstown in Nelson County off US-62 and Hardin-Leslie Road. The 4,000-acre unit is managed by state foresters under a lease agreement with the Isaac W. Bernheim Foundation. There are about 12 miles of dirt roads in the forest.

Pennyrile State Forest
Mailing address: Forest Administrator, Pennyrile State
    Forest, Kentucky Division of Forestry, Route #4,
    Box 106, Dawson Springs, Kentucky, 42408
Telephone: (502) 797-3241

Pennyrile State Forest, comprising 14,821 acres, was established in July of 1954 when the U. S. Department of Agriculture deeded 15,260 acres of woodlands to the Commonwealth of Kentucky. Part of the original acreage is now a wildlife refuge. The largest unit in the state forest system, Pennyrile State Forest adjoins Pennyrile Forest State Resort Park in Caldwell and Christian counties, reached via Ky-109 and Ky-672. There are six developed trails suitable for day-hiking or horseback riding in the unit, and miles of unmarked logging roads.

Six Mile Island State Forest
Mailing address: Division of Forestry, 618 Teton Trail, Frankfort, Kentucky, 40601
Telephone: (502) 564-4496

Six Mile Island, northeast of Louisville, is 78 acres of woodlands in the Ohio River above Cox Park in Jefferson County. The island was purchased on October 11, 1974, to save it from commercial development.

Kentucky Ridge and Kentenia State Forests
Mailing address: District Forester, Kentucky Division of Forestry, P.O. Box 31, Pineville, Kentucky, 40977
Telephone: (606) 337-3011

Kentucky Ridge State Forest is west of Pineville, Kentucky, in Bell County off US-25E and Ky-190. The forest consists of two units with a combined area of 11,940 acres which virtually surround Pine Mountain State Resort Park.

Kentenia State Forest comprises 3,624 acres in seven tracts, all east of Harlan, Kentucky, off US-119 in Harlan County. The mountaintop units are south of the Little Shepherd Trail (Ky-1679), a 46-mile gravel road atop Pine Mountain which extends northeast from Harlan to Whitesburg, Kentucky. There's one developed campground at the Putney Lookout Tower on Little Shepherd Trail, reached via Ky-2010 from Laden, Kentucky, on US-119. Open year-round, the campground has tent pads, picnic grills, shelter house, pit toilets, and drinking water.

Dewey State Forest
Mailing address: District Forester, Kentucky Division of Forestry, Box 85, Prestonsburg, Kentucky, 41653
Telephone: (606) 886-8562

Dewey State Forest is located off Ky-3 in Floyd County, east of Prestonsburg. The 7,350-acre unit along Dewey Lake is leased to the Commonwealth by the U. S. Army Corps of Engineers. There are eight miles of logging roads in the unit.

Daniel Boone National Forest
Mailing address: Ranger District Headquarters,
    Daniel Boone National Forest, U.S. Forest Service,
    100 Vaught Road, Winchester, Kentucky, 40391
Telephone: (606) 744-5656

Stretching for more than 120 miles from the Kentucky-Tennessee boundary northward to Lewis County, just south of the Ohio River, Daniel Boone National Forest appears on maps of Kentucky as a green corridor of land separating the Bluegrass Region from the Cumberland Mountains. Daniel Boone National Forest, at the western edge of the Cumberland Plateau, is a land of narrow valleys surrounded by rock cliffs and knob-like foothills clothed in dense forests. The Commonwealth's most spectacular scenery and most remote lands are within the forest—raging white water rivers, cascading waterfalls, rock arches, and tractless woodlands.

Kentucky's only national wilderness area and national geological area, five Kentucky Wild Rivers and three sizeable roadless areas, identified under the National Forest Service's Roadless Area Review and Evaluation program (RARE II), are within the boundary of the forest. Of the two million acres within the forest's demarcation boundary, more than 660,000 acres in 22 counties are under public ownership.

In part because of its vastness, there are more outdoor recreational opportunities in Daniel Boone National Forest than anywhere else in Kentucky. The diversity of recreational pastimes available in the forest includes hiking, white water canoeing, both stream and reservoir fishing, nature study, hunting, rock climbing, and family camping.

The Weeks Law, enacted by the U. S. Congress in 1911, enabled the Forest Service to purchase the lands, which had formerly been known as Cumberland National Forest. In the 1960s, the name of the forest was changed to honor frontiersman and settler Daniel Boone, one of the first white men to extensively explore the area.

Morehead Ranger District
Mailing address: Morehead Ranger District Headquarters,
    Daniel Boone National Forest, Box 10, Morehead,
    Kentucky, 40351
Telephone: (606) 784-5624

The Morehead Ranger District, the northernmost of the seven ranger districts in Daniel Boone's National Forest, comprises 116,630 acres in Ro-

wan, Menifee, Morgan, and Bath counties. The major recreational drawing
card in the district is the Pioneer Weapons Hunting Area, a 7,300-acre
tract of woodlands west of Cave Run Lake in Menifee and Bath counties,
reached via US-60, Ky-211, Ky-801, and Forest Service Roads 129 and
918. Hunting seasons at Pioneer Weapons Hunting Area run concurrently
with Kentucky's statewide hunting seasons. The area has good populations
of whitetail deer, wild turkey, squirrel, and ruffed grouse. Hunting is limited to primitive weapons—longbow, crossbow, flintlock and percussion
cap pistols, rifles, and shotguns. There are seven day-hiking trails in the
heavily wooded Pioneer Weapons Hunting Area.

Camping is permitted at Clear Creek Furnace Recreation Area on FS
Road 129, south of Salt Lick, Kentucky, off Ky-211. Open April 1 to December 31, the campground/picnic area has four primitive campsites, pit
toilets, drinking water, picnic tables, and grills. Maximum length for RVs is
22 feet.

The only other developed campground in the district is at Rodburn
Hollow northwest of Morehead, off US-60 on FS Road 13, adjacent to the
district ranger headquarters. Open April 1 to November 1, the 11-site
campground and adjacent picnic ground with shelter have flush toilets and
drinking water, picnic table at each site, and grills. There's one day-hiking
trail that leads from the campground.

Stanton Ranger District
Mailing address: Daniel Boone National Forest, Ky-15, Stanton, Kentucky, 40380
Telephone: (606) 663-2852

The Stanton Ranger District of Daniel Boone National Forest encompasses
55,000 acres of forestlands under public ownership in parts of Menifee,
Wolfe, Powell, Estill, and Lee counties. The district's major recreational
attraction is the Red River Gorge Geological Area, 25,600 acres east of
Stanton, Kentucky, reached via Ky-15, Ky-715, and Ky-77.

In the late sixties and early seventies, a controversy raged over a proposal by the U. S. Army Corps of Engineers to build a 5,000-acre impoundment on the North Fork of the Red River. Many residents of Clay City,
Kentucky, argued that the dam was needed for flood control; proponents of
the project in nearby Lexington sought a new water supply for their growing
metropolitan community. Environmentalists pointed out that rare communities of plants and animals and the scenic, archaeological, and geological
integrity of the region would be destroyed if the impoundment were built.

The Red River Gorge controversy was intense. There were marches on Kentucky's State Capitol complete with speakers and folk singers, fund-raising drives, court suit, and counter suit. Eventually, after months of thorough investigation by appointed groups finally determined that the cost benefits did not warrant the building of the dam, the proposal was killed in October 1975.

The next important development for the area came when nearly 26,000 acres in the gorge were formally designated as a national geological area, giving the region a special, protective status and a place on the register of important scenic and natural areas in America. But the controversy and subsequent national designation that brought the area to the public's attention had a dramatic impact on the once obscure region. Millions of persons flocked to the gorge to hike its trails and canoe and kayak its boulder-strewn white water, and the area was nearly loved to death at the height of its popularity during the controversy. As a result, the area suffered from overuse—trampling of plant life, careless fire building, litter, and a general disregard of backcountry ethics by many of the visitors, most of whom were novice outdoorsmen.

Presently, the numbers of people visiting Red River Gorge have subsided somewhat to tolerable levels, but millions of persons still camp, hike, and sightsee there each year. The Koomer Ridge campground and the 23 hiking trails in Red River Gorge Geological Area are perhaps the most publicized and popular, and by far the best known to out-of-state visitors, of any recreational facilities in Daniel Boone National Forest.

Red River Gorge lies in the Pottsville Escarpment at the western edge of the Cumberland Plateau. Known for its rugged topography, the gorge is characterized by an abundance of rock arches and palisades, deep V-shaped valleys, cascading waterfalls, sandstone cliffs, and dramatic overlooks that provide sweeping vistas of heavily forested land. It features the largest concentration of natural rock arches in the eastern United States; more than 80 are known to exist in the drainage of Red River, including 18 major arches in the drainage of the North Fork alone. A glance at the topographic map quadrangles of the gorge reveals such unusual names as Red Byrd Arch, Whistling Arch, Rock Bridge, Grays Arch, Sky Bridge, Princess Arch, Castle Arch, and Half Moon Arch. In addition to the rock arches, other points of geological interest include Tower Rock, Raven Rock, Hen's Nest Rock, Angel Windows, Indian Staircase, and Chimney Top Rock—a palisade that affords visitors a spectacular overlook of the wooded river valley and bordering rock cliffs.

The geological story of Red River Gorge began during Mississippian times, more than 340 million years ago. The major geological formations are conglomerate sandstones, limestones, and siltstones, overlaid by shale. Stream erosion and weathering processes formed the gorge on the North

Fork of Red River in much the same way that the Grand Canyon was cut by the Colorado River.

Red River is a tributary to the Kentucky River, one of 10 major drainages in the state. The river rises in the southwest corner of Wolfe County and flows generally westward for 95 miles. The serpentine path of the Red and its tributaries has sliced portions of the drainage into narrow, irregular valleys divided by steep ridges. Hilltop elevations range up to 1500 feet above sea level and may rise up to 500 feet above the valley floor. Today, layers of sandstone that have resisted the crumbling effects of the water and the weathering process stand out boldly as cliffs above the surrounding forests of the river valley.

An intensive examination of the flora of the Red River Gorge in 1970 revealed that 555 species of vascular plants from 100 families and 304 genera are found in the area. Forest types can be classified as those associated with ridge tops, slopes, and streambanks.

In general, the ridge tops of Red River Gorge support an oak-pine community that consists of three species of pine and five species of oak. Other hardwoods associated with this community are pignut, sweet pignut hickory, and shagbark hickory.

Below the cliffs, the canopy layer of the forest consists of American beech, tulip poplar, American and white basswood, sweet birch, sugar and red maple, eastern hemlock, and yellow buckeye. The understory layer of plant in this community consists mainly of American holly and magnolia. Common shrubs of this forest type are rose bay rhododendron, spice bush, hazelnut, and mountain laurel, a shrub whose pinkish bloom flowers in profusion throughout eastern Kentucky in late May.

The stream bank components of the forest include American hornbeam, river birch, hazel, alder, black willow, sycamore, and elm. In a short section of the Red River valley below Copperas Creek, immediately below the highway Ky-715 bridge, there is an extremely rare association of beech (a constituent of the slope forest), sycamore, and cottonwood.

The list of wildflowers in the region is exhausting; species occurring frequently are trailing arbutus, bent trillium, rue anemone, rattlesnake plantain, partridge-berry, bloodroot, hepatica, scouring rush, yellow trout lily, squirrelcorn, violets, bluet, spring beauty, foam flower, Allegheny spurge, dwarf ginseng, and wild geranium.

Generally pollution-free, Red River supports what is described as a high-quality stream fishery. Game fishes include smallmouth bass, muskellunge, suckers, Kentucky (spotted) bass, rock bass, and other sunfishes. Some of the tributaries of Red River are populated with difficult-to-find chubs, minnows, and stream darters.

Wandering hunting parties of Shawnee were among the early visitors to the gorge. They came from the north to hunt the buffalo, elk, and deer that once inhabited the lowlands west of the gorge.

The most famous white hunter to explore the region was Daniel Boone. Historians say he probably visited the Red River Gorge area between 1769 and 1771. During the winter of 1769-70, while his brother Squire returned to North Carolina for supplies, Boone lived alone in the wilderness, dangerously low on powder, lead, and provisions, sleeping in canebrakes and rock shelters to avoid capture by wandering bands of Shawnee.

In 1968, a crude hut of short split planks overlaying a framework of poles was discovered in a rockhouse in Red River Gorge. The hut is about the size of a pup tent, contains a small stone fireplace, and was definitely meant for no more than one person. One of the planks bore the carved name: "D. boon." There is some controversy over whether or not it was really built by the famous explorer. Today, the hut can be seen at Natural Bridge State Resort Park, a mile and a half south of the Slade interchange of the Mountain Parkway on highway Ky-11.

Native wildlife in Red River Gorge includes the gray fox, two species of squirrels, white-tailed deer, wild turkey, mink, beaver, muskrat, and gray fox. In all, 59 species of fish, 31 species of amphibians, 105 species of resident birds, and 36 species of mammals have been identified in the area.

The 30-mile loop drive through the gorge begins at Nada, Kentucky, one and one-half miles west of the Slade interchange of the Mountain Parkway on Highway Ky-15. At Nada you turn north (right) onto highway Ky-77 and continue west on highway Ky-715. Eight miles of paved highway parallels the river. Ky-715 connects with Ky-15 at Pine Ridge.

Highway Ky-77 passes through Nada Tunnel, which was cut by hand through a rocky ridge in 1877. Picks and shovels were used to excavate the 800-foot-long tunnel that provided railroad access to the giant timber of the area. Logging here was intense from the 1880s to the turn of the century.

In the summer of 1975 an information station was opened to assist visitors in learning more about the fascinating region and its recreational facilities. The information station is open April 1 to October 31; it is located at the intersection of Rock Bridge Road (FS Road 24) and Ky-715, just off the Pine Ridge exit of the Mountain Parkway.

Sky Bridge Picnic Area, Rock Bridge Picnic Area, Grays Arch Picnic Area, and Chimney Top Rock Overlook are open year-round. The 44-mile trail system consisting of 23 separate trails is also open year-round.

There are three National Forest Service-managed campgrounds in the Red River Gorge Geological Area. The Koomer Ridge Recreational Area, a fee area, is three and one-half miles southeast of the Slade exit of the Mountain Parkway on Ky-15. Open Memorial Day to Labor Day, the campground, currently under expansion, has 70 primitive campsites, pit toilets, drinking water, picnic tables, and grills; maximum length for RVs is 22 feet. The Tunnel Ridge Road Group Camp and Chimney Top Rock Group Camp, both with primitive campsites and pit toilets, are available year-round for church, civic, Scout, and other such groups through special arrangements with the National Forest Service.

There are two day-use areas in the southern reaches of the district, both at the sites of old iron furnaces. The Cottage Furnace Picnic Area (open April 1 to October 31), on FS Road 227 off Ky-213 in Estill County, is at the site of an open hearth pig iron furnace which operated in the era prior to 1900 when Kentucky was one of the leading iron-producing states, before the invention of the Bessemer process for making steel. The ruins of the Fitchburg Iron Furnace are on Ky-975, east of Ravena, Kentucky, off Ky-1571 in Estill County.

Berea Ranger District
Mailing address: Daniel Boone National Forest,
 Berea, Kentucky, 40403
Telephone: (606) 986-8434

The Berea Ranger District encompasses 73,000 acres of Federally-owned lands in Lee, Estill, Owsley, Jackson, and Rockcastle counties. The two points of interest in the district are the Turkey Foot Recreation Area and the S-Tree Campground.

Turkey Foot Recreation Area is in Jackson County northeast of McKee, Kentucky, on FS Road 4, off Ky-89. The campground is on the banks of the War Fork of Station Camp Creek, a high-quality mountain stream stocked with rainbow trout that supports good native populations of smallmouth bass and sunfishes. Open Memorial Day to Labor Day, the campground has 15 primitive campsites (16-foot maximum length for RVs), pit toilets, drinking water, picnic tables, and grills. South of the recreation area off FS Road 4 is a day-hiking trail that connects with Ky-587.

The S-Tree Campground, in Jackson County southwest of McKee, Kentucky, is reached via Ky-89, FS Road 43, and FS Road 20. There's a lookout tower on the grounds. Open year-round, the campground has 15 campsites, pit toilets, drinking water, picnic tables, grills, and shelters. Maximum length for RVs is 22 feet.

Somerset Ranger District
Mailing address: Daniel Boone National Forest, Route #2, Box 507, Somerset, Kentucky, 42501
Telephone: (606) 679-2018

The Somerset Ranger District encompasses 64,000 acres under Federal ownership in McCreary and Pulaski counties. This district of Daniel Boone National Forest includes some of the prime recreational areas in all of eastern Kentucky: Beaver Creek Wilderness, the Narrows of the Rockcastle, Natural Arch Scenic Area.

Bee Rock Campground, east of Somerset, Kentucky, in Pulaski County on Ky-192, is situated on the western bank of the Rockcastle River, one of Kentucky's most celebrated white water rivers that was designated by the Kentucky Legislature as one of eight "Wild Rivers." The campground, open April 1 to October 31, is one mile downstream from the Narrows of the Rockcastle, a jumble of house-sized boulders that constrict the raging river into a tight chute. The river valley is flanked by rock cliffs. There are 20 campsites (22-foot maximum length for RVs), pit toilets, drinking water, boat launching ramp (on eastern bank of the river across from the campground), picnic tables, and grills. Bee Rock Campground sits amidst some of Kentucky's most spectacular scenery.

Approximately 12 miles southwest of Bee Rock Campground is the Little Lick Campground, reached via Ky-122 (Old Whitley Road) from Mt. Victory, Kentucky in Pulaski County. The campground, open April 1 to October 31, is on the northern bank of the Cumberland River. There are seven primitive campsites, pit toilets, drinking water, picnic tables, and grills.

The Eastern Wilderness Areas Act of 1974 established 16 national wilderness areas in the eastern United States and 17 study tracts which could later be admitted to the National Wilderness Preservation System, if the guidelines for inclusion outlined in the bill were met. The 251,388-acre package of Federally-owned lands included a 5,500-acre unit east of Alpine, Kentucky, reached via US-27 and FS Road 50. The near roadless area in McCreary and Pulaski counties was named Beaver Creek Wilderness.

Forest types in Beaver Creek Wilderness can be classified as those associated with slopes and stream banks. Below the cliffs, the canopy layer includes American beech, yellow poplar, ash, American and white basswood, sweet birch, several varieties of oak and hickory, red maple, elm, and eastern hemlock—all constituents of the mixed mesophytic forest, the oldest and most diverse forest type in the eastern United States.

Broad-leaf magnolia, dogwood, and American holly are generally prevalent in the understory of the slope forests of Beaver Creek; common shrubs include rose bay rhododendron, spice bush, hazelnut, and mountain laurel.

Before the white man settled the land, bands of Choctaw, Cherokee, and Shawnee Indians roamed over this part of southeastern Kentucky, living off the game-rich land, sometimes growing crops by a crude method of agriculture that was later adopted by mountaineers. The Indians left pottery, flint arrowheads, scrapers, pendants, and spear points, and mussel-shell beads as evidence of their habitation of the area.

Settlers first came to Beaver Creek in the early 1800s, most by flatboat down the nearby Cumberland River. In the following 100 years, the land was settled, farmed, and timbered. Mud-chinked cabins were built on the main creek, garden patches and stock lots were cleared for use below the cliffline. Some of the mountaineers grew corn on the ridgetops; often surplus was made into "moonshine." Most activity around Beaver Creek ended rather abruptly in the early 1900s when commercial timber operations ceased. By then, only scattered pockets of timber remained in the steep, narrow side hollows where loggers found access difficult. Abandonment of the land by the loggers and subsistence farmers gave way to several decades of undisturbed forest renewal. Federal ownership of Beaver Creek came in 1937, when Cumberland National Forest was established.

In the Beaver Creek area, there has been little human impact for about 70 years. Some sections of the creek drainage have not been substantially altered since the times of the first settlers. Only four gravel access roads and a number of wildlife openings, maintained to promote huntable populations of whitetail deer under a state game management plan, stand as evidence of man's impact in the Beaver Creek region.

In secluded hollows, where sandstone cliffs border steep, narrow valleys, the land is remarkably wild and fresh. In these hard-to-reach backcountry sections of Beaver Creek, the character of the land comes forth: sparkling waterfalls tumble into clear, pebble-bottomed pools amid fern-draped boulders shaded by stands of eastern hemlock and slick-leaved rhododendron.

Spring comes to this Appalachian plateauland with a parade of wildflowers that continues until October, when the first frosts set the valleys ablaze with autumn color. Wildflowers are abundant everywhere in the woodlands of Beaver Creek. In late March and early April, trailing arbutus, rue anemone, spring beauties, bluets, and hepatica add color to the damp mat of leaves on the forest floor. Later, crested dwarf iris, large-flowered trillium, bent trillium, and violets spring up on sunny hillsides. May brings warmer, longer days and such wildflowers as jack-in-the-pulpit; pink lady's slipper; false Solomon's seal; stone crop, with its fleshy leaves and white blossoms matted on ledges and boulders in the woods; wild geranium; partridge-berry; wild pink; and May apple, with its large, umbrella-like leaves.

By May, spring fern fiddleheads begin uncurling into wide, delicate fronds—Christmas ferns, rock cap ferns, maidenhair ferns, royal ferns, and the stately cinnamon fern, with its three-foot spread. The frequent rains and warm nights turn the sparse winter woodlands green and lush, shaded by a dense canopy of leaves.

Summer wildflowers include ox-eye daisy, striped pipsissewa, red catchfly, wood betony, and rattlesnake plantain. By late July, blueberries are plentiful, ripe for the backpacker's taking.

From the Three Forks Overlook on the edge of the gorge-like valley, the hiker gets a commanding view of surrounding valleys and ridges. From the woods below comes the sound of Little Hurricane and Middle Forks converging. In the distance, the narrow, cliff-lined valley of Freeman Fork stretches to the horizon.

The surrounding cliffline was formed over 300 million years ago during the Pennsylvanian period of geological history. Major geological formations of the area are sandstones and siltstones, overlaid by shale. Weathering processes have eaten away the softer layers of rock, exposing iron deposits and strata of colored gravel called conglomerates. In the evening light, these cliffs sometimes take on an orange or golden cast. Scraggly, weatherbeaten pines cling precariously to the ridgetop edges.

The 16,474-acre Beaver Creek management unit has gained considerable attention not only because it contains Kentucky's only wilderness area, but also because of a test suit initiated by the Greenwood Land and Mining Company, in which the company tried unsuccessfully to gain permission to prospect for coal on lands under public ownership in and around the Beaver Creek Wilderness. The Franklin County Court upheld the ruling of the Kentucky Department of Natural Resources and Environmental Protection to deny a surface mine permit. Kentucky law prohibits strip mining on public lands, even though a private company owns the mineral rights.

Beaver Creek is a high-quality mountain stream supporting a good population of smallmouth bass and sunfishes. Access to the creek is by foot only. There are two day-hiking trails in the wilderness, and extensive exploration means cross-country hiking through rhododendron thickets and dense forests. The upper reaches of the Beaver Creek drainage may be reached via FS Roads 130 and 839 off US-27 and FS Roads 128 and 46 off Ky-90 east of Parker's Lake, Kentucky.

West of Beaver Creek Wilderness on US-27 at Alpine, Kentucky, there's a seasonal (April 1 to October 31) picnic grounds. Picnic tables, grills, pit toilets, and drinking water are available. Northeast of Beaver

Creek Wilderness, upstream of the mouth of Beaver Creek on the southern banks of the Cumberland River, is the Sawyer Recreation Area, reached via Ky-90, Ky-896, and Ky-1609 from Parker's Lake, Kentucky, on US-27. Open April 1 to October 31, the campground has 10 primitive campsites, pit toilets, drinking water, picnic tables, and grills. A boat launching ramp at the recreation area is open year-round.

Natural Arch Scenic Area, featuring a 90-foot-long and 50-foot-high rock span, is approximately two miles west of Parker's Lake, Kentucky, in Whitley County off Ky-927. A series of day-hiking trails encircles the rock arch and the surrounding woodlands in Gulf Bottoms and Buffalo Canyon. An adjoining picnic grounds with pit toilets, drinking water, picnic table, and grills is open April 1 to October 31. The trail system and access to the rock arch are open year-round.

London Ranger District
Mailing address: Daniel Boone National Forest, Box G,
     London, Kentucky, 40741
Telephone: (606) 864-4163

The London Ranger District encompasses 88,694 acres of Federally-owned lands in Laurel, Rockcastle, and Whitley counties. The recreational drawing cards of the district are Laurel River Lake and the system of day-hiking trails, shelters, and a campground along the eastern bank of the Cumberland River between the mouth of Rockcastle River and the Cumberland Falls State Resort Park.

The Baldrock Picnic Area, open April 1 to October 31, is approximately 10 miles southwest of London, Kentucky, in Laurel County in Ky-192. Pit toilets, picnic tables, and grills, and a day-hiking trail are located at the roadside picnic grounds. Five miles further down the road, on Ky-1193 off Ky-192, is the Rockcastle Recreation Area. The campground, at the mouth of the Rockcastle River, is open April 1 to October 31. There are 37 primitive campsites (fee area), pit toilets, drinking water, picnic tables, grills, and a shelter. The boat launching ramp at the site is open year-round. The maximum size allowed for RVs in the campground is 16 feet.

The London Boat Dock, open April 1 to December 15, weather permitting, is a privately-owned marina at the mouth of the Rockcastle. A restaurant on the dock has sandwiches, breakfast, coffee, and soft drinks for fishermen. The three completely furnished housekeeping cottages on the grounds rent for $14 to $16 a night per couple, $2 for each additional person. One cottage sleeps eight, the other two sleep four each.

The marina has 150 buoy line tie-downs for boats. Fourteen-foot fishing boats rent for $5 a day, $15 a day with 5- or 7-horsepower outboard (gas and cushions included). There's also one houseboat that rents for $50 a day (two-day minimum) plus gas. The 40-foot houseboat is powered by a 50-horsepower outboard, and is fully equipped (silverware, linens, etc.). Other facilities at the marina include regular and mixed gas, live bait (minnows and nightcrawlers), artificial bait, boating supplies, mechanic on duty (seasonally), and boat launching ramp. Mailing address: London Boat Dock, Box 653, London, Kentucky, 40741. Telephone: (606) 864-5225.

A loop hiking trail beginning at the Rockcastle Recreation Area follows the eastern bank of the Cumberland River to the Twin Branch Shelters, one mile below the mouth of the Laurel River. The trail and shelters are convenient for fishermen. At the mouth of the Laurel there's another marina, Little Marina, open April 1 to November 31 (open 24 hours a day in the summer). There are 40 buoy tie-downs for boats, and soft drinks, hot sandwiches, and candy are available. Fourteen-foot fishing boats rent for $4 a day, $15 with 6-horsepower outboards (12-hour day). Regular gas, live bait (minnows and nightcrawlers), ice, tackle, and boat launching ramp are available. Three sleeping rooms, each with two beds, rent for $11 per day; the two fully-furnished housekeeping cottages rent for $16 a day. Mailing address: Little Marina, P.O. Box 42, Corbin, Kentucky, 40701. Telephone: (606) 528-9888.

The Moonbow Trail connects the mouth of the Laurel River with Cumberland Falls State Resort Park. Another overnight shelter, ideally situated for fishing trips, is located at Bark Camp Creek.

Stearns Ranger District
Mailing address: Daniel Boone National Forest, P.O. Box 459, Whitley City, Kentucky, 42653
Telephone: (606) 376-5323

The Stearns Ranger District consists of 130,000 acres of land under public ownership in Whitley, Wayne, and McCreary counties. The southernmost of the ranger districts in Daniel Boone National Forest, the Stearns unit has some of Kentucky's most remote woodlands and several fine fishing/canoeing streams.

Rock Creek begins in Pickett State Park in Tennessee, just across the state line from McCreary County. It flows northeastward before emptying into the Big South Fork of the Cumberland, near Stearns, Kentucky. There are one campground, one picnic area, two hiking trails, and two natural arches along Rock Creek, a designated Kentucky Wild River, long known for its good rainbow trout and smallmouth bass fishing.

The Great Meadow Campground, on FS Road 139, is reached via Ky-1363 and FS Road 566 from Yamacraw, Kentucky (five miles west of Whitley City, Kentucky, on Ky-92). Open year-round, the campground has eight campsites, pit toilets, drinking water, picnic tables, and grills. Maximum length for RVs at the campground is 22 feet. A hiking trail which passes Gobblers Arch connects the campground with Rock Creek and Hemlock Grove (on the eastern bank of the creek), a pack-in, pack-out picnic area open year-round. The other hiking trail in the area connects FS Road 137 (on the western bank of Rock Creek) to Buffalo Arch and FS Road 562.

The South Fork of the Cumberland River is one of the most celebrated white water runs in the eastern United States. A Kentucky Wild River, the Big South Fork heads up in Tennessee and flows northward to Lake Cumberland through McCreary County. The section of the river best for canoeing and kayaking is from the Tennessee-Kentucky line to Blue Heron, Kentucky. Devil's Jump, a spectacular rapids west of Stearns, Kentucky, is reached via Ky-92 and FS Road 706.

There are two recreational points of interest on the lower end of the Big South Fork of the Cumberland River at the headwaters of Lake Cumberland. Alum Ford Campground is reached via US-27 and Ky-700 southwest of Parker's Lake, Kentucky. The campground, open year-round, has seven primitive campsites, pit toilets, drinking water, picnic tables, grills, and a boat launching ramp. Two hiking trails lead to Yahoo Falls Scenic Area, farther downstream. One hiking trail begins on Ky-700 two miles east of Alum Ford. The second trail begins south of Whitley City off Ky-1651 and parallels the South Fork of the Cumberland River to Alum Ford, then continues northward to Yahoo (pronounced Yea-hoe) Falls Scenic Area. The pack-in, pack-out picnic grounds at Yahoo Falls is also open year-round, and drinking water and pit toilets are available. There's an overnight shelter for hikers on the riverside trail, just south of Alum Ford Campground.

The only other development in the Stearns Ranger District is the Bon Hollow Picnic Area, open April 15 to October 31. Bon Hollow Picnic Area is west of Williamsburg, Kentucky, on FS Road 554 off Ky-92.

Redbird Purchase Ranger District
Mailing address: Daniel Boone National Forest, P.O. Box 1, Big Creek, Kentucky, 40914
Telephone: (606) 598-2192

The Redbird Purchase Ranger District comprises 140,000 acres of Federally-owned lands in Clay, Knox, Perry, Bell, Owsley, Harlan, and Leslie counties. The compartments of land were purchased in 1964, 17 years after the United States Forest Service made its initial acquisitions for Cumberland National Forest.

There is currently only one developed area in the Redbird Purchase Ranger District, the Big Double Creek Picnic Ground, south of Peabody, Kentucky, on FS Road 1501 off Ky-66. Open year-round on a pack-in, pack-out basis, the picnic ground has picnic tables, grills, pit toilets, and drinking water.

Annual eagle census. Photograph by Tennessee Valley Authority.

7
Nature and Scenic Areas

Introduction

A three-year study recently completed by the U.S. Fish and Wildlife Service on wildlife-associated recreation for the calendar year of 1975 revealed that record numbers of Americans are participating in wildlife observation and study. Almost 50 million persons (55 percent men and 45 percent women) observed wildlife that year, while nearly 14 million of them (58 percent men and 42 percent women) took either still or motion pictures. Together they spent nearly 1.6 billion days afield.

These figures help to substantiate the belief that more and more Americans are trying to learn about nature by birdwatching, plant and animal study, day-hiking, and nature photography. Evidence of man's impact on plant and animal communities has aroused a spirit of preservation, and environmental education has increased the popularity of nature and scenic areas, those lands set aside especially for study, rather than consumptive uses such as hunting and fishing.

The seven nature and scenic areas discussed in this chapter were created with funds provided by the state, private colleges, state-funded universities, private foundations, and nonprofit nature organizations. Lilley Cornett Woods, which contains stands of virgin hardwoods, was purchased by the Commonwealth of Kentucky to save the trees from being cut. Berea College Forest, although actively managed for timber, is a living model of proper watershed management and water resource utilization. The Clyde E. Buckley Wildlife Sanctuary, intended as a living heritage of the natural environment and a center for study, is one of the few Audubon Society sanctuaries in the interior of the United States. The foresight of a German immigrant has forever preserved Bernheim Forest, a 10,000-acre tract of woodlands in the Knobs region of central Kentucky, so that city dwellers can have a place to learn about nature.

Murphy's Pond, a 280-acre slough containing the only stand of virgin cypress trees in Kentucky, was saved from draining by the efforts of a family who fought to save the area's natural qualities. Reelfoot Lake, although lying mostly in Tennessee, and heavily visited by campers, fisher-men, and hunters, should be included in the list of important nature and scenic areas because of its unique beginnings and large concentrations of wildlife. The natural lake was formed during the New Madrid Earthquake of 1811-12 and is an important rest stop on the Mississippi flyway for migrating waterfowl and bald eagles. Historical Pilot Knob is the center of interest in the Spencer-Morton Preserve, made possible through funds from the Nature Conservancy.

Kentucky's nature and scenic areas showcase the rich natural re-sources of the Commonwealth and will remain forever as monuments to geology, plant and animal communities, and their complex relationships which man is just beginning to understand.

Lilley Cornett Woods
Mailing address: P.O. Box 78, Skyline, Kentucky, 41851
Telephone: (606) 633-5828

Lilley Cornett Woods, one of the last remaining tracts of virgin timber in the eastern United States, is a prime example of a climax forest at its best. Untouched for thousands of years except by the forces of nature itself, this 554-acre tract of woodland on Linefork Creek in Letcher County, near Whitesburg in eastern Kentucky, offers the visitor a first-hand look at the last remaining climax portion of one of the greatest forest types of all time, the mixed mesophytic, which was at its finest in the Cumberland Moun-tains of eastern Kentucky.

Named for the man who spent most of his life personally guarding the forest against intruders, Lilley Cornett Woods (Lilley's Woods, as they were known to his friends and neighbors) is located on Ky-1103 and may be reached via Ky-15 from the Mountain Parkway at Campton or by US-25E and US-119 from Interstate-75 at Corbin.

Trees in the virgin portion of the woods are more than 400 years old. Their recent survival is attributed to Cornett, whose intense devotion prompted him to insure their safety from fire by sending crews into the woods at his own expense when the danger was great. Cornett steadfastly refused to allow any logging in his woods, even during World War II when lumber was scarce and all his neighbors were selling their trees.

In 1915, Lilley Cornett saw the woods and decided they were worth protecting. He knew that if the trees were cut, Kentuckians would probably never have another opportunity to view such a majestic stand of hardwood trees. Between 1915 and 1933, Cornett bought up the land and began a lifelong vigil to preserve for all time the last remaining tract of virgin eastern timberland. At his death in 1958, his four sons decided to carry on their father's wish. When mining interests attempted to strip the area in 1969, Cornett's sons sold the land to the Commonwealth of Kentucky, with the provision that the land would remain untouched forever. The mining companies subsequently agreed that as long as the woods remained the property of the state and were managed as a forest preserve, they would relinquish their mineral rights.

Lilley Cornett Woods, designated a national natural landmark, is open to visitors from April 1 to October 31, 9:00 a.m. to 4:30 p.m daily. Since January 1977, Eastern Kentucky University has been responsible for the protection and management of the forest, which now serves as an environmental study area for graduate students at the university. Guided tours of the woods are conducted daily.

There are two day-hiking trails in Lilley Cornett Woods. Shop Hollow Trail is a short 45-minute walk. The longer Big Everidge Trail, takes about four hours to hike. Big Everidge Trail has a 900-foot gain in elevation and numerous switchbacks through narrow, steep valleys and ridges. Along the hiking trails are many fallen trees, among them several 100-foot-tall chestnuts. Huge white oaks that have stood for nearly 500 years are dwarfed by hickory trees which reach 170 feet in height. The downed trees are matted with mosses and ferns.

In the lower, moist areas, eastern hemlocks grow so densely that the forest floor is deeply shaded, allowing only shade-tolerant herbaceous ground plants to grow in rich soil. The black walnut also thrives at the lower elevations; some reach 60 or 70 feet into the air before their trunks branch. At the higher elevations, pitch and scrub pine and chestnut oaks live in the drier sites atop ridges. Smooth-barked beech abound as one of the most common trees in the hillside, slope forest community. In all, there are some 90 species of trees and shrubs, a large variety of animal life, and a profusion of wild flowers—trilliums, partridge berries, pink lady's slipper, trailing arbutus, and May apples. Songbirds and predatory birds, such as the broad-winged hawk and barred owl, are common in Lilley Cornett Woods.

Botanists speculate that the forests of eastern Kentucky were the seed producers for all the great American forests. Ice ages destroyed most of the northern forests, while the plateauland of eastern Kentucky, with a relatively southerly climate and hilly terrain, was a buffer against the advance of glaciers. Pockets of trees survived the onslaught of ice age after ice age to become the seed producers after the cold climate drastically changed more than 10,000 years ago. Lilley Cornett Woods is the last remnant of the great forests which stretched from the Big Sandy to the Mississippi River in Kentucky, the "progenitors" of all the diverse forest types of this country.

Berea College Forest

Berea College Forest, 5,500 acres in Madison, Rockcastle, and Jackson counties of eastern Kentucky, is an outdoor laboratory for forestry students and an integral part in a demonstration project of water and timber management in the Appalachians. Berea College was a pioneer school of forestry education in America. The first general forestry course was offered by the college's agriculture department in 1898.

After the turn of the century, Berea College embarked on a land acquisition program. By 1910, sizeable tracts of valuable timber and year-round reliable water sources were purchased. The woodlands east of the city of Berea, bounded roughly by Blue Lick Creek on the north, US-421 on the east, Ky-21 on the south, and Davis Hollow on the west, are today called Berea College Forest. In addition to providing land for recreational uses and forestry research, Berea College Forest protects the watershed from which the city of Berea gets its domestic and industrial water.

A liberal arts college, Berea College was founded to provide educational opportunities to mountain youths with ability but limited economic resources. There is no tuition; every Berea College student must work to help meet the expense of bed and board. Since the school's founding in 1855, concern for the "dignity of labor and the preservation of Appalachian crafts" has led to establishment of college-operated student industries offering more than 60 different kinds of jobs, many of which are in such Appalachian crafts as weaving, wood turning, antique furniture reproduction, broommaking, ceramics, baking, and cooking homestyle candies and jams.

The nonsectarian, interracial college was founded to promote the ideal of Christian brotherhood. The college, with its attractive tree-lined campus in downtown Berea, is the cornerstone of the historic community, a model for all Appalachia. Berea is a center for the mountain arts with museums, galleries, and Boone Tavern, which offers fine accommodations and wholesome home-cooked regional foods.

There are 13 day-hiking trails of varying lengths in the Berea College Forest. The forest types are representative of those in the Cumberland Plateau. Virginia and short leaf pine, yellow poplar, hickory, and mixed oaks grow in drier sites atop ridges, with rich stands of yellow poplar in the moist cove sites at 1400 feet. At lower elevations in the creek valleys, there's a multitude of herbaceous ground plants, mosses, ferns, and wildflowers. Basswood, walnut, ash, sugar maple, white oak, and hickory trees thrive under these conditions. Most of the timber in the area was cut in the 1880s but reforestation took place rapidly. Berea College Forest is now actively managed for timber through a cooperative program between the college and the United States Forest Service. Geologists estimate that the rock formations and soil types (heavy clay soils derived from carboniferous shales, gray-shale clay zone, and limestone soils) range from the Devonian to the Holocene period. Geological points of interest in Berea College Forest include Devil's Slide, Devil's Kitchen, and Fat Man's Misery.

The Pigg House, south of Ky-21 near the Indian Fort Theatre, can be reserved for Girl Scout, civic, religious, and nature study groups. The log home was donated to the college in the 1920s. Wooded hillsides surround Indian Fort Theatre, the setting for "Wilderness Road," the summertime outdoor drama about mountain families caught in the turmoil of the Civil War. The drama, filled with dancing and singing, mountain music, colorful costumes, and thunderous battles, is a stirring testimony to the Civil War's tragic impact on the isolated and proud people of the Appalachians. Performances are at 8:30 p.m. nightly except Sundays. The 1978 season runs from June 28 to Labor Day; admission prices range from $1.25 to $5.

Each May and October, the Kentucky Guild of Artists and Craftsmen, a nonprofit organization devoted to the preservation and development of Kentucky's arts and crafts, holds its semiannual craft fairs in Berea's Indian Fort Theatre. The fairs bring together as many as 100 exhibitors to display their Kentucky products: pottery, woven items, quilts, chairs, baskets, jewelry, paintings, prints, woodwork, sculpture, and candles. Daily craft demonstrations at the three-day fairs include the wheel-throwing of pottery, vegetable dyeing, silk screen printing, carving, and broommaking. Performances of Kentucky's music—ballads, bluegrass, folk, and country—are also presented during these seasonal craft fairs.

Although the Berea College Forest is primarily a day-use area, camping is allowed by special permission. There's a state-maintained roadside picnic area on Ky-21 near the Indian Fort Theatre. Permission for camping and reservations for accommodations in the Pigg House must be arranged through the Office of the Business Vice-President, College Post Office Box 3204, Berea College, Berea, Kentucky, 40404. Telephone: (606) 986-9341.

Clyde E. Buckley Wildlife Sanctuary
Mailing address: Route #3, Frankfort, Kentucky, 40601
Telephone: (606) 873-5711

Atop the bluffs of the Kentucky River in northwest Woodford County, Kentucky, is the Clyde E. Buckley Wildlife Sanctuary, 285 acres of wooded hill country and open fields, rich in native plants and wildlife. The sanctuary is intended to preserve a living heritage of the natural environment and serve as a center for study. Operated by the National Audubon Society, on land donated by Mrs. Clyde E. Buckley of Lexington, Kentucky, as a memorial to her late husband, this wildlife refuge is one of the Audubon Society sanctuaries located in the interior of the United States.

Points of interest in the sanctuary include the Marion E. Lindsey Birdwatching House, an all-weather, glass-enclosed observation building near bird feeders; the Ray Harm Nature Center, named after the Kentucky wildlife artist-naturalist; and a bird-watching shelter overlooking Apollo Pond and its adjacent wetlands. From these observation points, or while walking the six miles of color-coded nature trails in the sanctuary, visitors may see a wide variety of wildlife, including whitetail deer, cottontail rabbit, raccoon, red and gray fox, woodchuck, and birds of wide variety.

The sanctuary lies in the path of the spring and fall migration of many species of birds—herons, black and mallard ducks, Canada geese, warblers, and kingfishers. In spring and summer, the woodlands and fields are filled with the calls of colorful songbirds busily building nests and rearing young. Warden Naturalist, Tim Williams, conducts programs open to the public at no cost on Saturdays and Sundays, beginning at 2:00 p.m. with nature walks, followed by slide presentations and special programs at 4:00 p.m. The sanctuary is closed Mondays and Tuesdays; the hours the rest of the week are Wednesday through Friday 9:00 a.m. to 5:00 p.m., Saturdays and Sundays 1:00 to 6:00 p.m., and Saturdays 9:00 a.m. to 12 noon by reservation only for groups up to 30 persons.

The displays in Harm House include medicinal herbs, wildflowers, bird nests, lichens and fungi, local marine fossils, coal-age fossils, the water cycle of condensation and evaporation, food chains of plants and animals, insect collections, local high school science projects, and a near complete collection of prints and miscellaneous sketches by the man for whom the environmental education center was named.

In addition to these permanent displays and representative prints by other wildlife artists such as Coheleach, Eckelberry, and Ruthven housed in the nature center, the sanctuary staff prepares traveling exhibits for local county fairs and career days at high schools. The newest development in the day-hiking trail system is the self-interpretive status of the White Trail, with a brochure for better understanding of each stop along the way.

The Clyde E. Buckley Wildlife Sanctuary, 12 miles west of Versailles in Kentucky's Bluegrass Region, is reached via US-60 and the Glenns Creek-McCracken and Germany roads.

Bernheim Forest
Mailing address: Clermont, Kentucky, 40110
Telephone: (502) 543-2451

Bernheim Forest, 10,000 acres in Nelson and Bullitt counties, Kentucky, is just a 45-minute drive south of Louisville. Opened to the public in 1950, the 10,000-acre area is managed by the Isaac W. Bernheim Foundation as a nature preserve and study area. Reached via US-31 E, US-150, Ky-245, Ky-61, and Ky-245, or Interstate-65 and Ky-245 (the Bernheim Forest ramp four miles south of the Sheperdsville Plaza), Bernheim Forest is open daily from 9:00 a.m. to sundown, March 15 to November 15.

Isaac W. Bernheim immigrated to the United States from Germany when he was 17 years old. When he reached New York he had $5 in his pocket. He peddled hardware goods to colonies of German immigrants in Pennsylvania, and eventually moved to Paducah, Kentucky, where he founded a wholesale whiskey business operated in partnership with his brother. In 1872 Bernheim moved to Louisville and incorporated the Bernheim Distillers. Bernheim retired from business at the time of Prohibition and died in 1945 at the age of 96.

Bernheim grew up near Germany's famous Black Forest, and had a deep love of wild things. About 1928, he purchased 13,000 acres of woodlands and set up a foundation to protect and develop the acreage so that city dwellers could learn about nature. A trust fund provided money for maintenance and the construction of day-use facilities, including an arboretum center, picnic grounds, two small lakes, paved access roads, extensive gardens and arboretum, nature trails, and fire roads.

Continuous programs, workshops, lectures, bird censuses, nature walks, and wildlife seminars are conducted through cooperation with universities, the National Audubon Society, the Sierra Club, and other nature-oriented groups. Research projects on wildlife, forest ecology, and horticulture have been conducted on the grounds. About 2,000 acres of Bernheim Forest are landscaped. The 225-acre arboretum has flowering trees and hardwoods—crabapples, hollies, nut trees, beech, ginkgoes, oaks, horse chestnuts, and buckeyes.

Picnic grounds are located at Toms Town, Guerilla Hollow, on the north side of Cedar Lake in a pine grove surrounding the forest office east of Rock Run Bridge. Visitors are asked to keep their speed under 25 miles per hour on paved roads. No swimming or boating is allowed on either of the two small lakes. Fishing, under Kentucky Fish and Wildlife regulations, is not permitted on Sundays or Federal holidays. Acceptable bait includes artificial lures or crickets, red worms, nightcrawlers, meal worms, cut bait, or dough balls; no minnows. Picnic tables and grills are available at most picnic grounds; visitors may use their own portable grills, tables, and lawn chairs in the Pines Picnic Area. Since Bernheim Forest is a nature preserve, hunting is not permitted, and unleashed dogs, air rifles, guns, and molestation of wildlife are strictly prohibited.

Overlooking Big Meadow is a grove of dogwoods and azaleas surrounding the original bronze statue, "Let There Be Light," by George Grey Barnard. All plants are labeled and grouped by seasonal interest; plant collecting is not allowed. Holly Hill is another point of interest in the landscape arboretum. American, Japanese, and deciduous holly surround the plaque, "Justice."

Most of the day-hiking trails in Bernheim Forest are located in the 8,000 acres of woodlands, undisturbed since the forest was established in 1928. Only the Sun and Shade Trail in the arboretum center, which demonstrates shade tolerances of plants, and a self-guided nature trail adjacent to the Nature Center are outside the extensive woodland holdings. Driving from the Nature Center to the fire tower overlooking Wildcat Hollow, the trailheads of six day-hiking trails are passed. These trails and their lengths are: Poplar Flat, .75 miles; Rocky Run, 1.0 mile; Boulder Hill, 1.5 miles; Pine Point, .5 miles; Tower Loop, .5 miles; and Overall Fork, 3.5 miles. There are also numerous unmarked footpaths in the forestlands south of the fire tower. All trails are for foot travel only.

Murphy's Pond
Mailing address: c/o Dr. W.J. Pittman,
    Department of Biology, Murray State University,
    Murray, Kentucky, 42071
Telephone: (502) 762-2786.

The complex aquatic ecosystems called wetlands are a fast-disappearing resource threatened by channelization and the advance of agriculture. One such unique area in far western Kentucky is Murphy's Pond, a 280-acre cypress slough southwest of Fancy Farm, Kentucky, off Ky-307 at the Hickman-Graves county line. The pond, fed by the waters of Obion Creek, is said to have been formed by the 1811-12 earthquake that was centered along the Mississippi River where Kentucky, Tennessee, and Missouri meet.

Murphy's Pond is now owned by Murray State University and is used as a biological study area, safe from man's infringement. The university's acquisition of the land, 150 acres of which are an open pothole, was made possible by the Nature Conservancy, a nonprofit, Washington-based organization that purchased the pond and adjoining timberlands in 1961 for $67,000, protecting Kentucky's only virgin stand of cypress trees and the surrounding wetlands from destruction. The university bought the wetland area from the Nature Conservancy, but through partial return of the purchase funds and a matching grant from the U.S. Bureau of Outdoor Recreation, Murray State's actual expenditure was about $5,000.

Intensive study of the area has taken place almost since its initial purchase from the heirs of George Allen Courtney, who was praised for realizing the potential threats to such a resource and agreeing to sell it to the Nature Conservancy. Biologists have identified at least 45 species of mammals, 40 reptiles (including cottonmouth water moccasin, *Agkistrodon piscivorus*), 30 species of amphibians, and 200 species of birds (including large concentrations of migratory waterfowl).

Murphy's Pond is open to the public anytime, but it's advisable to write or call prior to visiting to insure that you have exact directions on how to find it. There are many wetlands in the area, and it's easy to get lost.

Reelfoot Lake
Mailing address: Northwest Tennessee Tourist Council, P.O. Box 63, Martin, Tennessee, 38237

In December of 1811, sparsely populated sections of western Kentucky, Tennessee, and eastern Missouri territory were rocked by an earthquake, believed to have been as much as 15 times as intense as the one which hit San Francisco 95 years later in 1906. One settler in a river town in the New Madrid Bend of the Mississippi River, where the quake was centered, later wrote that the quake hit in the middle of the night and that he was awakened by a groaning, creaking, and rumbling from the earth. The ground was rising and falling like a choppy lake, and clouds of foul-smelling sulphur fumes blackened out the moon. Fearing for his life, he fled to the woods as his cabin chimney crashed through the roof. The tremors and thundering after-shocks continued for more than a month. Landslides swept huge chunks of riverbank into the water, trees were violently uprooted, and deep cracks were opened up in the earth. Islands in the river disappeared and new ones were formed.

For a 48-hour period, the Mississippi River ran backwards, filling in miles of sunken cypress forest. Out of all the destruction came the creation of Reelfoot Lake, one of western Kentucky and Tennessee's most impressive natural wonders. A fishhook-shaped slough-like natural lake 25 miles long from its upper reaches in Fulton County, Kentucky, to Blue Basin, west of Samburg, Tennessee, Reelfoot Lake is part swamp, part shallow lake encircled by magnificent stands of cypress trees, a precious wetland ecosystem rich in aquatic plants, fish, birdlife, and mammals.

The 18,000-acre lake in Lake and Obion counties, Tennessee, and Fulton County, Kentucky, is reached via Ky-94 and Tn-78 from Hickman, Kentucky, and US-45W, US-51, and Tn-21 from Fulton, Kentucky/Tennessee. The wetland areas surrounding the lake are managed as Reelfoot National Wildlife Refuge, Reelfoot Lake State Resort Park (state of Tennessee), and Reelfoot Wildlife Management Area (Tennessee Fish and Wildlife Resource Agency).

For many years, there was a dispute over who actually owned Reelfoot Lake. Through the courts, the state of Tennessee gained control in 1914. Ten years later, the state purchased most of the property surrounding the lake for a proposed park and public hunting area. Development of the state park began in 1934; in 1977 the facilities were improved and the park took on "resort park" status.

Reelfoot Lake State Resort Park is 10 miles north of Tiptonville, Tennessee, on Tn-78 overlooking the Upper Blue Basin. The 20-unit Airpark Inn and restaurant are open year-round except Christmas Eve to New Year's week. A smaller five-unit motel (three housekeeping units) operated by the state of Tennessee is located one mile southwest of Samburg, Tennessee, on Tn-21/22. The park's facilities and services include a museum, auditorium, 120-site campground with water and electrical hookups, picnic table and grill at each site, RV dump station, and bathhouses complete with showers, commodes, and lavatories. There's a wading pool at the Airpark Inn for use of lodge guests and Airpark Campgrounds guests only. Scenic cruises on the lake are available April through October (weather permitting), 9:00 a.m to sunset daily. A historical and nature talk is given during the cruise. Recreational facilities at the park include tennis, softball, horseshoes, archery, shuffleboard, badminton, and indoor table games. Mailing address: Reelfoot Lake State Resort Park, Route #1, Tiptonville, Tennessee, 38079. Telephone: (901) 253-7756.

Reelfoot Lake has long been known for its bounty of wild animals and plantlife. The haunting cypress tree with its broad base and "knees" extending from the water is the symbol of Reelfoot Lake. In spring and summer the waters are abloom with yellow and white waterlilies, saw grass, and other aquatic vascular plants. Birdlife includes red-winged blackbirds, cowbirds, many species of warblers and wrens, ospreys, and wading birds like herons, grebes, and terns. The swampy woodlands surrounding the lake are filled with raccoon and opossum, foxes, beaver, and whitetail deer. The fall and winter seasons bring virtually millions of mallards, wood ducks, and Canadian geese. Ducks flock to the lake to feed on the rich beds of wild rice, celery, and duckweed. Adjacent to the lake's northern end is the Reelfoot National Wildlife Refuge, U.S. Fish and Wildlife Service, Samburg, Tennessee, 38354. Telephone: (901) 538-2481.

One of the top attractions to nature enthusiasts, photographers, field biologists, and ornithologists is the annual migration of bald and golden eagles to Reelfoot Lake. Almost two hundred years ago, on June 20, 1782, the bald eagle became the official emblem of the United States, "a living symbol of our nation's strength and freedom." At present its numbers are drastically low. The bald eagle is found only in North America and is one of America's largest birds of prey. A fully matured female may measure 36 to 40 inches from beak to tail and weigh up to 16 pounds, while the male (which is smaller) will weigh 5 to 10 pounds. Wingspans of both average 6 to 8 feet.

Most people recognize the bald eagle by its white head, but until the bird is three years old it is almost entirely brown. Between the ages of three and five years the bird will begin to get a small amount of white on its head and tail, and by the time the eagle is five years of age it will have acquired the characteristic white head and tail.

These birds have declined in number primarily due to the use of DDT and other persistent pesticides which concentrate in the fish the bald eagle eats. This causes the eagle to lay weak-shelled eggs which are easily broken during incubation. In June of 1972 the United States banned most uses of DDT but other pesticides, such as Dieldrin, are still being used.

Bald eagles have been coming to Reelfoot Lake since the lake was formed, and up until 1962 they nested there. The increase in the number of people on the lake and the opening of ditches to some of the more remote areas of the lake have probably been instrumental in keeping the eagles from nesting there in recent years.

Most of the bald eagles that come to Reelfoot Lake nest in Canada and the Great Lakes region. During the winter months bald eagles are found all along the Mississippi River. Reelfoot Lake is one of their major wintering areas. Since a bald eagle's diet is about 95 percent fish, it needs ice-free water in which to feed.

Bald eagles begin coming to Reelfoot Lake around the first of November and leave around March 15. They reach their peak in January and February when 100 or more eagles can be found on the lake. These birds can be found at almost any location on the lake during the winter months. You are likely to see them perching in the cypress trees along the shoreline or soaring over open water. A leisurely drive around Reelfoot Lake along Tn-21 and Tn-22 will generally result in sightings of our nation's symbol.

Fishing is a favorite spring, summer, and fall recreational pastime. There are numerous boat docks and guide services available to visiting anglers. The traditional "stump jumper" fishing boat at Reelfoot resembles a cross between a canoe, a dory, and the dugout canoe used by Indians in South America. Its bottom is flat, both ends are pointed, and the narrow boat is about 16 feet long. A special double-lock oar system enables the rower to face the way he is traveling. Some of these boats are equipped with small inboard motors about the size and power of a lawn mower engine.

Reelfoot Lake is quite shallow (two to three feet in most places), but in some of the canals and holes it's as much as 20 feet deep. Extremely fertile, Reelfoot Lake produces large populations of rough and game fishes. The fishing for bass, crappie, and bluegill is done over stump beds, lily pads, and around cypress roots (knees). Wide channels are cut through the sawgrass and lily beds. In the early spring, good stringers of bass and crappie are taken. In early summer (May to July), the bluegill run is especially good. Reelfoot bluegills are hand-sized and full of fight when taken on cane poles or ultralight tackle.

An interesting legend surrounds the formation of the lake, and local people accept it as a part of the interesting region's past. Before the white man came, tribes of Choctaw and Chickasaw Indians lived along the Mississippi River in what is now southwest Kentucky and northwest Tennessee. The legend recounts that a Chickasaw chief's only son was born deformed with a club foot. He was given the name Kalopin, which meant Reelfoot.

When Kalopin grew to manhood and became the chief of his father's tribe, he ventured southward to a village of the Choctaw, where he met and fell madly in love with the chief's daughter. The Choctaw chief, Copiah, refused Kalopin's plea for her hand in marriage because of the warrior's deformity. The Great Spirit warned Reelfoot that if he stole his neighbor's daughter he would cause the waters to swallow up his village and send his people to a watery grave. Reelfoot was frightened but his love got the best of him. Returning to the Choctaw village, he secretly stole away with the maiden, and took her to a cypress grove near the banks of the Mississippi River. When he saw what Reelfoot had done, the Great Spirit stomped his feet in anger. The Father of Waters heard the Great Spirit and flowed over Reelfoot's country, creating the lake.

Spencer-Morton Preserve
Mailing address: c/o William H. Martin, Director,
   Division of Wild Areas, Eastern Kentucky University,
   Richmond, Kentucky, 40475
Telephone: (606) 622-3122

History recounts that Daniel Boone first viewed Kentucky's Bluegrass Region in June of 1769 from Pilot Knob, a rocky perch on the western edge of the Cumberland Plateau. Today, the sandstone bluff rising 730 feet above the surrounding countryside is the center of interest in the 320-acre Spencer-Morton Preserve, a nature study area managed by Eastern Kentucky University. In 1976 the Kentucky Chapter of the Nature Conservancy purchased the land four miles northwest of Clay City, Kentucky, in Powell County off Ky-15.

Spencer-Morton Preserve is open year-round to day-use only, including picnicking, day-hiking, and nature study. No overnight camping is allowed, and guests are asked to register at the main gate to the preserve before entering. On a clear day buildings on the campus of Eastern Kentucky University, 30 miles to the southwest, can be seen from Pilot Knob.

The geology of the area is that of claystone, siltstone, and sandstone rocks formed during Mississippian and Pennsylvanian periods of geological history, approximately 200 million years ago. The protected forest is composed of communities of trees—white oak, tulip poplar, and black oak on the lower and middle slopes of the knob, and Virginia pine and chestnut oak at the higher, dry sites. Wildflowers grow in profusion throughout the forest. The plant and animal communities of the preserve are studied by students at Eastern Kentucky University.

Sailing on Kentucky Lake. Photograph by Kentucky Department of Public Information.

8
Special Interest
Recreational Activities

Introduction

The outdoor recreation experience encompasses a mind-boggling variety of pursuits, and the special interest activities which follow represent the most challenging. These are sports for only the most adventuresome persons. They are physically demanding, and are sometimes spiced with the element of danger; thus, many consider them the most rewarding of all outdoor pursuits, because they afford the opportunity to discover hidden abilities and realize experiences which most people only dream about.

In this chapter, the equipment outlets, training schools, and organizations in Kentucky for hang-gliding, scuba diving, sailing, bicycling, sport parachuting, and snow skiing will be discussed. These sports are certainly not for everyone, but are nonetheless a valid part of the broad range of outdoor pursuits available in the Commonwealth.

Snow Skiing
Mailing address: Louisville Ski Club, 924 Oakland Drive, New Albany, Indiana, 47150
Telephone: (812) 948-9338

Although there are no downhill ski resorts in Kentucky, and Kentucky's winters aren't always snowy, there is a growing number of persons interested in both cross-country and downhill skiing. Ski clubs are the primary boosters of the sport and are responsible for virtually all the organized trips to downhill ski resorts in neighboring states. When snow does fall in Kentucky, some of the local equipment outlets sponsor informal cross-country skiing outings in city parks and golf courses.

The Louisville Ski Club, founded in 1950, is the largest and most active skiing organization in Kentucky. The 700-member club meets the second and fourth Tuesdays each month at the Holiday Inn Central, 1921 Bishop Lane; telephone: (502) 458-9592. The Louisville Ski Club is an all-volunteer organization that sponsors year-round social and athletic activities—volleyball and softball tournaments, picnics, water skiing and houseboating trips, backpacking and rafting excursions in the summer months, and package ski trips in the winter to resorts in nearby states (West Virginia, North Carolina, Ohio, Michigan), plus one major western trip to either California, Colorado, Utah, or Nevada. A membership in the Louisville Ski Club is $20 a year, and includes monthly newsletter and biannual roster.

OUTLETS IN KENTUCKY FOR CROSS-COUNTRY SKIING EQUIPMENT

Cherokee Cyclery, 128 Breckinridge Lane, St. Matthews, Kentucky, 40207. Telephone: (502) 897-2611. Sponsors local cross-country outings and a few weekend trips out-of-state. Informal classes on basic technique.

Viking Canoe and Mountaineering Center, 3308 Preston Highway, Louisville, Kentucky, 40213. Telephone: (502) 361-8051. Informal class sessions and local outings.

The Great Outdoors, 3824 Wilmington Avenue, St. Matthews, Kentucky, 40207. Telephone: (502) 895-7353. Local informal outings and training sessions, out-of-town trips, and ski service department.

Sage School of the Outdoors, 209 East High Street, Lexington, Kentucky, 40507. Telephone: (606) 255-1547. Informal outings locally.

OUTLETS IN KENTUCKY FOR DOWNHILL SKIING EQUIPMENT

Allied Sporting Goods, Shelbyville Road Plaza, St. Matthews, Kentucky, 40207. Telephone: (502) 897-3253.

Brendamour's Sporting Goods, Inc., Jefferson Mall, Louisville, Kentucky, 40219. Telephone (502) 966-8278 (502) 966-8279.

Scuba Diving

Diving waters in Kentucky are limited, but several enthusiastic organizations have led the way in discovering the best places. Their unanimous choice for the best scuba diving lake in Kentucky is Dale Hollow, the

35,000-acre impoundment on the Obey River in south central Kentucky and Tennessee.

Visibility in Dale Hollow is dependent on water levels and time of year. Normally, visibility is 20 to 25 feet, sometimes as much as 50 to 60 feet, with a minimum never less than 10 feet. The best diving is off rock ledges in the old river channel, where current keeps silt to a minimum, thus clearing the water. Spring-fed coves are usually good spots, too. Some popular sections of the lake for scuba diving are Wolf Creek, Sulphur Creek, and First Island. An air station is located at Eagles Cove Marina, Byrdstown, Tennessee, 38549. Telephone: (615) 864-3456.

There are two retail stores/instructional schools in Louisville, as well as one in Lexington, and a club for advanced divers whose members are primarily from Louisville and southern Indiana. The Kentucky Diving Headquarters (KDH) offers beginners instruction (classroom, pool, and open-water training) that leads to certification. In addition to basic instruction, KDH has special classes in dive rescue and recovery and underwater photography. Kentucky Diving Headquarters publishes a bimonthly newsletter, *Bottom Times,* to inform interested divers about weekend outings and special trips to the Bahamas and the Caribbean. Tanks and regulators can be rented through the shop, where many of the major lines of scuba gear are sold. For more information, contact co-owners E. J. Snider or Ron Lipman, Kentucky Diving Headquarters, 3928 Shelbyville Road, St. Matthews, Kentucky, 40207. Telephone: (502) 897-6481.

Another instructional/retail sales sport scuba diving organization in Louisville is Diver's, Incorporated, owned and operated by Bob Coffey and Joe Elkins. Diver's, Inc., is the only scuba organization in Kentucky that has its own on-premise pool for instruction. The basic certification courses include lecture sessions, pool work, and open-water training at Dale Hollow Lake, where the organization keeps a 40-foot houseboat with onboard air compressor. The professional staff of Diver's Inc., teaches courses in commercial diving, cave diving, dive rescue and recovery, underwater photography, and all advanced certifications. They also dive commercially all over the U.S. A monthly newsletter keeps interested divers up to date on sponsored trips to local quarry sites, as well as to Florida, the Great Lakes, the Caribbean, and the Bahamas. Mailing address: Diver's, Inc., 4807 Dixie Highway, Louisville, Kentucky, 40216. Telephone: (502) 448-7433.

The Lexington Dive Shop is the main supplier of equipment and air for scuba divers from central Kentucky. Owner Tom Weller and his staff offer instructional clinics with classroom and pool sessions and open-water dives leading towards sport diving certification. Repair facilities, rental equipment, retail sales, and a schedule of trips to local waters as well as to the Bahamas are available. Mailing address: The Lexington Dive Shop, 819 Euclid Avenue, Lexington, Kentucky, 40502. Telephone: (606) 266-4703.

The Kentuckiana Underwater Explorers Society is a loose-knit organization of advanced divers who promote the sport by sponsoring dive trips, diving seminars, and social activities. The organization is similar in objectives to small clubs in the Fort Knox, Lexington, and London areas. Mailing address: Kentuckiana Underwater Explorers Society, c/o Tom Wills, 5021 Invicta Drive, Louisville, Kentucky, 40216. Telephone: (502) 447-6248.

Hang-Gliding

Hang-gliding may be the closest man has ever come to flying "like a bird." Strapped in a harness to an aluminum-framed kite with nylon "wings," the hang-glider sails with the wind high above forests and rocky cliffs, experiencing flight in its truest sense, a freedom that transcends jet planes and skydiving.

Hang-gliding is a small but growing sport in Kentucky. It is estimated that between 1,000 and 1,500 persons have received hang-gliding training and are pursuing the adventurous sport. Anyone of average strength and balance can become a hang-gliding pilot; young and old alike participate in this non-polluting, fascinating sport. Safety is a growing concern to hang-gliding enthusiasts, and through the leadership of the U.S. Hang-gliding Association of Los Angeles, backup systems, such as drag chutes, are being developed in efforts to make the sport safer.

There are two certified hang-gliding schools in Kentucky. Bob White operates the Appalachian Hang-gliding School, which holds classes (ground school includes basic aerodynamics and launching and landing techniques), conducts flight sessions at local training hills, and organizes monthly trips to higher sites in Tennessee, West Virginia, and North Carolina. The four- to five-hour instructional sessions cost $35; this fee includes instruction, glider, helmet, and harness. Mailing address: The Great Outdoors, 3824 Wilmington Avenue, St. Matthews, Kentucky, 40207. Telephone: (502) 895-7353.

Derby City Kite Sales, operated by Ron Oakley, offers sales, service on seven brands of hang-gliders and tow kites, and an instructional school. Hang-gliding ground school classes and training flights are held every weekend. The $30 cost includes ground school (basic aerodynamics, assembly, kite handling on the ground and in the air, and takeoff and landing procedures), use of harness, safety helmet, and glider, and first flight from a 30-foot training hill. Training facilities in either eastern Jefferson County, central Kentucky, or southern Indiana are used, depending on wind directions. Students can sit in on two additional ground school and training exercises after their first flight. Persons under 18 years of age must have notarized permission from a parent or guardian; injury release forms must be signed by all participants in the school's training. Ron Oakley is also the contact for information regarding the Louisville Hang-gliding Association. Mailing address: Derby City Kite Sales, 8400 Blue Lick Road, Louisville, Kentucky, 40219. Telephone: (502) 969-6295.

Sport Parachuting

The plane levels off at 2800 feet. You've gone over everything you learned in the training classes for the last time. The jumpmaster gives the command to "sit in the door," and your heart is pounding in your chest. Below you there's nothing but wide open spaces, miles of countryside that resembles a patchwork quilt.

"Out on the strut," commands the jumpmaster, pointing to the wing brace. Standing on the step, looking straight ahead, you are riding the wind. The seconds seem like hours. "Go!" Your feet leave the strut and you're falling, spread-eagle, gathering speed fast. The whine of the airplane's motor fades in the distance, and there's nothing but growing silence. You're falling free, mysteriously free for the first time, a feeling independent of any sensation of time or space. A tug at the cord, and your parachute opens; you begin maneuvering the steering lines. The earth is slowly getting closer, but you don't want it to end. Feet and knees together, you brace for the landing.

Chutes are blossoming in the sunshine above you. Somehow there is a strange, new-found bond between you and that ocean of air, the sky. And there's a sense of accomplishment, and deep-down pride. You've discovered a part of yourself you've never known before.

Sport parachuting is an intense personal experience. The training, the flight up in the light plane, and the jump itself require immense concentration and mental alertness. It is estimated that there are more than 35,000 sport parachutists, making over one-and-a-half million jumps each year. In Kentucky, there are several thousand active sport parachutists, according to the U.S. Parachute Association. There is one training school in the state.

The Greene County Sport Parachute Center is five miles west of Bardstown, Kentucky, on Airport Road, off US-62, and is open year-round, seven days a week, from 9:00 a.m. to dusk. Beginner jump classes are held on Saturdays and Sundays, weather permitting. The Greene County Sport Parachute Center is one of many centers operated by the Xenia, Ohio-based firm. The Greene County Sport Parachute Centers throughout the country have the largest membership of any parachuting club in the world. Each year, thousands of first-time "jumpers" get their training from this organization, whose licensed and professional jumpmasters and instructors have earned more than eight national competitive titles, and made as many as 2500 jumps over the years. The course cost (including first jump) is $45. Training, gear, club membership (no dues), log book, plane ride up, and jumpmaster's services are included in this cost; after the first time, the cost is $9 per jump. In most cases a static line (which opens the parachute automatically when the jumper goes out the door) is used for the beginner's first five or so jumps. Groups of five or more get special first-time rates, $35 per person. Anyone from 16 to 60 in reasonably good physical condition can enroll in the program; 16- and 17-year-olds must have notarized parental consent. Special arrangements for training during the weekdays are available. The training period lasts from three to five hours and covers familiarization with parachute equipment, aircraft orientation, exiting the aircraft and stable falling techniques, possible malfunctions and corrective actions, steering the parachute, and parachute landings. Mailing address: Greene County Sport Parachute Center, Route #2, Box 140, Bardstown, Kentucky, 40004. Telephone: (502) 348-9981 or 348-9531.

Bicycling

The bicycle is a freedom machine. One of the most popular recreational pastimes of today's freedom-loving generation, bicycling is a freewheeling world of long rides in the country with wind and sunshine on your face, backroad attractions of farms and small towns, and a closeness with nature that comes from exploring under your own power, at your own pace.

Bicycling is economical in the sense that after you've made the initial purchase, there's little upkeep and no cost for operating your bike, as the only fuel needed is a strong pair of legs, "pedal power." Bicycling is a nonpolluting, nonconsumptive activity that sedentary city dwellers and physical fitness buffs alike have found to be great exercise.

Bicycling is a relaxing activity that can be pursued casually for an hour or two after supper as a way of forgetting the pressures of the day, or taken seriously as a way of discovering rural America on long multistate tours. Around the next curve could be the challenge of a steep climb or a rough road, or the exhilaration of a long downhill stretch. It's a recreational activity for the adventuresome that fosters a strong sense of camaraderie. Bicycle racing, while conducted on a limited scale, is nonetheless very popular with Kentucky's most enthusiastic bicyclists.

History

Bicycle design has changed a great deal since 1816, when Baron Karl von Drais built a crude all-wood machine with two equal-sized wheels connected by a bar. His primitive Draisine, or Pedestrian Hobby Horse, was unsteerable in its earliest version, but its rider could balance himself and propel the crude bicycle by alternately paddling against the ground, first with one foot, then with the other. Between 1835 and 1839, a Scottish blacksmith named Kilpatrick MacMillan built the first self-propelled bicycle. Then, in 1861, the Michaux family in France improved on earlier designs with their iron and wood velocipedes, propelled by means of crude pedals. The Boneshaker, Pennyfarthing, and other "suicide wheels" (one huge pedalled wheel trailing a tiny one in the rear) were next on the scene. It was another highwheeler, the Ordinary, that introduced the bicycle to America at the Philadelphia Exposition in 1876. America's first bicycles, made in 1877, cost $313 and weighed over 70 pounds.

By the 1890s bicycles looked much as they do today, and bicycling was booming, both as a recreational pastime and as an economical means of transportation. At the turn of the century, touring clubs were extremely popular. The League of American Wheelmen (LAW) was one of the first major clubs established, and affiliated groups were formed in towns throughout America. On weekends, club members set out on 100-mile tours, called Century Rides. It was the era of America's first big bicycle craze.

By 1910, the automobile age was underway and bicycling was on its way out, a victim of the new motorized mobility. For the next half century the bicycle, whose engineering breakthroughs had been largely responsible for the development of the automobile, motorcycle, and airplane (the Wright Brothers were bicycle mechanics), was regarded as a child's toy. It was not until the 1960s, when the physical fitness and ecology movements began, along with trends towards more leisure time, that the bike came back into favor. Today, America is experiencing a second big bicycle boom, not unlike the one at the turn of the century when the bicycle had just been invented.

Bicycling Organizations

The League of American Wheelmen is still going strong, more than 80 years after its founding. Its national headquarters is located at 19 South Bothwell, Palatine, Illinois, 60067; telephone: (312) 991-1200. The regional representative is Dr. Grace Donnelly, 611 Buckingham Lane, Lexington, Kentucky, 40503; telephone: (606) 227-9576. LAW has two strong affiliates in Kentucky, the Louisville Wheelmen and the Bluegrass Wheelmen.

Louisville Wheelmen.   The Louisville Wheelmen trace their origin back to 1897 during the first big bike boom. That year, Wheelmen's Rest was built in Louisville just south of Churchill Downs in Wayside Park at Third and Southern Parkway. It was from this landmark—a 15-foot semicircular stone bench—that the Louisville Wheelmen's first Century Rides embarked. The rides, to Elizabethtown and back, were held every Sunday.

"Louisville was the country's dead center of cycling activity at the turn of the century when we had three velodromes here. At one time, every land speed record was made here," says Dave Spitler, president of the 200-member Louisville Wheelmen. Spitler also tells of a turn-of-the-century LAW convention bicycle parade down Broadway in Louisville that had 10,000 participants all carrying small lanterns.

Family membership in the nonprofit Louisville Wheelmen is $10 a year and individual memberships are $7. Members are entitled to participate in all club-sponsored events—rides, meetings, rallies, and races; they also receive a bimonthly newsletter. Louisville Wheelmen members range in age from small children to senior citizens.

Nonmembers are invited to join the Louisville Wheelmen on their rides simply by showing up at the announced starting point and introducing themselves to the ride captain. Ride schedules are published in local newspapers each weekend, as well as in the club newsletter. Louisville-area bicycle shops are also good sources of information for Louisville Wheelmen activities.

At least one group ride is held every Saturday and Sunday of the year, including an annual January 1st, 10-mile Polar Bear Ride. Louisville Wheelmen rides are rated according to how strenuous they are, ranging from easy to difficult. A CB-equipped sag wagon accompanies Louisville Wheelmen on long rides, carrying supplies and, occasionally, sagging riders who overestimated their ability. Louisville Wheelmen hold an annual 248-mile TOTS (Tour of Three States) ride from Louisville to Cincinnati and back each September. Sixteen- to twenty-hour Double Century rides are also held frequently.

Inaugurated in 1972 by the Louisville Wheelmen, the two-day Kentucky Derby of Cycling is one of the top attractions of Kentucky Derby Festival Week in Louisville. The Wheelmen also sponsor time trials and preliminary races leading up to the big one.

One of the Louisville Wheelmen's biggest goals is to get a modern velodrome built in the area again. At present, the Wheelmen's racing facility is a hill-and-dale road course in Cherokee Park. Sponsoring charity bike-a-thons and bike safety promotions, promoting biking for health, ecology, and pleasure, working with city officials in the planning of commuter bikeways, and holding family picnics and outings are among other Louisville Wheelmen activities. Mailing address: Louisville Wheelmen, c/o

David Spitler (President), P.O. Box 35541, Louisville, Kentucky, 40232. Telephone: (502) 893-2403.

Bluegrass Wheelmen. The Bluegrass Wheelmen were organized in central Kentucky in the summer of 1970 and now have over 100 members, including LAW regional representative Dr. Grace Donnelly. Bluegrass Wheelmen fees are $6 per family membership and $4 for individuals. Like their Louisville counterpart, Bluegrass Wheelmen sponsor rides open to the public every Saturday and Sunday with schedules published in the local newspapers each weekend, as well as in the organization's newsletter. A sag wagon accompanies long trips. Informal races are held occasionally. In addition, the Bluegrass Wheelmen work with bike promotions and safety programs, charity bike-a-thons, and bikeway planning. The Bluegrass Wheelmen's Century Ride is a scenic six-county loop through the cities surrounding Lexington and outlying Bluegrass farmlands. The annual Red River Rally is also a favorite ride. Held on an October Sunday, the invitational rally travels from Lexington to Natural Bridge State Park with an optional ride through the spectacular Red River Gorge Geological Area. Mailing address: The Bluegrass Wheelmen, c/o Mike Staton (President), P.O. Box 1397, Lexington, Kentucky, 40591. Telephone: (606) 272-0236 (vice-president Don Burrel).

Other Biking Organizations.
    The following organizations also sponsor rides and other bicycle-related activities in Kentucky:

International Bicycle Touring Society, 846 Prospect Street, La Jolla, California, 92037. This organization sponsors some 20 tours annually, some international and some stateside. One frequently scheduled trip is a two-week tour through Kentucky's Bluegrass section. Area representative is Dr. Richard Nave, 4005 Lime Kiln Lane, Louisville, Kentucky, 40222; telephone: (502) 426-2266.

United States Cycling Federation, Box 669, Wall Street Station, New York, New York, 10005. Area representative is Bob Zeman, 835 W. Jefferson, Louisville, Kentucky, 40203; telephone: (502) 459-3208.

River City Road Club, 128 Breckinridge Lane, Louisville, Kentucky, 40207. Telephone: (502) 897-2611. A bicycle racing club; Carson Torpey, president.

Bicycle Federation, Box 68, Silver Springs, Maryland, 20709. Telephone: (301) 587-6110.

Bicycle Manufacturers Association, 1101 15th Street NW, Washington, D.C., 20005. Telephone: (202) 452-1166.

Tours

Of the following ten tours, the Louisville Wheelmen suggested five, the Bluegrass Wheelmen suggested three, and two were mapped out by local IBTS representative, Dr. Richard Nave. They represent only a handful of the many good tours available to Kentucky bikers.

Blue Grass Tour #1: Lexington-Midway-Georgetown Loop.   To see parts of Kentucky's Bluegrass horse farm region, as well as some fascinating historical sites, bike from Lexington northwest out Ky-1681 (Old Frankfort Pike). Turn right on Ky-1967 in Woodford County and follow it 1.7 miles, then turn left on Craigs Mill Road and follow it for three miles. Turn right on US-62 and follow it one mile to Midway. Midway is a sleepy rural Kentucky town, one of the state's oldest. A few years ago a row of old rundown buildings on Railroad Street was renovated into bright-colored, gingerbread-trimmed boutiques and specialty shops. You'll love browsing through its many small shops with names like The Red Brick House, The Caboose, Potpourri, La Cortisanne, The Walnut Basket, Something Special, and The Twig. In Midway you can lunch at an elegant tea shop or a town cafe.

After you leave Midway, stay on Ky-62. Turn right on US-421, then make a quick left onto Ky-341 and follow it 2.3 miles. Make a right onto Ky-1973 (Iron Works Pike), which will take you to the new Kentucky State Horse Park. Everything you always wanted to know but didn't know who to ask about the equine world and horse farm operation is the best way to describe what you will find at this new state park scheduled for opening in late summer of 1978. You can take rides in horse-drawn vehicles or go horseback riding, see movies explaining the state's number one industry, visit a horse museum, admire the larger-than-life bronze statue of Man O' War, or just walk around the stables and observe thoroughbreds, standard-breds, and saddlehorses in the daily training routines.

After leaving the Horse Park continue down Ky-1973 to Ky-353 (Russell Cave Pike) and turn left. You'll pass Castleton and Spindletop farms. Go less than half a mile, then turn left on Huffman Mill Pike, which will take you across the north fork of Elkhorn Creek, and make a left onto Lemons Mill Road. Lemons Mill Road is a beautiful road that parallels the north fork of Elkhorn Creek. The scenery includes farms, tree-lined roadways, and a picturesque dam. Follow Lemons Mill Road into Georgetown.

Georgetown, another of the state's oldest towns, is full of interesting historic sites—Royal Spring; Georgetown College; the spot where pioneer Baptist minister Elijah Craig invented bourbon; Choctaw Academy; old iron storefronts; historic homes; and nearby the town of Stamping Ground, named for the buffalo herds that once pawed the ground at the springs waiting for their turn to drink. Here, too, is the old farmhouse where U.S. chess champion, J. W. Showalter, and his equally talented chess-playing wife lived at the turn of the century.

Take US-460 west out of Georgetown to Cane Run Road where you turn left and come to the tiny town of Great Crossings, where buffalo forded a stream and gave the town its name. (For a short side trip to Stamping Ground, take a right on Ky-227, but be alert for a narrow bridge hidden in a sharp curve.) Turn left off Cane Run Road onto Moore's Mill Road, then right on US-62, which is not heavily travelled. Turn left on Ky-1681 to bring you bring you back to your starting point.

Bluegrass Tour #2: Lexington-Paris Loop.   This tour also goes through the heart of horse country and will take you past several thoroughbred farms. Take Ky-353 (Russell Cave Pike) northeast out of Lexington and turn right on US-460 which will lead you into downtown Paris. Paris is the home of Claiborne Farm and Triple Crown winner Secretariat, one of the all-time great thoroughbreds. The largest thoroughbred farm in the world, Claiborne is home of about 25 equine heroes of the racing world, now standing at stud. Golden Chance Farm, who raced 1970 Kentucky Derby winner Dust Commander, is also near Paris. Stoner Creek Stud the home of standardbred great Meadow Skipper, is also the burial place of thoroughbred Count Fleet who won the Triple Crown in 1943. Duncan Tavern, built in 1788, is now a museum operated by the DAR (open Tuesday through Sunday, 9:00 a.m. to 12 noon and 1:00 to 5:00 p.m.). Cane Ridge Shrine, built in 1794 and the founding site of the Christian Church, is also a noteworthy attraction.

The Colville Covered Bridge, Millersburg Military Institute, and the ancient Ionic columns of the Paris Fine Arts Center are also points of interest. Take Ky-627 out of Paris past Claiborne Farm to Ky-956 where you turn right and come back to your starting point. Do *not* take the picturesque but hazardous Paris Pike. It is one of the most scenic roads in the state but is too narrow, shoulderless, and too heavily traveled by big trucks for bicyclists.

Red River Gorge Geological Area Tour.   The rugged rock cliffs and sweeping forest vistas of eastern Kentucky make this route one that geology buffs and outdoorsmen alike will find fascinating. The tour begins at the Lexington home of Kentucky's most famous statesman, Henry Clay. The historic home, called Ashland, is open 9:30 a.m. to 4:30 p.m. daily except Mondays.

From Ashland, take US-421 (the Richmond/Athens-Boonesboro Road) to Jack's Creek Road where you take a right and go four miles, then turn right onto Spears Road. After 1.6 miles on Spears Road turn left onto Tates Creek Road and then go straight on Ky-169 to the Kentucky River which you cross via Valley View Ferry. Take a left onto Ky-1156 and go 4.5 miles, then take a left and follow Clay's Lane for 2.3 miles. Next, turn left onto US-25. After about a mile, turn left into the White Hall State Shrine. White Hall was the home of fiery abolitionist Cassius Clay, the Lion of White Hall. It's open from 9 a.m. to 5 p.m. daily from April 1 through October 31.

Leaving White Hall, backtrack a bit on US-25 and take a right onto Ky-627. Follow it for 5.7 miles, then turn right onto Ky-358, which will take you to Fort Boonesborough State Park, a recreated version of the stockade Boone and his men built in 1775. This replica of Daniel Boone's fort is complete with costumed craftsmen working at soap making, blacksmithing, and other pioneer tasks. Open April 1 to Labor Day.

From Boonesborough, go back .3 of a mile and make a right onto Ky-627, then ride about seven miles to Winchester. From Winchester, turn right on Ky-15 and go 11.7 miles, then turn left on Ky-974 for 2.4 miles and right on Ky-646 for 4.6 miles. A right onto Ky-11 will take you into Clay City where you may want to visit the Red River Historical Museum. The featured display is a collection of LAW member Joe Bowen's photographs and memorabilia of his 14,000-mile Discover Bicycle America tour. Follow Ky-11 into Stanton and all the way to Natural Bridge.

After overnighting at the park, bike the 40-mile Red River Gorge triangle by taking Ky-11 south, then turning left onto Ky-715. Next, turn left onto Ky-15 and follow it about a mile; then turn right, back onto Ky-715. Follow Ky-715 to its intersection with Ky-77 and make a left onto Ky-77, which will take you through the picturesque old railroad logging tunnel at Nada. Turn left onto Ky-11 then and return to Hemlock Lodge at Natural Bridge State Park.

Covered Bridge Tour.   No one is exactly sure why early American bridges were covered. One theory suggests that covering made it easier to drive animals over streams, since the bridge entrances resembled barn entrances. Kentucky has about 15 covered bridges still standing and you can see four of them on one bicycle tour through Fleming County. From Lexington, take Ky-57/956 (Briar Hill Road) to North Middletown and Moorefield, where you turn right onto Ky-36. A left onto Ky-11 will take you to the first covered bridge at Sherburne. The Sherburne bridge crosses the Licking River at the boundary between Bath and Fleming counties. Built in 1867, the 266-foot-long bridge was privately owned, and toll was collected from stagecoaches that crossed it en route between Maysville and Mt. Sterling. It may be the state's most unusual bridge since it is a semisuspension bridge as a result of the steel cables and beams added in 1951 for strength.

Continue on Ky-11 to Ky-156, where you turn right. Turn right again onto Ky-32 and you will come to the White Bridge at Goddard, so called because it was once painted white, a rarity in Kentucky. White Bridge carries a country road just off Ky-32 over Sand Lick Creek nine miles east of Flemingsburg and is just 63 feet long. An especially photogenic bridge and the only covered bridge in Kentucky of town lattice construction, it was moved from an original site 10 miles away and rebuilt at Goddard in 1968. Its date of construction is unknown, but it was built in an era when wooden pegs were used to hold planks together.

A roadside park a couple of miles down Ky-32 on the right is a good place to stop for a picnic lunch. Then continue 4.7 miles further down Ky-32 and turn right onto a gravel road. Make a right onto Ky-158. The Ringos Mill Bridge carries Ky-158 across Fox Creek at Ringos Mill. Of multiple king post truss construction and some 158 feet long, Ringos Mill Bridge was built around 1865. Turn left onto Ky-111 which will take you to the tin-covered Grange City-Hillsboro Bridge, 82 feet long and of multiple king post truss construction. The bridge was probably built in the late 1860s, and carried Ky-11 across Fox Creek until recent replacement with a new concrete span. Backtracking is the best return route to Lexington.

Mammoth Cave National Park Tour.   Louisville is a good starting point for this trip. Take Ky-61 south out of Louisville to Boston, then Ky-52 south to New Haven. Then take a right on US-31, and go east to White City. Follow Ky-470 to Buffalo. (An alternate route takes you via Ky-155 out of Jeffersontown, in suburban Louisville, to Taylorsville. Pick up Ky-55 to Bloomfield, then follow Ky-162 into Bardstown where you can visit My Old Kentucky Home State Park. Take Ky-49 south from Bardstown to Ky-527 and turn right on Ky-52 to get to New Haven. Then go left on US-31 east to White City and follow Ky-470 to Buffalo.) At Buffalo, take a right onto Ky-61 to visit the Abraham Lincoln Birthplace National Historic Site.

After overnighting at historic Hodgenville, take US-31E .2 of a mile south and make a right onto the Bikecentennial 76 Route. Ride about 2.5 miles to Ky-357. Take a left and go to Munfordville, then take US-31W south to Cave City. A right on Ky-70 will take you right to the park entrance. Cave tours are available, featuring such wonders as Frozen Niagara, Fat Man's Misery, and Jenny Lind's Armchair. Tours by lantern light, history-oriented tours, and the Wild Cave Tour are also favorites of visitors. The best way back to your Louisville starting point is to backtrack.

Sleepy Hollow Ride.   Kentucky's largest city, Louisville, is a bustling metropolitan area with a lot of heavily traveled roads. Within a few miles of the city, however, are fine biking backroads. Several good Louisville area tours have been published in a free Louisville Wheelmen booklet called "Cycling." A Wheelmen favorite and one that is included in the book is the Sleepy Hollow Loop, a hilly ride over 25 miles long. This tour is not for novices. Start from Louisville's Cox Park and ride upriver on River Road which offers a fine view of the Ohio. Turn right on Wolfe Pen Branch Road and left onto Chamberlain Lane, then right onto Sleepy Hollow Road and left onto River Road, which will lead you back to your starting point.

Long Run Tour. Louisville Wheelmen's Long Run ride is about 25 miles long through rolling rural hills. It starts from the fire station on LaGrange Road in Anchorage, a small city just outside Louisville's east end. Cross the railroad tracks and take Ridge Road, bearing right at Avoca Road. Turn left onto Aiken Road, then right onto Flat Rock Road which leads you into Long Run Park on the left. If you want to make a loop of it rather than an out-and-back, however, try coming to the park by another route: turn left from Avoca Road onto English Station Road, right onto Old Henry, left onto Factory Lane, right on Old Henry, left on Reamers Road, right on Pine Bluff Road, right on Aiken, left on Flat Rock Road, and right into the park, then continue the loop by reversing the out-and-back route given·above.

Tour de Gil. The Louisville Wheelmen's Tour de Gil is named for the owner of the Highland Cycle Shop in Louisville, Gil Morris, who hosts a different ride each year. The following Tour de Gil is one of the most popular with local riders. It takes you over 22½ miles of rolling hills and scenic valleys. Start from Chenoweth Park and ride out Marydale to Billtown Road. Turn left on Billtown Road and left onto Seatonville Road. Make a right onto Brush Run (this is really more or less just a continuation of Seatonville Road), which will lead you into Routt Road. Turn right on Routt which will take you to Dawson Hill Road where you again turn right. Dawson Hill Road leads into Back Run Road which leads to Seatonville Road. Then left on Seatonville and follow it to Shaffer Lane. A right turn takes you back to Billtown Road where you turn left onto Marydale and go back to your starting point.

Locust Grove Tour. The Wheelmen's Locust Grove Tour starts at Eastern Parkway and Bardstown Road in Louisville. Ride east down Eastern Parkway to the Daniel Boone statue at the entrance to Cherokee Park. Ride through Cherokee Park via Hogans Fountain and Big Rock to Seneca Park. Go straight through Seneca Park which will lead you to Willis Road, a continuation of the Seneca Park Road. Ride out Willis Road and turn left onto Breckenridge Lane, then right on Westport and left on Hubbards Lane. Turn right onto US-42 and left on Blankenbaker. On Blankenbaker, you can stop and tour the Locust Grove Historic Home Museum, the circa-1700 plantation home where Louisville's founder George Rogers Clark lived his last years. The museum is open daily from 10 a.m. to 4:30 p.m. except Sundays when it opens at 1:30 p.m. and closes at 4:30 p.m. Turn left on River Road to Zorn Avenue, passing Cox Park. Turn left on Zorn and as you're turning, you'll see the Louisville water pumping station which is a famous local landmark. Its engine room, built in the 1850s, is designed like a Corinthian temple and ornamented with elaborate Grecian statuary. Cross US-42 next, then continue on Zorn (here it picks up the name Hillcrest). Bear right into Frankfort Avenue and then turn left onto Stilz to Grinstead. Turn right on Grinstead and follow it into Cherokee Park where you turn left to Bardstown Road and your starting point.

Wheelmen's Bench Tour.   If you'd like to see the historic Wheelmen's Bench and at the same time take a good look at Louisville, try this ten-mile ride over flat city streets. Start at Wheelmen's Bench at Third and Southern Parkway near Churchill Downs and turn right riding south out Southern Parkway to the Iroquois Park entrance. Follow the park road to the stone overlook at the summit where you can see the city stretched out below you.

Bikeways

Bikeways have three classifications. Class I bikeways are separate facilities for the exclusive use of bicycles. They are paved, are usually at least eight feet wide, and often run parallel to a motorist route. Class II bikeways are a separate lane on an ordinary street or sidewalk, indicated by a stripe or curb or traffic buttons. Class III bikeways are ordinary streets or sidewalks that are shared with motorists or pedestrians. They are marked with Kentucky Department of Transportation "Bike Route" signs.

Louisville Area

Kentucky's first partially Class I bikeway, a $350,000 national prototype in Louisville largely financed by Federal funds, is scheduled for use by the end of summer 1978. A direct route to the center of town for people who want to ride bicycles to work, the new, nearly four-mile-long Beargrass Creek Bikeway will link the Cherokee-Seneca Park area with the downtown riverfront. It is part of a comprehensive plan for Louisville that includes a network of bikeways to be completed in three stages during the next quarter-century. The program's short-range plans call for over 144 miles of bikeways in Louisville and the Jefferson County suburbs by 1985, while its long-range plan for the year 2000 proposes bikeways that will serve more than 100 schools, 37 recreation areas, and 21 major employment/shopping center areas.

Beargrass Creek Bikeway is a mixture of Class I, II, and III. It begins as

Class I, a separate roadway for bikes. From the entrance of Cherokee Park it crosses Grinstead Drive and Lexington Road along Beargrass Creek. It then crosses the creek and runs alongside the I-64 right-of-way to Locust Street. The bikeway continues down Locust to Spring as a Class III route. For a section of Spring to Story it becomes Class II, then from Story to Quincy it reverts to Class III. At Quincy the bikeway becomes Class II along Adams Street to a point where it nears the right-of-way of I-71. Here the roadway becomes a separate 10-foot-wide Class I roadway for bikers which follows the south side of I-71 to First Street. Finally, it crosses River Road under the I-64 ramps and follows the public wharf to the Belvedere.

The plan includes a paved parking lot at the park entrance, as well as bicycle lockers and information kiosks at both ends of the bikeway. Although basically a commuter route, Beargrass Creek Bikeway will also offer good recreation potential since it goes through Louisville's historic Butchertown area and passes close to Bakery Square, a bakery renovated into a complex of boutiques and specialty shops. Butchertown Pub is a well-known watering hole for cyclists in the area. The riverfront plaza at the end of the bikeway is also a fun-filled spot, especially during the summer when the city's free ethnic heritage weekend festivals are held. During French Heritage Week, Louisville Wheelmen sponsor a bicycle Tour de Louisville.

Louisville has several Class III bikeways, basically just signed streets throughout the city that are light in traffic and fair for biking if you don't mind intersection lights and stop signs that keep you from building up any speed. "Bike It," a booklet/map showing many of these city routes with their green "Bike Route" signs, is available free by writing to the Louisville and Jefferson County Traffic Engineering Department, 601 West Jefferson, Louisville, Kentucky, 40202; telephone: (502) 587-3241. In addition to these nearly 100 miles of Class III bikeways already in the city, Louisville anticipates some 150 more miles by 1985. The following are three of the oldest Class III bikeway routes, which were designated in 1973.

Bikeway #1: Iroquois Park-Churchill Downs. A five-mile ride curving around from Iroquois Park to Wyandotte Park and then to Churchill Downs, this route begins on the old horse bridle path near Iroquois Park, takes a left at Brookline Avenue, then a sharp turn onto Sixth and winds its way back to the bridle path. The route then goes through residential neighborhoods to Churchill Downs, and Kentucky Derby Museum where the great race's memorabilia are housed—a saddle used by five-time winner jockey Eddie Arcaro, the colorful silks of Derby winners, and other racing mementos. The museum has free guided tours in the summer and is open daily from 9:30 a.m. to 4:30 p.m. except during racing season when the hours are shortened to 9:00 to 11:00 a.m.

Bikeway #2: UL-Louisville Zoo/Cherokee Park. This seven-mile trail takes you from the University of Louisville to your choice of two destinations, the Louisville Zoo or Cherokee Park. The trail starts at Brandeis Avenue on the University of Louisville campus. Cross the railroad track to Texas avenue; then turn right at Burnett for the zoo, via a tough hill on Illinois Avenue, or continue on Texas to the park.

Bikeway #3: McAlpine Dam-Chickasaw Park. This six-mile route takes you from the locks at McAlpine Dam to Chickasaw Park. When you reach Vermont Avenue, follow it straight to South Western Parkway and Shawnee Park, then take South Western to Chickasaw Park from which you can see the Ohio River in the distance.

Lexington Area

Lexington, Kentucky's second largest city, expects to have two new Class I bikeways completed within the next year or so. Both will be eight-foot-wide paved routes separate from the roads they parallel. The proposed Richmond Road Bikeway, 2.6 miles long, will run from Todds Road past the Jacobson Park entrance to Walnut Hill Road. The proposed Tates Creek Bikeway, 2.2 miles long, will run from Gainesway Drive to Lakewood Drive. Still in the initial planning stage are two more Class I bikeways, one along Versailles Road and the other beside Harrodsburg Road. A portion of the Trans-America Bikecentennial Trail marked by ''76'' signs also runs through Lexington. Bluegrass Wheelmen also have hopes of turning an abandoned railroad right-of-way in the Bryan Station and Winchester Road area into a bicycle recreational facility, as has been done with other un-used railroad rights-of-way in other states.

Lexington already has three bikeways, all of which are near the campus of the University of Kentucky. A Class I separate bike facility at the university, eight-feet-wide and paved, runs alongside Stadium Access Road ''D'' from Access Road ''C'' to Tates Creek Road. The Class-III South Limestone Bikeway, on which bicyclists and pedestrians share sidewalks with curb cuts, runs from Southland Drive to UK where it links up with the extensive campus system of sidewalks and curb ramps. The Cooper Drive Bikeway, also Class III, consists of sidewalks shared by bikers and pedestrians. It runs from Chinoe Drive to connect with the UK system and utilizes curb ramps for easy bike entry.

The Bikecentennial Trail

As part of our country's recent 200th birthday party, a 4,000-mile, 80-day coast-to-coast bicycle route through ten states was established. The

190   Special Interest Recreational Activities

bicentennial is officially over now, of course, but the Transamerica Bikecentennial Trail is still marked with the easy-to-follow "76" signs, and the trail offers some fine biking through the Bluegrass State. Guidebook-and-map sets, including the history, geography, climate, and detailed descriptions of the country you'll be biking through, are available for $5 per set by writing Bikecentennial, P.O. Box 1034, Missoula, Montana, 59801, or calling (406) 721-1776. Lodging facilities, campgrounds, water sources, restaurants, grocery stores, and tourist attractions are included in the guidebook.

The purpose of the Bikecentennial Trail, its planners stress, is not just a celebration of the nation's bicentennial but the promotion of bicycling as a recreational life-style. Bicyclists on this trail enjoy a feeling of tracing their country's development through the two centuries since its beginnings, and "trailblazing" this development on two wheels. Although the Bikecentennial Trail occasionally wanders onto major highways or dirt roads, it stays mostly on blacktopped country roads close to major cities or recreational areas so bikers can leave the trail for supplies when necessary.

The Ohio River Ferry from Cave-In-Rock, Illinois, is the Bikecentennial Trail's doorway into Kentucky. A large cave with a gaping 25-foot high entrance, originally the site of ancient Indian councils, Cave-In-Rock was a landmark to settlers and early 1800s flatboatmen. By the time of our nation's western expansion, the cave had become an infamous hideaway for a dangerous band of river pirates who counterfeited money and plundered passing rivercraft, murdering the boats' passengers and selling the pilfered cargoes downstream. Cave-In-Rock State Park in Illinois is a good rest spot for cyclists prior to beginning the cross-Kentucky route.

Once into Kentucky via the ferry, the Transamerica Bike Trail swings down Ky-91 to Marion in Crittenden County, then on into the small towns of Clay, Dixon, and Sebree in Webster County, passing through the western coal field region. The trail then winds through wooded hills past the coal mines, oil fields, and tobacco farms of McLean, Ohio, and Daviess counties. Crossing Green River, the trail passes through the towns of Beech Grove, Guffie, Glenville, Utica, Whitesville, Deanfield, Fordsville, Ellmitch, and Shreve.

At Falls of Rough (population 45) in Breckinridge County, which you'll reach after crossing Rough River via a narrow wood-floored bridge, the guidebook calls your attention to the site of one of the first paddle-driven lumber mills in the country. The lumber mill was destroyed by a flood; later, in 1823, a grain mill which still stands was built at the site. The mill, operated for 140 years by the Green family, ground corn and other grains for people in seven counties. Rough River Dam State Resort Park, located on the Bikecentennial Route Ky-79, is a good rest stop. The 130-foot high dam borders Breckinridge and Grayson counties.

Hardin County's portion of the trail goes through Hardin Spring, crosses US-62, then continues on to Four Corners and Sonora. You're traveling through the Knobs Region now, a crescent-shaped area in the Bluegrass Region that was named for the dome-shaped hills that separate the Pennyrile from the Bluegrass on the west. Larue County and the town of Hodgenville, birthplace of Abraham Lincoln, are next on the trail.

At Hodgenville, the Transamerica Bikecentennial Trail briefly parallels another famous trail, the tristate Lincoln Heritage Trail. West of Hodgenville is the Abraham Lincoln Birthplace National Historic Site, where the humble log cabin in which Lincoln was born in 1809 is displayed inside a large marble mausoleum on his father Thomas's 300-acre Sinking Spring Farm. Lincoln's birthplace is near the Bikecentennial route on US-31E, four miles south of where the trail turns off onto Ky-61. Also on US-31E, 10 miles north of Hodgenville, is the Knob Creek Farm, and a replica of the log cabin in which the Lincolns lived when Abraham was two, before the family moved to Indiana.

After passing through the towns of Buffalo, Leafdale, and Lebanon, the Transamerica Trail then carries you into Nelson County and the historical city of Bardstown, home of the Rowan family's Federal Hill estate immortalized by songwriter Stephen Collins Foster in "My Old Kentucky Home." The estate is now a state park and the site of an annual outdoor summer musical that recreates Foster's life through song, dance, and drama. In Bardstown you'll also want to visit St. Joseph's, the oldest cathedral west of the Alleghenies, built in 1819. Talbott Tavern in the courthouse square was built in 1779 and is believed to be the oldest continuously-operated hotel in America. Besides good country cooking, the tavern also boasts walls of murals said to have been painted by attendants to the court of Louis Phillippe, exiled King of France, who was said to have stayed there. Holes in the paintings are allegedly the result of outlaw Jesse James's target practice during his stay at the old stagecoach stop. The monument on the courthouse lawn memorializes steamboat inventor John Fitch.

The Transamerica Trail then leaves Bardstown and goes into Washington County. Near Springfield, the trail's route along Ky-258 takes you to Lincoln Homestead State Park, the site where Abraham Lincoln's father, Thomas, and his mother, Nancy Hanks, grew up and courted. The Francis Berry House where Nancy Hanks lived has been moved here from its original site a mile away. A replica of the cabin where Thomas lived and the carpenter and blacksmith shops where he learned his trades are also on the grounds. The cabin in which Thomas and Nancy were married, however, has been moved about 25 miles east to Harrodsburg's Fort Harrod State Park where you can see it in the massive Lincoln Marriage Temple.

Harrodsburg is, in fact, your next important stop on the Bikecentennial Trail. Founded in 1774, Harrodsburg in Mercer County was not only Kentucky's first settlement, but also the first English settlement west of the

Alleghenies. Its biggest attraction is the replica of Fort Harrod; also, during the summer, the outdoor drama, "Legend of Daniel Boone," is performed at the park amphitheatre. You'll also enjoy following the town's Pioneer Red Arrow Tour of old pioneer and pre-Civil War homes.

Seven miles northeast of Harrodsburg is Shakertown at Pleasant Hill, a charming restored Shaker village. The Shakers were a religious group known as the United Society of Believers in Christ's Second Appearing, but because of the trembling dances used in their worship, they were called the Shakers. The colony began in 1820. The flat broom, the clothespin, the circular saw, washing machines, and metal point pens were only a few of the ingenious inventions made by these industrious people during the 100 years their experiment lasted. The last member of the colony died in 1923. Today, authentically-costumed craftspersons recreate the life-style that thrived in early America. While the Shakers believed in separation from the world, they were always hospitable to "the world's people." Their tradition of wholesome meals and fine lodgings has been preserved. Meals are served by long-aproned "sisters" who assure you that you "are kindly welcome."

Danville's Constitution Square Shrine, and the Perryville Battlefield State Park, where the bloodiest single-day battle of the Civil War in Kentucky was fought, are near enough for an interesting short detour off the Transamerica Trail at this point.

An alternate route, the Lexington Loop, departs from the regular trail at Burgin and takes you northeast, passing near High Bridge, a 308-foot-high railroad bridge, one of the highest in the world, which spans the Kentucky River. The Lexington Loop continues north through Troy (named for Kentucky's famous horse painter of the last century) and Keene into Lexington, and Fayette County, the heart of the Bluegrass Region.

You may want to "stay another day in Lexington" (the Chamber of Commerce motto) to see such local attractions as Ashland; the Hunt-Morgan House where the Thunderbolt of the Confederacy, John Hunt Morgan, is said to have ridden his horse through the beautiful fan-windowed front door, kissed his mother, and then ridden out the back door with the Union hard on his heels; Waveland Pioneer Life Museum; Headley Museum with its unique collection of jeweled bibelots and seashells; Keeneland, the nation's only nonprofit thoroughbred race course (open in April and October); Red Mile Trotting Track (open for a spring and fall meet); historic Gratz Park; and other historic sights.

Leaving Lexington, the Transamerica Trail's alternate loop leads to Winchester and through Stanton to eastern Kentucky's scenic Natural Bridge State Resort Park and nearby Red River Gorge Geological Area in the Daniel Boone National Forest.

The regular route of the Transamerica Trail will take you to Berea via

Burgin and across Herrington Lake. When you get to Berea, you'll be at the end of the Bluegrass guidebook section and the beginning of the Appalachian guidebook section.

Berea is a perfect rest stop for catching your breath before taking on the Appalachian adventure. If any one thing symbolizes Kentucky other than horses, bourbon, tobacco, and caves, it's oldtime mountain arts and crafts—east Kentucky's heritage. Berea is Kentucky's center of arts and crafts activity and a mecca for those who appreciate simple old-fashioned handmade items and the pride derived from hard work. The Kentucky Guild of Artists and Craftsmen, whose headquarters are in Berea, sponsors a semiannual (April and October) arts and crafts fair at Indian Fort Amphitheatre north of Berea.

Several arts and crafts shops and galleries in Berea offer crafts by Berea College students as well as local artisans. Crafts activities, from quilting to woodworking to dulcimer-making, are on display at student industries. Berea College (a mountain school devoted to the preservation of Appalachian culture and mountain heritage) is open to tours by the public. Accommodations and meals are available at Boone Tavern.

From Berea the trail continues past Bighill into the Daniel Boone National Forest via Estill and Owsley counties and through the towns of Jinks, Arvel, Levi, Booneville, and Arnett to Buckhorn Lake State Park via Ky-28.

Nearing its end in Kentucky, the trail crosses the Kentucky River, enters Perry County, and passes through the towns of Hazard, Bulan, and Dwarf, then wanders through the Knott County towns of Fisty, Carrie, Hindman, and Pippa Passes. At Pippa Passes, you may want to pause long enough to visit Alice Lloyd College. Another major attraction in the Hazard area is the Lilley Cornett Woods, with over 500 acres of virgin forest. Guided tours are available. After traversing Pike County (Kentucky's largest county) and Elkhorn City, the trail in Kentucky ends at the Breaks Interstate Park on the Kentucky-Virginia border.

For further information on the Transamerica Bikecentennial Trail, write Bikecentennial, P.O. Box 1034, Missoula, Montana, 59801, or call (406) 721-1776.

Fishing on Kentucky Lake. Photograph by Kentucky Department of Public Information.

9
Fishing

Introduction

There's no shortage of fishing in Kentucky. Boasting more miles of water than any state except Alaska, Kentucky has enough fishing opportunities for everyone. Ten manmade lakes over 5,000 acres and innumerable small lakes (both public and privately-owned) have been impounded from Kentucky's 10 major rivers. Farm ponds, small creeks, and oxbow lakes also contribute to the variety of angling opportunities in Kentucky.

Fishing is a year-round sport in Kentucky, and only during the coldest winters are Kentucky's waters iced over. The number-one fish in Kentucky is the largemouth bass (and his cousins, the spotted and smallmouth bass), followed closely by the crappie, white bass, bluegill, rough fishes (catfish, carp, buffalo, suckers, and bullheads), rainbow trout, walleye, sauger, and the rockfish and muskellunge, whose numbers have increased drastically in the past few years, due to vigorous management programs by fishery biologists of the Kentucky Department of Fish and Wildlife Resources. Chain pickerel, fliers, bowfin, and brook trout also are found in Kentucky, but their habitat is restricted.

In this chapter the Kentucky game fishes, tackle and techniques for catching them, and a rundown on statewide hotspots will be discussed. Whether you prefer the big sprawling impounds or the quiet secluded streams, Kentucky is a great place to wet a line!

Largemouth Bass

The largemouth bass (*Micropterus salmoides*) is the most sought-after of the "black basses" in Kentucky waters. He's cagey, and can grow to enormous size. "Ole bigmouth" knows every trick in the book to throw a lure; he's a terrific brawler in close quarters, able to break even the stoutest monofilament with sudden dives and gill-rattling acrobatics. The current state record in Kentucky is 13 pounds, eight ounces, taken in 1966 from Greenbo Lake.

Largemouth bass are highly predacious fish who prefer forage fishes as their main food, although just about anything that walks, hops, swims, or flies, and will fit into their gaping mouths, is taken with great relish. Snakes, frogs, baby ducks, insects, and small fish of any species are all part of the largemouth's diet.

The largemouth bass is an ideal quarry. His vicious strike is one of the most thrilling freshwater angling experiences. The largemouth is the most adaptable and highly available of the three species of "black basses" found in Kentucky. The largemouth can withstand and thrive in a number of adverse water conditions—summer's heat and low water, moss-choked shallow farm ponds, stripmine pit lakes, and watershed lakes, sources of water for agricultural use. The Kentucky Department of Fish and Wildlife Resources raises the state's stocking supply in the Minor Clark Hatchery near Morehead, Kentucky, and stocks largemouth fry in ponds barren of fish as a service to landowners. Fishery biologists estimate that it takes two to two and one-half years on the average for a largemouth bass to reach the harvestable size of 12 inches in Kentucky, although in some highly productive bodies of water in western parts of the state where the climate is milder, and the growing season longer, the largemouth is known to grow faster.

The largemouth is easily distinguished from the smallmouth. The largemouth's mouth is considerably larger, and the upper jaw extends well behind the eye on the largemouth. In addition, the spinous and soft portions of the dorsal fin that are separate on the largemouth are well connected on the smallmouth.

Although the largemouth's color characteristics are similar to those of the Kentucky spotted bass, the largemouth usually lacks the rows of conspicuous black dots below the lateral streak. The spotted bass's head is more pointed and pike-like in appearance. The largemouth also lacks the small patch of burr-like teeth on the tongue, one of the more easily distinguished physical differences between the spotted bass and his cousins.

Bass are taken by a greater variety of techniques than any other fish. Fly rod devotees, plug casters, and spin fishermen all take their share. Bass will hit spinners, plastic worms, jig and eels, crank baits, surface propeller baits, and popping bugs.

As a general rule, artificial lure and live bait selection are determined by the season of the year. Certain methods seem to outproduce the others during each season. Bass are readily taken year-round in Kentucky, no matter whether it's hot or cold, rainy or dry.

Because there are more similarities than differences between the three species of bass, techniques do not vary widely. Although it is possible to specialize to some extent, the selective angler often takes the other two species in spite of his efforts to go after just one species. It is not unusual for anglers to string all three species on the same outing, especially in those areas where their habitats overlap.

Winter is slowpoke time in Kentucky. Because the bass is a cold-blooded creature, frigid water temperatures slow his metabolism down, but they certainly don't shut it off. Many of the largest fish of the year are taken in the dead of winter.

Jig fishing is an extremely productive method during the colder months. The tackle requirements for jigging are simple, crude, and very effective. The jigging pole is usually a two-piece, telescoping fiberglass rod 10 to 14 feet in length. A small reel for storing extra line is affixed to the butt section, and the line is run through the hollow rod's tip end. The line used must be up to 40 pounds in test, and strong, heavy hooks are needed to withstand the extreme amount of force a big fish can exert in close quarters.

Live bait is the traditional favorite, and a large, squirming gob of night-crawlers or a lively shiner minnow has been the undoing of many cagey lunkers. Jigging is most productive in muddy waters; the muddier it is, the shallower you fish.

Big, prespawn female bass love to lurk in and around heavy cover at this time of the year. Jigging is one of the best methods available for teasing them out of log jams, tree tops, and the like. It is a slow, thorough, and very deadly angling technique.

People who prefer to take their bass by casting lean heavily toward jig and eel combinations. This deadly duo has just the right amount of action at the slow speeds that winter fishing calls for. Spinner baits and crank baits account for their share then, too.

Spring fishing calls for different tactics altogether. The bass are hungry, active, and ready to fight. Medium running baits and topwater plugs are good choices. The bass are constantly cruising the shallows, gorging themselves in preparation for the energy demands of spawning. Spinners are especially productive when the water is murky to muddy.

Summertime bass angling calls for a search for water in their preferred temperature range. The bass will retreat into deep water, shaded areas, anywhere they can find comfort. The best place to begin your search is submerged creek channels.

Plastic worms and deep running lures are especially productive when fished in this structure. Submerged stump beds, underwater delta areas, and steep rock walls are excellent places for trolling or casting deep running lures. Largemouth bass are especially fond of floating vegetation. They can hover under its canopy in the shade, lying in wait for any delicious morsel that may happen along. Small plastic worms, frogs, or weedless spoons will often prove irresistible to these bushwhacking bass. Night fishing is another deadly tactic when pleasure boaters and water skiers take over the lakes by day.

In the fall of the year, water temperatures begin dropping again. Bass feed voraciously to fatten up for the long winter and the action is often fast and furious. Bass can be taken at almost any depth, and a variety of techniques produce well.

Live-bait fishermen using large minnows or small crayfish take a lot of hefty stringers from rocky points on big lakes. Although some live-bait enthusiasts prefer to let the bait rest on the bottom, most of them work the bait along slowly. Smallmouth bass are particularly vulnerable to this approach.

Large schools of bass often gang up and feed in the "jumps" in the major reservoirs in the fall. By herding schools of shad minnows to the surface, they are able to feed heavily in a relatively short span of time. When the bass tear into the shad, boiling and churning the water, they are vulnerable to almost any shadlike lure or spoon tossed into the melee.

Crank baits and spinners come into their own again at this time of the year. The bass are shuffling to and from the shallows in order to procure food, and these lures are ideal for intercepting them. Shallow to medium running lures are usually the best bet in the early fall period.

Bass fishing is a year round sport in Kentucky. There is a season and technique for every angler. Bass fishermen will find Kentucky a wonderful place to fish, one with a variety of situations to suit their personal fancy.

Spotted Bass

The spotted bass has found a home in Kentucky. Even the state legislature seems to have a soft place in its heart for this remarkable fish because it quickly passed a bill which declared the spotted bass Kentucky's state fish. In fact, it even went as far as to rename the fish, calling it the Kentucky bass, the common name it is most known by now. The fish is abundant in Kentucky's northern boundary, the Ohio River, and all of the streams that are tributaries to it.

Fisheries biologists didn't recognize it as a separate species until 1927, although many Ohio River commercial fishermen recognized it as such long before then. Spotted bass are usually considerably smaller than largemouth or smallmouth, and individuals that weigh in excess of three pounds are rare. The state record for the species is seven pounds, 10 ounces. The spotted bass faintly resembles a cross between the largemouth and smallmouth. Both its physical characteristics and habitat preferences lie some-where between those of its two more widely distributed cousins.

Ichthyologists have taken spotted bass from every major river in Kentucky except for the Little Sandy, and the fish seems to have adapted well to living in large bodies of water. They are present in all of Kentucky's major lakes.

A member of the family *Centrarchidae,* the spotted bass *(Micropterus punctualatus)* has two major physical characteristics which differentiate it from its cousins. The first is a small patch of teeth on the tongue, but the most prominent is the longitudinal rows of "dark spots" which form definite stripes on its pale belly.

In streams, spotted bass are found in deep sluggish pools, and seem to move towards mud bottom areas during highwater periods when water is turbid. Spotted bass, like largemouths, often feed in schools, and are taken in the "jumps" as well. They seldom feed alone; catch one and chances are there's another close by. Small groups of these fish like to suspend themselves beneath docks, piers, and boathouses. Spotted bass love cray-fish, and will feed on them whenever they can. Minnows, though, are their predominant food source. Sometimes large insects are taken.

Underwater humps or ridges next to the river channel are good places to fish for Kentucky bass. Small shad-like lures will often tempt them from these underwater lairs.

Another peculiarity of the spotted bass is their propensity for deep water. They consistently locate at depths deeper than other black bass, often as deep as 100 feet or more if adequate dissolved oxygen is present. Fishermen can often locate schools of Kentucky bass by fishing the deepest fish-holding structures in the area. Spotted bass are extremely strong for their size. They are very agile and leap well when hooked. In clear, cool water they take on a greenish-bronze color and their "spots" become more distinctive.

Smallmouth bass

"Inch for inch, pound for pound, the gamest fish that swims." That's how Dr. James Alexander Henshall, the father of bass fishing, described the smallmouth. Dr. Henshall, a native Kentuckian, gained much of his knowledge of bass fishing from angling in the smallmouth-rich streams in central Kentucky.

Kentucky is a smallmouth bass fisherman's dream come true. A majority of the 13,000 miles of streams in Kentucky contain smallmouths, and because the Commonwealth is at the extreme southern edge of the small-mouth's range, they grow bigger there than anywhere else in the United States. In fact, Kentucky's state record smallmouth, an 11-pound, 15-ounce lunker taken July 11, 1955, is the current world record for the species.

A member of the sunfish family, *Centrarchidae,* the smallmouth bass *(Micropterus dolomieui)* is considered by many anglers as the "cream of the crop." A fat and sassy "bronzeback" is a prize that any sportsman can feel proud to harvest. Smallmouth are more particular in their eating habits than their kin, the largemouth and spotted "Kentucky" bass. Their food consists mainly of crayfish and small fishes, and smallmouth are highly selective about the size of their prey. Small lures and spider-web-thin line are a must for enticing the smallmouth to strike, in part because they prefer crystal-clear waters.

Before the impoundment of several important smallmouth rivers, smallmouth fishing was restricted exclusively to streams in Kentucky. The Licking, Cumberland, Green, Nolin, and Rockcastle river systems were, and still are, good smallmouth producers. Some of the state's smaller streams, like Elkhorn Creek, made famous by Dr. Henshall, produce excel-lent catches. Although these stream "smallies" do not attain the size of their lake counterparts, they make up for it in spunk and aerial acrobatics.

Smallmouth prefer streams with a gradient of 7 to 25 feet per mile, and avoid more sluggish bodies of water. Streams with a bedrock, or sand and gravel bottom, usually produce the best smallmouth fishing. A healthy abun-dance of crayfish usually goes hand in hand with most good-quality streams.

The damming of the Cumberland and Obey rivers, which formed Lake Cumberland and Dale Hollow Lake, respectively, has been important to the smallmouth because these deep, cool lakes provide smallmouths a more productive system in which to grow and reproduce, waters where they can reach trophy size more easily.

Smallmouths in the seven- and eight-pound class are taken from Lake Cumberland and Dale Hollow every year. Barren River Lake and Nolin Lake are two other consistent smallmouth-producing impoundments.

The smallmouth is a terrific gamefish, agile, strong, and possessed of terrific endurance. His heart-stopping leaps and frantic, drag-screeching runs will quicken the pulse of any bass fishing enthusiast.

Bluegill

The bluegill is one of the most popular panfish. This scrappy gamester hardly needs an introduction. He is the most widely distributed of the seven sunfishes of the genus *Lepomis* found in Kentucky waters.

Although the bluegill (Lepomis macrochirus) lacks the size and glamour of some other Kentucky fishes, he's certainly nothing to sneeze at. If bluegill grew as large as bass, I doubt if you could land them on conventional bass-fishing tackle. Bluegill grow to a healthy size in Kentucky ponds and lakes. The current state record is three pounds, six ounces. Bluegill will feed on just about anything that will fit into their mouths, and often try to eat things that will not; insects, fish eggs, crustaceans, mollusks, and fry are all in danger when this finned marauder is cruising for food. Despite their ravenous appetites, bluegills can at times be selective feeders. To take big, hawg-size bluegills (one pound or more) consistently, an angler must know to adapt his technique to their feeding preferences and seasonal wanderings.

The best live baits for bluegill fishing are crickets, red worms, meal worms, horseweed worms, grasshoppers, and wax worms, and occasionally they will take small minnows. The angler forever searching for the one bait which will yield big bluegill consistently has on occasion even tried catalpa worms, or tiny bits of saltwater shrimp baited on lead-head jigs.

Bluegills prefer shallow water throughout the spring and early summer, when they are most easily taken. They usually spawn in late May or June when water temperatures reach into the 70s. Their nests are saucer-shaped and clustered in colonies. Because of their ability to reproduce in large numbers, overcrowding and stunting are management problems, especially in ponds and small lakes.

Bluegill can be taken on a variety of artificial baits. Fly-rod fishermen take them readily on poppers, small wet and dry flies, sponge spiders, and crickets. An especially productive method for fishing with spinning gear is the clear bobber, with an 18-inch trailing leader. A fly or small jig is attached to the leader. The bubble allows for enough weight to cast the rig. Fly-spinning rigs are especially effective when "gills" are on the nest, as adult males will attack anything that comes close to the nest. By varying the length of the leader it's possible to keep the lure at the proper depth. It's important in bluegill fishing to match the lure with the predominant food source whenever possible.

During periods of extreme hot and cold it is often hard to catch big bluegills; they're more selective feeders and harder to locate then. They seek out deepwater holes, creek channels, and the protection of bedrock shelves. It is during these "dry spells" that specialized technique comes into play. Some die-hard bluegill fishermen use short rods tipped with piano wire and bait-casting reels, similar to ice-fishing rigs, to jig the depths with live bait, flies, or grubs. The technique of jigging off the bottom is especially effective because it imitates the natural actions of benthic organizations.

The bluegill is a stillwater panfish, whose favorite home is a pond or lake, although they are found in slow-moving big rivers. The bluegill's cousin, the longear sunfish *(Lepomis megalotis)*, is the predominant stream panfish. The bluegill is best recognized by the dark opercular flap and the red belly prominent in adults.

Bluegill are taken in all of the major lakes in Kentucky, and most of the small lakes. The redear sunfish *(Lepomis microlophus)* or "shellcracker," has in some cases replaced the bluegill as the primary panfish in some of the small lakes managed by the Kentucky Department of Fish and Wildlife Resources. The green sunfish *(Lepomis cyanellus)*, as well as the pumpkin-seed *(Lepomis gibbosus)*, are found in association with the bluegill in larger streams of major rivers, although the green sunfish is far more plentiful.

Crappie

There are two species of crappie found in Kentucky, the white crappie *(Pomoxis annularis)* and the black crappie *(Pomoxis nigromaculatus)*. The two species are members of the sunfish family, *Centrarchidae,* and are distinguished from one another by coloration and the number of dorsal spines. The white crappie, "newlight," is silvery-olive shading to darker olive-green on its back and has six dorsal spines, five in rare cases. The black crappie, commonly known as the calico bass, is also silvery-olive, but with dark green to black worm-like markings; the black crappie usually has seven or eight dorsal spines that are equal in length to the anal fins.

Both species of crappie occur in all river drainages in Kentucky, and thus are found in all major impoundments and most of the state-managed small lakes. Crappies feed on a wide variety of organisms—invertebrates such as crustaceans and insects, and small fishes. They are strictly carnivorous, and their preferred food is young minnows. They never seem to get enough of them.

Crappie reach maturity in about three years. Their nests are shallow depressions in three to eight feet of water; they spawn in the spring when water temperatures reach into the 60s. One female may produce up to 100,000 eggs in one season. The state record crappie in Kentucky is four pounds, three ounces. White crappie are more abundant than black crappie.

Most crappie are taken from Kentucky waters on live bait—spinners, skipjacks, or shad minnows. The crappie, one of the most sought-after of Kentucky fishes, is taken on cane poles or telescoping fiberglass rods and ultralight tackle. The key to catching crappie is finding the right depth. They prefer to school around heavy cover, submerged stump rows, and brush.

The Kentucky Lake crappie rig allows an angler to fish two minnows at once, each at different depths. One hook is tied to the end of the line and a one-ounce barrel sinker is attached to the line 10 inches above the hook. A three-eyelet swivel is attached 10 inches above the sinker, with a leader and hook suspended off it. Heavy leader, preferably 20-pound test, and a #3 lightwire hook are used so that the hook will straighten out and the rig won't break when it's hopelessly snagged on the bottom. An equally successful rig is basically the same, with the sinker on the bottom and either a single or tandem hooks suspended above. The sinker on the bottom allows the angler to "bottom bounce" in deep water, without the rig's continually hanging up in heavy cover.

In April and May, when crappie spawn, they head for shallow water. They congregate under drift and shoreline brush submerged by high water. They will readily take minnows in the spring; jiggling the bait will often entice them to strike.

Once a couple of fish are taken from one spot, drop anchor and go to work. This drift-fishing technique is essential in locating fish. Once you've found them, quietly drop your minnow into every nook and cranny in the brush, for crappie will rarely go far to take a minnow. This type of fishing demands a long rod (such as a flyrod rigged for crappie fishing) or a cane pole. Crappie are rarely taken close to the surface, except in extremely shallow water; they prefer to stay close to the bottom.

Springtime is also an excellent time to fish for crappie with artificials on ultralight gear, grubs, white and yellow do-jigs, and spinners. Cast along brush adjacent to deep dropoffs, or jig the tiny lures up and down in brush, as you do with live minnows.

Knowing crappie movement throughout the year in lakes and rivers is the real key to angling success. You've got to find them to catch them. Crappies will usually bite all day. They seem to bite best just before a front moves in and during light rain. A drop in water level will virtually shut off crappie feeding sprees; a rise in water levels usually means good fishing. In summer (June, July, and August), when the crappie return to their deep-water haunts in old river channels of manmade impoundments, nightfishing is a particularly effective technique. The strong light from the lantern draws insects, which in turn draw minnows and crappie.

During the winter months of January and February the crappie are in the deepest water. At that time of the year they're finicky feeders and must be coaxed into striking. Their bite is so slight that many crappie experts put a short section of piano wire on the top of their rods to detect even the slightest tugs. Crappie prefer smaller minnows in the winter. During the spring and summer, progressively larger minnows work best. During early spring and fall, crappie move to the mouths of creeks. The best fishing is often along the high ridges adjacent to deep water. Contour maps and a depthfinder are almost always needed to pinpoint such potential hotspots.

By far the best crappie fishing lakes in Kentucky are Kentucky Lake and Lake Barkley. Lake Cumberland, Barren River Lake, and Green River Lake are also good. Adequate cover is a must for good populations of crappie. The Blood River and Jonathan Creek embayments of Kentucky Lake are perhaps the best crappie waters in Kentucky as the structure and cover are ideally suited. Kentucky Lake is known regionally as a producer of "slab-sized" crappie weighing up to three pounds.

Rockfish

The rockfish is one of the real success stories of fishery management in Kentucky. A saltwater relative of the white bass, the rockfish (*Morone saxatilus*) is a member of the true bass family, *Serranidae*.

The rockfish closely resembles the white bass, but its body form is more elongate, less compressed, with a nearly straight back. Its coloration is dark greenish to bluish above, sometimes with a brassy tinge, becoming paler on its sides and silvery below. The predominant feature of the fish is seven to eight narrow longitudinal stripes, which accounts for its common name, striped bass.

The rockfish stocking program has been a real shot in the arm to angling opportunities in Kentucky. From the first 12 rockfish stocked in Lake Cumberland in 1957 from the Santee-Cooper Reservoir in South Carolina, the project has grown immensely. Originally an anadromous species that lived in salt water (Atlantic Ocean and Gulf of Mexico) but spawned in fresh water, rockfish became land-locked in the coastal reservoir. In the five years after the initial stocking, 2,792 more rockfish, many of them under 13 inches, were introduced into Herrington Lake, Cumberland Lake, and Kentucky Lake. The stocking of rockfish fry began in 1965 when 540,000 were placed in Lake Cumberland. During those early years fry were also introduced into Dewey Lake, Lake Barkley, and Green River Lake. After 1969 nearly all of the rockfish introduced into Kentucky waters were fingerlings raised from fry in the Frankfort National Fish Hatchery. Biologists believe that the fingerlings have a better survival rate when stocked, although the one problem in raising them up to a couple of inches in brooder ponds is that they have narrow tolerances for changes in water temperature.

Rockfish in the 30-pound class now being taken from Lake Cumberland and Herrington Lake, which support the largest number of rockfish in Kentucky, were from the 1969 stocking class. Scale samples sent in by anglers help biologists study the age and growth of these remarkable fish.

The rockfish program in Kentucky entered a new era in the summer of 1978 when the acquisition of broodfish through netting began. Biologists began raising fry from captured fish, inducing the mature male and female to spawn in circular tanks because rockfish don't spawn naturally in Kentucky waters. Thus, the program became independent, as biologists no longer have to rely on outside sources for rockfish fry. A mature female rockfish that weighs 13 pounds will produce approximately one and one-half million eggs, which means that the output of several fish will easily supply the fry that are introduced into Kentucky waters as fingerlings, thus sharply accelerating the program in the future.

Rockfish, feeding almost exclusively on gizzard shad, are a valuable predator fish because they grow big enough to take fish that are too large for other prey species.

Rockfish are outstanding sport fish. They are big, brawny fish that take line in long, screeching runs. Trolling or casting in the jumps with large shad-like lures or a plunker and fly rig are the preferred angling methods. Some fishermen swear by the use of live bluegills as bait, but you have to locate a feeding school first. The use of a graph-recorder is a big help in locating marauding schools of rockfish in open water.

Rockfish have a terrific potential as Kentucky's gamefish of the future. The current state record is 45 pounds, eight ounces, taken April 17, 1978, from Lake Cumberland.

Sauger and Walleye

The sauger and walleye are both members of the family *Percidae,* the perches and darters. They closely resemble one another and are often misidentified by fishermen. Both are found in all of Kentucky's major rivers, and consequently are also caught from the impoundments created by these rivers. They are coldwater fishes who begin spawning runs as early as February when the warmwater species are still inactive. They live and feed in deep water throughout most of the year, and specialized fishing techniques are needed to catch them.

At one time walleye and sauger were an important gamefish in Kentucky. Their annual runs were a grand occasion. Today the average angler knows little about these fishes and how to catch them. For the most part, they're a neglected resource.

The walleye has captured the attention of fishery biologists to a greater extent than the sauger, and stocking programs have contributed to success in bringing back the walleye. Unfortunately, increased turbidity of rivers, the blocking of spawning routes by high-rise dams, and a general lowering of water quality in such important rivers as the upper Cumberland, Tennessee, Kentucky, and Barren have severely limited the potential of both species. However, the walleye and sauger have adapted somewhat to the changes in their habitat.

The walleye *(Stizostedion vitreum)* spawn when water temperatures reach 45 degrees Fahrenheit. The fry eat crustaceans and insect larvae but turn to small forage fish when they reach fingerling size. The state record walleye was taken from Lake Cumberland in 1958, and weighed 21 pounds, eight ounces. Walleye are taken by fishing doll flies, crank baits, spinners, and jigs in the Rockcastle River (as far upstream as the Narrows) and the Big South Fork of the Cumberland River near Yamacraw, Kentucky (Ky-92 bridge), upstream of Lake Cumberland. Large catches of walleye were taken from Lake Cumberland in the 1950s not long after the lake was built, but the good fishing played out. Fishery biologists from the Kentucky Department of Fish and Wildlife Resources are seeking to re-establish a population of walleyes in Lake Cumberland through stocking and the study of the fish's food and reproduction habits. More than a million one-and-one-half-inch walleye have been stocked in Lake Cumberland since 1973. The program has met with some success, as spawning runs in Lake Cumberland's headwaters have been better in recent years.

A sluggish fish, the walleye responds best to lures presented at a slow retrieve. The best fishing spots are often deepwater structure, since walleye are bottom feeders. Laurel River Lake, impounded in 1974, was initially stocked with walleyes, as well as rainbow trout. Barren River Lake is another Kentucky impoundment where the walleye potential has been extensively studied and large stockings have been initiated. Both Barren River Lake and Rough River Lake now have self-sustaining populations of walleye. In 1977 more than 300,000 walleye fingerlings were stocked in Rough River Lake. During a four-year period between 1973 and 1977, more than four million walleye fry were stocked in Barren River Lake. The earlier stockings were river walleye, but biologists discovered that the hardier northern strain of lake walleyes seems to survive better. Eggs of the lake variety walleye are now being hatched at the Minor Clark Hatchery and the fry are being raised to fingerling size for stocking.

Walleye fishing demands deepwater tactics, a thorough probing of submerged creek channels, underwater ridges, and gravel points. Trolling bottom-bouncing lures and casting with jigs and doll flies, as well as still fishing with nightcrawlers and minnows, are proven methods for catching walleyes.

It's not easy to distinguish between a walleye and a sauger; not only do they inhabit nearly the same waters across North America, but they look amazingly alike. The main difference is that the walleye has a whitish lower lobe on the caudal fin, which is missing in the sauger. The sauger also has a black spot on the basal portion of the pectoral fin, saddle-like blotches on the body, and five to six pyloric caeca (finger-like structures where the intestines leave the stomach).

The sauger *(Stizostedion canadense)* is a smaller cousin of the walleye. He's excellent tablefare. Like the walleye, the sauger is a school fish; when one is taken, it's a good possibility there are more in the area. The slender, toothy fish is rapidly gaining popularity among fishermen, especially those who fancy trolling. The Kentucky state record sauger weighed six pounds, 11 ounces.

Sauger are taken in great numbers from the lower Tennessee and Cumberland rivers and Kentucky Lake. In summer, sauger are taken by deep-water trolling and night fishing with minnows in the Barkley Canal. Good catches of sauger are also taken each spring by casting do-jigs in the discharge below Kentucky and Barkley dams. The dams halt the fish's upstream migration and concentrate populations in the tailwaters. Populations in Kentucky Lake congregate in the lake's feeder tributaries.

The sauger experts have perfected a unique trolling method in which a 16-ounce elongated sinker is attached to one eyelet of a three-eyelet swivel. From the other eyelet a stout leader and minnow-like lure is attached. No rod is used; instead, the line is simply stored on an automatic fly reel which is attached to the boat with a common "C" clamp. The heavy sinker keeps the lure down deep, "bouncing the bottom." The anglers sit on the rear seat of the boat, usually fishing in pairs. Steel line or heavy braided line in preferred, and the rig is hand-fished. Even the most subtle strikes can be felt when the line is in your hand. Hooked fish are simply brought in hand over hand, the slack taken up with the reel. Sometimes spinners and spoons are trolled instead of minnow-like lures. The secret of success is keeping the lure right on the bottom where sauger feed.

White Bass

The white bass is the most widely distributed of the three species of true basses, family *Serrandiae,* found in Kentucky. A predominantly marine family whose members are widely distributed in tropical and warm temperate seas, there are few true basses which are totally freshwater. The white bass *(Morone chrysops)* is found in all medium to large rivers in Kentucky, and consequently in all major lakes. While most true basses are anadromous—that is, they spawn in fresh water and live in salt water— white bass migrate seasonally from small streams where they spawn in the spring to large pools in rivers or lakes in the summer.

The white bass is a silvery rocket with fins. Constantly on the move, white bass school up by the thousands. They are voracious feeders, so aggressive that the schools of shad they rip into will literally beach themselves if trapped against the bank. White bass are like finned wolves. Their run-and-gun feeding sprees, called "jumps," make the surface bubble and froth. White bass in the two- to three-pound class are magnificent fighters when taken on light tackle. The state record white bass in Kentucky weighed five pounds. Although forage fishes make up the bulk of their diet, white bass will also feed on insects and crustaceans.

To be successful in white bass fishing, anglers must capitalize on the seasonal movements of the fish. March, April, and May are the months during which most of our gamefishes in Kentucky spawn, and therefore these are our best fishing months. White bass are the earliest spawners on the gamefish timetable. They begin to congregate when the water temperatures reach the upper 50s, their optimum spawning temperature being 60 degrees Fahrenheit. The old saying, "The white bass run when the dogwoods are in bloom," has considerable substance to it, as the same kind of weather that brings out the blooms in these flowering trees also warms the water enough to induce spawning.

White bass don't need current to spawn, but they prefer it to calm water, although, curiously enough, they are a pelagic species—that is, they live and feed in open water. The annual spawning run on the Dix River is a prime example of the migrational pattern. Schooling in calm water, the white bass travel as far as 15 miles against the current from the upper reaches of Herrington Lake. Good strings of these fish are also taken before the optimum 60 degree temperature is reached. A good access point to Dix River is the Highway Ky-52 bridge between Lancaster and Danville.

The headwaters of Lake Cumberland, Nolin Lake, and Barren River Lake also have white bass runs each year. White bass are also taken in large numbers from tailwaters below Kentucky Dam, Barkley Dam, Wolfe Creek Dam (Lake Cumberland), and to a lesser extent below all the dams of Kentucky's major impoundments. Spinners, small shad-like crankbaits, spoons, white lead-headed jigs, and live minnows are the preferred bait for white bass. One rig which has been highly effective for years is the "plunker and fly" combination, said to have been perfected by white bass fishermen on Herrington Lake back in the 1930s. A floating hookless plug with a popper lip (often a plunker is made by removing the hooks from a bass stick bait) gives the rig weight so it can be cast long distances. An 18-inch leader of 25-pound test monofilament is tied to the rear eyelet of the plug so that a jig or small spoon (anything flashy and white) can be trailed. The plunker and fly rig is simply cast over a working jump and retrieved through it rapidly. The popping action of the plunker imitates a feeding white bass on the surface and the trailing fly is a shad. The rig is also effective for blind casting when the fish have gone down after a jump. The noise on the surface often draws white bass to the surface, and they see the trailing fly jig. The heavy leader keeps the line from twisting; the heavy "plunker" plug can be cast a country mile, and that's important when white bass fishing in the jumps because you never know where the fish are going to resurface. Long casts are usually the rule.

In the summer, after the spawning run and jumps, many anglers in Kentucky take white bass trolling and night fishing. During the "dog days" of August white bass are often taken in deep, open water by trolling deep with a heavy spoon or deep diving plugs with a trailing fly. The night-fishing technique is also effective during this time of the year. White bass are a popular summertime fish with houseboaters, as still fishing is one of the most successful methods for catching them. The bass are found in deep water (15 to 30 feet) off rocky points and steep rock walls along the old river channels. Nightfishing over gas lanterns is productive because when the strong light draws plankton, which in turn draws schools of shad, the white bass are not far behind. The trick in locating the depth at which the fish are feeding is to lower your bait to the bottom and begin reeling it up slowly, remembering the number of cranks of the reel from the point where you got the most strikes. Then fish at that level.

Rainbow Trout

The rainbow trout (Salmo gairdneri) is one of the two species from the family Salmonidae that have been introduced into Kentucky's waters. Rainbow trout stocking began in earnest in 1946 when the first truckload of fingerlings was hauled from the Smoke Mountain National Fish Hatchery in North Carolina and placed in several small streams in Bell County near Pine Mountain State Resort Park. Earlier efforts had failed because biologists didn't recognize the strict requirements of rainbows. They must have clear, cool waters that seldom exceed 65 degrees Fahrenheit. The ravages of mining, lumbering, and road building apparently wiped out the isolated populations of native trout in eastern Kentucky and today continue to contribute to keeping those trout which have been reintroduced into favorable waters from finding suitable spawning grounds.

Today, Kentucky's rainbow trout fishery is a "put-grow-and-take" proposition. The completion of Wolf Creek Dam, which impounded Lake Cumberland from the Cumberland River, was the most important development in bringing high-quality rainbow trout fishing to Kentucky. The cool waters below the dam, unsuitable for many warmwater species, were extensively stocked with rainbows and the results were nothing short of phenomenal. During the late fifties and throughout the sixties the tailwaters yielded rainbows in the five-pound class, and on September 10, 1972, a 14-pound, six-ounce state record lunker was taken.

The success of the project helped convince biologists that trophy-class rainbows could be harvested from stocked fingerlings on a put-and-take basis. With the availability of more trout from Federal sources, the trout stocking program expanded to Kentucky creeks and other tailwaters which had never produced good populations of warmwater fishes because the water was too cold. In effect, the purpose of the rainbow trout stocking program became apparent—to complement the sport fishery already available and to fill an important niche in waters with sport fishery potential not being realized.

Through the years fishery biologists have been cataloging streams which meet the rainbow's strict requirements, and the stocking program has proceeded as new waters were given a clean slate after careful monitoring. Kentucky receives its trout from the U.S. Bureau of Sport Fisheries and Wildlife through the Dale Hollow National Fish Hatchery in Celina, Tennessee. With the completion of the Wolf Creek National Fish Hatchery on the Cumberland River below Lake Cumberland, there will be more rainbows available for stocking in Kentucky's waters. In addition, the fact that the Wolf Creek hatchery is closer to the stocking sites in Kentucky means that the survival rates for stocked fish will be higher.

Since 1971 trout fishermen in Kentucky have been required to have a trout stamp in addition to regular fishing licenses. The funds from these stamps make funds available for the transportation costs and expenses of the personnel who actually stock the trout. In 1978, Department of Fish and Wildlife personnel stocked 330,000 rainbow trout in Kentucky waters, and U.S. Bureau of Sport Fisheries and Wildlife personnel stocked 52,000 rainbows in streams in Daniel Boone National Forest.

Worms and nightcrawlers are effective bait, especially when they are allowed to drift freely in the current. Kernel corn, small bits of cheese, and salmon eggs are also good baits. Small ultra-light spinners and spoons are particularly effective in the tailwater sections where the trout feed on shad minnows.

Laurel River Lake is fast becoming one of Kentucky's premier trout waters. More than 5,000 rainbows are stocked in Laurel each year, and the fishing is good. Anglers report that still fishing with worms and minnows along steep rock walls and spinner-casting in shallow tributaries are the best winter and early spring tactics. Laurel River Lake is stocked each year in early March with six- to eight-inch trout. The first year Laurel was impounded, 1974, trout grew at a phenomenal rate; six-inchers stocked in the spring were up to 16 inches in the fall.

The best rainbow trout fishing stream in Kentucky by consensus is Rock Creek in Daniel Boone National Forest. A Kentucky Wild River, Rock Creek is in McCreary County, reached via Ky-92, Ky-1363, and FS Road 137.

Brook Trout

The brook trout *(Salvelinus fontinalis),* a member of family *Salmonidae,* is found in only two streams in Kentucky, both of which are in Cumberland Gap National Historical Park. There are approximately 20 miles of fishing waters, 14 in Martin's Fork (a Kentucky Wild River) and six in Shillalah Creek.

The brook trout were implanted into the two streams on November 26, 1968, under the supervision of Bureau of Sport Fisheries and Wildlife biologist Frank Richardson, who conducted studies on both streams and recommended the stockings. A total of 115 native brook trout from Indian Camp Creek, Smoky Mountain National Park, were released into Shillalah Creek; 500 Maryland-strain brook trout from streams in Pisgah National Forest were stocked into Martin's Fork.

Brook trout are known to have inhabited these waters before lumbering operations lead to unsuitable conditions for their survival. Brook trout require perfectly clear and clean waters in the temperature range of the low 50s to mid-60s. They cannot tolerate either turbidity or excessively high water temperatures. Brook trout feed on mayfly, caddisfly, helgramite, stonefly (larva), beetles, crayfish, salamanders, and the blacknose dace *(Rhinichthys atratulus).*

Brook trout are one of the most beautiful species of trout. Their back and head are an olive green with worm-like markings of tan. Their sides have numerous spots of green and red with blue borders. They are game fighters on ultralight gear and will readily take tiny spinners and flies.

The populations of brook trout in Cumberland Gap National Park are something special. They are a precious resource, as they are the only populations of trout that reproduce in Kentucky, and fishing for them is a true wilderness experience. Martin's Fork, the better fishing stream of the two, is a mountain stream of classic beauty. It is a bedrock and pebble-bottomed stream that winds through stands of towering hemlocks. The stream is in a gorge between Brush Mountain and Cumberland Mountain. Mosses, ferns, and wildflowers grow all along the stream, which is canopied with rhododendron and mountain laurel.

The National Park Service maintains strict fishing regulations on the populations of brook trout. The open season for fishing is May 15 to September 15, although during low-water periods or in the event of the annual limit being reached, the fishing may be closed any time during the season. All fishermen must have a Kentucky fishing license and trout stamp and must check in at the park headquarters before and after fishing. Harvestable fish must be 12 inches or more in length and there's a limit of two trout per day per fisherman. Live bait is not permitted, and only single hooks are allowed.

Muskellunge

The silver muskellunge (*Esox masquinongy ohioensis*) is the largest member of the pike family, *Esocidae*. The silver muskellunge and chain pickerel are the only species of the family important to fishermen in Kentucky. An elongated, cylindrically-shaped fish, the musky has a jaw shaped like a duck's bill and armed with numerous sharp teeth. The olive-greenish back usually has black vertical bars; the belly is white.

The most important development in regard to muskellunge fishing in Kentucky came in 1973 when the Minor Clark Hatchery was completed, and biologists from the Kentucky Department of Fish and Wildlife began raising the fish for an extensive stocking program. Prior to 1973 there had been only limited stockings of musky when they were available from hatcheries in other states. The survival of the stocked fry was not good and had little if any effect on boosting populations of musky in Kentucky streams. Now that musky can be raised to five or six inches before stocking, their survival rate is much better. The eggs hatch in tanks, and the fry are reared in brooder ponds. Stocking them at an intermediate size means that there's less chance that they will be preyed upon by other game fishes. Musky grow amazingly fast, as much as 11 inches their first year, which means that they become predators relatively early in life. Through age and growth studies, Kentucky Department of Fish and Wildlife biologists have determined that it takes four years for a musky to reach the harvestable size of 30 inches.

The availability of large numbers of musky fingerlings (a mature musky female can produce upwards of 115,000 eggs) has led to massive stockings in Cave Run Lake, currently Kentucky's best musky fishing waters. As many as 8,000 musky, approximately one fish per acre, have been stocked in Cave Run Lake each spring since 1973. The results have been incredible, and late spring and summer creel studies have shown that each successive class is reaching harvestable size at that time of the year. The upper end of the lake is considered the best fishing for musky. Other lakes stocked with musky since 1973 are Grayson and Green River (6,000 stocked in 1977).

In recent years musky have been taken from 27 streams in Kentucky. The native populations have been drastically limited, however, by man's advancement on their habitat. Lumbering, pollution, and dam building have taken their toll in reducing musky waters. Today, there are approximately 750 miles of streams which support musky, and in a typical year musky fishermen creel about 300 to 350 legal-size fish. The surpluses of musky raised at the Minor Clark Hatchery are stocked in streams to help bolster native populations. In recent years the Licking River, Kentucky, Green, Drake's Creek, Tygart's Creek, Triplett Creek, Little Sandy River, Red, Barren, Sexton Creek, Sturgeon, Kinniconnick, Big Goose, and Station Camp Creek have been periodically stocked with musky when surpluses from the hatchery were available. All these streams have native populations.

Musky have strict habitat requirements. They prefer cool water in the range of 35 degrees Fahrenheit in winter to 78 degrees Fahrenheit in summer. Since they depend primarily on sight for locating food, they cannot tolerate turbid waters. Also, excessively high water temperatures will cause them to stop feeding. Musky spawn in late March through April when water temperatures are between 54 degrees and 60 degrees Fahrenheit. They do not build nests and are believed to deposit their eggs in shallow areas where the bottom is composed of decayed leaves, detritus, or brush. The male and female fish swim side by side, and milt and eggs are deposited simultaneously. Limiting factors in survival of the young are cold water after the eggs have been deposited, predation, and the quantity and quality of zooplankton and small forage fishes.

Musky are by far the most exciting fish in Kentucky's waters. They are predators in the truest sense of the word—cunning, vicious, and voracious feeders. They will gorge themselves on 12-inch gizzard shad, redhorse suckers, frogs, ducklings, and even muskrats. They are loners who attack their prey from hiding. Musky prefer the cover of rock ledges, submerged brush, and logs. To the musky fisherman, it's the breathtaking, surging strikes of musky that tide them over the long hours of casting. There's a feeling you get when musky fishing that maybe the next cast will be the one to roll a trophy fish.

The musky is a savage fighter, capable of leaps, power dives, and other tackle-busting maneuvers. The best tackle for muskies is a stiff casting rod and level-wind casting reel equipped with 20- to 35-pound test line tipped with a wire leader, because musky can easily break line with their sharp pointed teeth.

Musky are taken by trolling, casting, and still fishing with live bait. Huge bucktail spinners, propeller baits, and diving lures are the best bet for casting. A steady, fast retrieve is preferred because musky like fast moving targets and can be intimidated into striking. The fast retrieve also insures good solid hooking. Trolling is also a good musky-producing method. Flashy lures work best and long bucktails which draw their attention are also effective. Tandem rigs utilizing an outlandish "teaser" lure often work well when trolled. Some fishermen jig the banks in the spring with live bait, huge suckers, and spinners. This method, too, is a proven musky-getter. The Kentucky state record musky weighed 43 pounds; the world record fish weighed 60 pounds, 15 ounces.

Catfish

There are seven species of catfish important to anglers in Kentucky. They are all from the Family *Ictaluridae*. The common names of Kentucky's "whiskered fish" are blue catfish, black, yellow, and brown bullhead, channel, white, and flathead catfish. The channel catfish is by far the most widely distributed.

Although catfish are found in all of Kentucky's major rivers and impoundments, as well as in many small lakes and farm ponds, the best fishing is in the tailwaters of major lakes, namely Lake Barkley, Kentucky Lake, Barren River Lake, Green River Lake, Rough River Lake, and Nolin Lake. The tailwaters below Kentucky Dam support unbelievable numbers of catfish, many that are real monsters. The reason is the large amount of food available—shad, skipjack herring, and minnows. During the generation of electricity, many of these forage fishes are chopped up by the turbines, and the catfish scavenge for their remains in the "boils." One very productive fishing method is to run a johnboat against the swift current near to the base of the dam and fish in the old river channel with cut bait. Fishing the "boils" requires the use of specialized gear—a short stout rod, heavy line, heavy weights to keep the bait on the bottom in the swift current, and a strong back to haul'em in. The current state record for the blue catfish is 100 pounds, taken from the Tennessee River below Kentucky Dam. The record flathead catfish was also a monster, tipping the scales at 97 pounds.

Catfish will take a wide variety of bait—chicken livers, minnows, small bluegill, nightcrawlers, crayfish, cut bait, and "stink baits," which appeal to the catfish's strong sense of smell. These evil-smelling concoctions may be made from any number of revolting ingredients such as chicken blood and intestines, carp dough, soap, cotton, clay, and any strong-scented kitchen preparations such as mustard and limburger cheese. Often the ingredients are mixed up and left to get rancid in a jar with the top tightly screwed on. Many stink baits are the results of many years of experimentation and are carefully guarded secrets.

Another technique for taking huge catfish in the boils is snagging. Stiff saltwater rods, heavy line, and saltwater reels are used. A weighted treble hook is jerked vigorously through the boils. The technique may be a bit unorthodox, but it's productive.

Catfish can occasionally be taken on artificial lures—plastic worms, spinners, and imitation frog lures—but most often it's an accident; live bait is much prefered. Whether fishing for bullheads in a creek, putting out setlines, or running a trotline for channel catfish in a major lake, catfish are good fun and a popular fish in Kentucky waters. The catfish may be short on looks, but he sure is tops at the dinner table.

Rough Fish

Rough fish are sought after because of their commercial value, although many of them have some importance to sport fishermen. The rough fishes are members of the sucker family, *Castostomidae,* and the minnow family, *Cyprinidae.*

Rough fish are found throughout Kentucky in nearly all rivers and small streams. Many species of rough fish find their ways into farm ponds and small watershed lakes. Tons and tons of rough fish are harvested from Kentucky's waters each year by commercial fishermen using nets; the sport fishing harvest by hook and line is considerably less.

The rough fishes of the most importance to sportsmen are: smallmouth buffalo *(Ictiobus bubalus);* bigmouth buffalo *(Ictiobus cyprinellus);* river carpsucker *(Carpiodes carpio);* quillback carpsucker *(Carpiodes cyprinus);* highfin carpsucker *(Carpiodes velifer);* white sucker *(Catostomus commersoni);* golden redhorse *(Moxostoma erythrurum);* and carp *(Cyprinus carpio).*

During the spring spawning runs, the carpsuckers, redhorses, and carp congregate in shallow, murky streams. These fish are taken by sport fishermen on dough balls, and when properly cleaned and smoked are quite delicious. The golden redhorse is often taken during a special gigging season in the spring from shallow rock-and-gravel-bottom streams in south central and eastern Kentucky. The carp, the most abundant species of rough fish, is of importance to archers, who shoot carp as an off-season tune-up for the autumn bow seasons for deer. Bowfishing during the spring in the shallows of major lakes, where the carp spawn, is quite popular in western Kentucky. The state record carp, taken in 1971 from the south fork of the Licking River, weighed 54 pounds, 14 ounces.

Rock Bass

The rock bass *(Ambloplites rupestris)* is technically not a bass at all. Ichthyologists classify the rock bass as a member of the sunfish family, *Centrarchidae*. Nevertheless, the rock bass, commonly known as a "goggle-eye" or "redeye," is a fighter that does justice to the name bass. Rock bass are found in all of Kentucky's 10 river systems, although they are rare in the purchase region. Because of his large mouth and rounded pectoral fins, the rock bass is often confused with the warmouth and green sunfish, but the rock bass has more anal spines, and his red eye is distinctive. The rock bass is to the stream angler what the bluegill is to the pond fisherman.

The rock bass is common in the high-gradient, rocky streams of the Cumberland, Kentucky, Little Sandy, Big Sandy, and Licking rivers. He is often found in association with the smallmouth bass and prefers cool streams with bedrock or loose gravel bottoms.

A formidable fighter, the rock bass is a heavy-bodied sunfish who puts up a real battle on ultralight gear. The state record rock bass in Kentucky weighed one pound, seven ounces. Streams that offer a series of pools and fast-flowing riffles are usually good places to fish for rock bass.

Rock bass usually try to stay out of the main current. Small spinners, jigs, small minnows, or crayfish should be cast into the side eddies of the riffles at the head of pools. Rock bass are particularly fond of these choice feeding locations.

Gar, Bowfin, Flier, and Chain Pickerel

The gar, bowfin, flier, and chain pickerel are all found in adequate numbers in exteme western Kentucky in oxbow lakes and streams of the lower Tennessee, Cumberland, Ohio, and Mississippi rivers. Their numbers certainly don't compare with other fish of value to sportsmen, but they are nonetheless important.

The spotted gar *(Lepisosteus oculatus)*, longnose gar *(Lepisosteus osseus)*, and the shortnose gar *(Lepisosteus platostomus)* are all fish-eaters of family *Lepisosteiformes*, who are found predominantly in western Kentucky. The longnose gar is by far the most abundant. Gar have little or no food value, but are excellent fighters. Gar surface often and can be caught on cut bait. They have numerous teeth, and heavy wire leaders and treble hooks should be used. Their bony mouths dictate vigorous hook setting.

The bowfin *(Amia calva)* of family *Amiformes* also inhabit sluggish streams of the Mississippi River drainage (Obion Creek, Mayfield Creek, and Bayou du Chien). Like gar, they are considered "trash fish," but if you've ever caught one, you'll understand why a few sport fishermen go after them. Bowfin are hardy fishes able to withstand the most adverse of conditions. Biologists have documented that they are able to breathe atmospheric oxygen by means of an air bladder. They feed on frogs, fish, snails, and insects, and can be taken on cut bait.

The flier (Centrarchus macropterus) of family Centrarcidae, and chain pickerel (Esox niger) of family Esocidae, are bona fide sport fish. Although they are found only in small numbers in exterme western Kentucky, they are taken by anglers who fish the oxbow lakes along the lower Ohio River and Mississippi. Both species are native to the oxbow lakes on the Ballard County Wildlife Management Area and Reelfoot Lake. Fliers will take baits similar to those used in bluegill fishing. The chain pickerel, a highly predacious fish, is often caught by bass fishermen and will strike crankbaits, safety pin-type spinnerbaits, and surface plugs.

Frog Gigging

During summertime, when the evenings are about the only time it's cool and the fireflies have returned, it's time to go frog gigging. There's something about prowling the banks of a creek or pond for those long-legged "Calaveras County jumpers" that has earned frog gigging a warm spot in the heart of many a sportsman.

The bullfrog (Rana catesbiana) is best known for its deep-voiced "jug 'o rum" calls, and unfortunately for the frog, the taste of his meaty legs. Fried frog legs are a delicacy of sorts, served in many restaurants throughout the South. They are fine eating with cole slaw and hush puppies for dinner, or fried up with eggs in the morning after a long night of fishing or gigging.

Frog gigging is done on Kentucky's major lakes and small streams, but most often in ponds. Frogs can be taken either by wading the banks wearing headlamps, or from inflatable rubber rafts or aluminum johnboats, where one person gigs and another holds the light.

Kentucky's frog season lasts from May 15 to October 31, a long five months during which there are likely to be a great many sleepless nights for the avid frogger. Between the fun of being out all night in the country and the good eating which is the reward for an honest night's work, frog gigging has a way of getting in your blood.

Frogs can legally be taken with gigs, knocked over the heads with scull paddles (a rather unorthodox style that's hard on scull paddles), or taken with .22s. You must have a hunting license if they're taken with firearms or bow and arrow; otherwise your fishing license will cover frogging.

Many froggers prefer a #2 hand-forged, four-prong gig mounted on a four-foot pole about the circumference of a broom handle. Some froggers mount their gigs on longer poles so they can easily get to the frogs way back in the brush at the water's edge. Many times I have taken a gig and strong flashlight with me when I was going to be out on the lake all night fishing for white bass over lanterns or plastic worming for bass. If the fishing gets slow, just head for the banks and gig a few. You'll be surprised at how it will keep the action going.

Frogs can get "gig-shy" especially if you're gigging in a small pond. Any big disturbance in the water when you're wading, like stepping in a hole and going in over your head, will send them jumping off the bank. You've got to keep your approach easy and slow, keeping the light in their eyes if you're going to get close enough for a good gig. It's best to wait till it's good and dark and the frogs have been out for some time. The limit for frogs is 15 per person for a 24-hour period, noon till noon.

As for cleaning frogs, a die-hard frogger friend of mine suggests: 1) cut the skin around the back and belly; 2) skin the legs with a pair of pliers; 3) cut the legs from the torso; and 4) cut off the toes. The job is done and they're ready for the skillet. Their tender, white meat is delicious eating and well worth all the effort of getting muddy and wet on a summer night; and after all, who worries about that?

Trotlines

The long, hot summer days have a way of melting the enthusiasm of even the most die-hard anglers, but there's a way to beat the heat and at the same time bring home some fish for the frying pan. Ever tried trotlining? It's a time-tested method of sport fishing that a lot of outdoorsmen have somehow overlooked.

Running a trotline is really fun when you grab hold of the line at the bank and feel a tug on it and you never know what you've got on the other end. Just the anticipation and guessing are enough to keep me interested.

A trotline differs from bank lines, in that a trotline has a series of hooks or "drops" spaced evenly on a long line. Bank lines are simply single drops tied to tree limbs or roots overhanging the water; they are often set in a row at points along the shore, but are not connected by one main line.

Trotlines should be set and baited in the late evening, run at midnight, rebaited, and run again in the early morning. This late evening, night, and early morning schedule is well suited to campouts, or, even better, to frog-gigging trips. Veterans use #3 hooks on their trotlines, make the drops plenty long (two to three feet), and space them farther apart than the 18 inches required by Kentucky Fish and Wildlife Resources regulations. The farther apart the drops are spaced, the less chance there is that a big fish will tangle up the line.

Trotlines can be set parallel or perpendicular to the bank. Most often they are stretched across narrow embayments, tied tree-to-tree, or secured to a fixed object on the bank at one end and sunk to the bottom at the other end with a heavy rock. If you want to keep the trotline off the bottom (which isn't a bad idea if you know the bottom where you are setting the trotline is a tangle of fallen trees which could really play havoc on those hooks), you might try experimenting with heavy rocks and plastic jugs, using the rock to anchor the trotline and spacing the jugs along the row of hooks in such a way as to exert upward pull on the main line just enough to keep the baited hooks near the bottom, but not resting directly on it. When running the trotline, it's a good idea to have one person scull-paddle the boat and keep it parallel to the line as much as possible, while the other takes off the fish and/or rebaits the hooks. Often it's easier to cut the drop and replace it with another than to try to unhook the fish if he's swallowed the hook. It's a good idea to bring along some extra drops already rigged up. The fish can simply be placed in a big bucket or wash tub to make running the trotline easier, quicker, and more efficient time-wise. Keeping a landing net in the boat is not a bad idea either, as there's always the chance of having a big catfish on the line.

Ponds, large reservoirs, and rivers are the best waters to run trotlines in, but some large creeks can be deceptively productive. The farm pond-reared channel catfish is perhaps the trotliner's most sought-after prize, although nearly all rough fish can be taken on trotlines if they're baited properly. Cut bait—shad and skipjack viscera—are always good bait for catfish. When trotlining in rivers, look for mussels on rocky shoals; they're good bait too. Nothing beats nightcrawlers, except perhaps catalpa worms, a caterpillar pest that feeds on the leaves of the catalpa tree.

How a trotline is rigged up and what kind of materials are used is a matter of personal preference for most avid trotliners. Hope Carleton of the Kentucky Department of Fish and Wildlife Resources stresses that there are different knots, and both nylon and cotton line are used in making trot-lines. Veteran trotliners like Carleton use 250-pound test line for the main line of the trotline, while a line of 90- to 150-pound test is preferred for the drops. Hope said that the "soft-laid nylon" line used by commercial fisher-men to knit nets was considerably more pliant than some other nylon line and that the softer cord was much easier to work with.

Trotlines can be stored in buckets, the hooks arranged over the lip and the line coiled inside. Some trotliners used pieces of styrofoam or cardboard to roll up the trotline in such a way that the hooks can be kept separate from the line and the whole rig can be easily unwrapped.

Twisted and knotted trotlines are a nightmare. Channel and blue catfish have a nasty habit of trying to twist themselves off the hook once they are caught, and in the process they can literally ruin a good line with twists and knots. Thus, it is a good idea to use swivels somewhere on the drop lines to keep the twisting of the line to a minimum. Barrel swivels are the best to use in contrast to snap swivels.

Some regulations to remember in connection with sport fishing with a trotline in Kentucky: 1) no more than 50 single or multibarbed baited hooks are allowed on any one trotline; 2) only two sports fishing trotlines may be used or fished at one time; 3) each trotline must be tended to at least once every 24 hours; 4) trotlines must be removed from waters when fishing is terminated; 5) trotlines are not allowed in state-owned and/or managed lakes of less than 500 acres; and 6) trotlines with more than 50 hooks are designated as commercial trotlines and must be tagged, to be fished only by persons holding commercial fishing licenses.

License Fees, and Creel and Size Limits

The following fishing license fees and creel and size limits are subject to change. They are presented as a guideline and do not include special regulations or permit fees. License costs and creel and size limits are subject to change annually.

FISHING LICENSES

License	Res.	Non Res.
Statewide fishing	$5.00	$10.00
3-day fishing		2.50
15-day fishing		4.00
Trout stamp	2.25	2.25

CREEL AND SIZE LIMITS

Species	Daily Limit	Poss. Limit	Size Limit
Black bass	10	20	12"
Rockbass	15	30	None
Walleye	10	20	15"
Sauger	10	20	None
Muskellunge	5	10	30"
White bass	60*	60*	None
Rockfish	5	5	15"
Crappie	60	60	None

*Singly or in aggregate

Rainbow Trout Streams

Note: Trout streams in Daniel Boone National Forest are listed separately at the end of this section.

Allen County

Trammel Creek, reached via US-31E, US-231, Ky-100, Ky-2152, Ky-265 (Old State Road), Ky-1332 at Butlersville (eight miles east of Scottsville, Kentucky), and Ky-240 at Allen-Warren County line west of Allen Springs, Kentucky. Stocked in March, April, June, July, August, and September.

Long Creek, reached via Ky-1578 at the junction of Napier Road and Ky-1578 at Amos, Kentucky; Beckham-Tracy Road; Ky-100 northwest of Holland, Kentucky, one mile southeast of Scottsville. A tributary to Barren River Lake, stocked March, April, June, and July.

Barren County

Beaver Creek, reached via US-68, US-31E, Ky-90, Ky-80, and Ky-1297 at Barren River Lake, southwest of Glasgow, Kentucky. Stocked in March, April, and June.

Peter Creek, reached via Ky-921 southwest of Dry Fork, Kentucky; north to Oilwell Road; Peter Creek Road 6 miles south of Haywood, Kentucky, and then flows into lake. Stocked in March, April, June, July, August, and September.

Breckinridge County

Sinking Creek, reached via Rosetta-Craysville Road at Rosetta, Kentucky; US-60; Clifton Mills Road, west of Webster, Kentucky; Ky-86/ 261 at Clifton Mills, Kentucky; and Ky-259. A tributary to the Ohio River, stocked in March, April, June, and July.

Casey County

Goose Creek, reached via Rock Road off Ky-1813 approximately one mile southeast of Dunnville, Kentucky. Stocked in March, April, June, and July.

Clark County

Boone Creek (see Fayette County).

Crittenden County

Claylich Creek, reached via Claylich Road off US-60 two miles northwest of Marion, Kentucky; Salem-View Road, US-60 approximately three miles west of Claylich Road; Ky-855, Claylich Road off Emmus Church Road. Stocked in March, April, June, July, August, and September.

Edmonson County

Beaver Dam Creek, reached via Ky-1749, 13.4 miles north of Bowling Green, Kentucky. A tributary to Green River, stocked in March, April, June, July, August, and September.

Elliott County

Caney Creek, reached via Frank Conn Road off Ky-649 east of Beartown, Kentucky; Dale-Fannin Road two miles east of Beartown, Kentucky, off Ky-649; Ky-504 at Little Sandy River. Stocked in March, April, June, and July.

Laurel Creek, reached via Carter's School Road off Ky-32 at Rowan County line; passes near Big Stone Road off Ky-556 and then Ky-567. A tributary to Little Sandy River, stocked in March, April, and June.

Estill County

Station Camp Creek, reached via Ky-1209 at Jackson County line, then Ky-89 to Irvine, Kentucky. Stocked in March and April.

Fayette County

Boone Creek, reached via Ky-1927, eight miles west of Winchester; Sulphur Well Road off Ky-1973 south of Nihizertown, Kentucky; Ky-418 east of Athens, Kentucky; Grimes Mill Road, and flows into Kentucky River at Clay's Ferry. Stocked in March, April, and June.

Green County

Big Brush Creek, reached via Ky-424 south of Taylor-Green county line near Bloyd, Kentucky; Ky-61 and Ky-569 west of Summersville, Kentucky. A tributary to Green River, stocked in March, April, June, and July.

Greenup County

Schultz Creek, reached via Ky-784 near South Shore, Kentucky; Peter Cave Road off Ky-784; Allen Church Road and flows into Tygart's Creek. Stocked in March and April.

Hardin County

Rough Creek, reached via Ky-86, 12 miles west of Elizabethtown; Pierce

Mill Road; Ky-84 at Hardin Springs, Kentucky. A tributary to Rough River Lake, also good white bass in spring. Stocked with trout in March, April, June, and July.

Harlan County

Laurel Fork Creek, reached via Abner Fork Road which intersects Ky-221 at Leslie County line. A tributary to Kentucky River, stocked in March and April.

Fugitt Creek, reached via Ky-179 at Louellen, Kentucky. A tributary to the Cumberland River, stocked in March, April, June, and July.

Harrison County

Raven Creek, reached via Ky-36 east of Renaker, Kentucky; Casey Mill Road and Ky-1054. A tributary to the South Fork of the Licking River, stocked in March, April, and June.

Hart County

Roundstone Creek, reached via Nancy Priddy Road, approximately seven miles south of Upton, Kentucky; Ky-1140 at Rider's Mill Road and into Nolin River, stocked in March, April, June, and July.

Lynn Camp Creek, reached via Ky-936 10 miles south of Hodgenville, Kentucky, off US-31E; Ky-569 off US-31E; Ky-566 off US-31E and flows into Green River. Stocked in March, April, June, and July.

Johnson County

Hood Creek, reached via Ky-201 to Lawrence County line, north of Kerz, Kentucky (as the crow flies, five miles north of Paintsville). Stocked in March, April, June, and July.

Lee County

Sturgeon Creek, reached via Ky-587 and Ky-399 east of Beattyville, Kentucky. Stocked in March and April.

Leslie County

Greasy Creek, reached via Ky-2008 and Ky-2009 which it parallels from Leslie-Harlan county border to Hoskinston, Kentucky. Stocked in March and April.

McCreary County

Little South Fork, reached via Ky-167 and Ky-92. A Kentucky Wild River, stocked in March, April, and June.

Pike County

Russell Fork, reached via Ky-80 between Elkhorn City and Nelse, Kentucky. Stocked in March and April.

Simpson County

Lick Fork Creek, reached via Ky-100, 4.0 miles east of Franklin, Kentucky; Ky-265; Ky-1171 east of Franklin. Flows into Drake's Fork, stocked in March, April, June, and July.

Sulphur Spring Creek, reached via Neosheo Road (Ky-11885), north of Neosheo, Kentucky; Brocken-Prices Mill Road and Eddison Lane, west of Prices Mill, Kentucky. A tributary of the Red River, stocked in March, April, June, July, and September.

Trigg County

Casey Creek, headwaters in Fort Campbell Military Reservation, reached via Ky-525 and Ky-1253. A tributary to Little River, stocked in March, April, June, July, August, and September.

Trimble County

Little Kentucky River, reached via Ky-157; US-421 at Ewingsford, Kentucky; Ky-316 and Ky-1335. A tributary to the Kentucky River, stocked March and April.

Wayne County

Beaver Creek, reached via Cooper Hollow Road at Oilton, Kentucky; Ky-200 and Ky-90 at Wayne County Sportsmen Club. A tributary to Lake Cumberland, stocked in March, April, and June.

Trout Stocking in Lake Tailwaters

Rough River, Nolin, Green, Cumberland, Buckhorn, Fishtrap, Grayson, Barren, and Carr Fork lakes are stocked with rainbow trout March through October.

Trout Streams in Daniel Boone National Forest

Clay County

Big Double Creek, reached via Big Double Creek Road off Ky-66. A tributary to Red Bird River, stocked in March, April, May, June, and October.

Jackson County

Buck Lick Creek, reached via Lime Kiln Lane off Lick Branch Road, approximately two miles west of Macedonia, Kentucky. A tributary to Station Camp Creek, stocked in November with sub-adults.

Indian Creek, reached via Ky-89 at McKee. A tributary to Rockcastle River, stocked in March, April, May, and June.

War Fork Creek, reached via Turkey Foot Recreation Area (FS Road 482). A tributary to Station Camp Creek, stocked in March, April, May, and June.

Clover Bottom Creek, reached via Clover Bottom Road off US-421 west of McKee, Kentucky. A tributary to Horse Lick Creek, stocked in November with sub-adults.

Laurel County

Cane Creek, located in roadless area north of Laurel River Lake; a tributary to Rockcastle River. Access by FS Road 119 at eastern bank of Narrows of Rockcastle River. Stocked in March, April, May, June, and October.

Hawk Creek, reached via Fall City Road, a logging road off Ky-80. Stocked in November with sub-adults; a tributary to the Rockcastle River.

McCreary County

Laurel Fork of Beaver Creek, reached via FS Road 130 off US-127 in Beaver Creek Wilderness. Stocked in November with sub-adults.

Rock Creek, reached via Ky-92, FS Road 1363, FS Road 566, and FS Road 137. A Kentucky Wild River; stocked in March, April, May, June, July, August, September, and October.

Menifee County

Brushey Creek, reached via Brushey Fork Road off US-460 approximately five miles east of Frenchburg. A tributary to Licking River; stocked in November with sub-adults.

East Fork of Indian Creek, reached via East Fork of Indian Creek Road off Ky-613, seven miles east of Stanton. A tributary to the Red River; stocked in March and June.

Leatherwood Fork of Indian Creek, reached via Leatherwood Road, from Ky-713 one mile west of Frenchburg off US-460. A tributary of the Red River; stocked in November with sub-adults.

Powell County

Middle Fork Red River, reached via Ky-15 west of Campton to Mill Creek Lake (Natural Bridge State Resort Park). Stocked in March, April, and May.

Rowan County

Craney Creek, reached via Craney Creek Road off Ky-1167 six miles east of

US-60 at Morehead. A tributary to Licking River; stocked in November with sub-adults.

North Fork Triplett Creek, reached via Ky-377 at Triplett, Kentucky. A tributary to Licking River; stocked in March, April, May, and June.

Whitley County

Bark Camp Creek, reached via FS Road 193 off Ky-90 and US-25W southwest of Corbin, Kentucky. A tributary to Cumberland River (downstream from Dog Slaughter Creek); stocked in March, April, May, and June.

Dog Slaughter Creek, reached via FS Road 193 off Ky-90 and US-25W southwest of Corbin, Kentucky. A tributary of the Cumberland River; stocked in March, April, and May.

Wolfe County

Parch Corn Creek reached via Chimney Top Road, off Ky-715 in Red River Gorge Geological Area. A tributary to Red River; stocked in November with sub-adults.

Swift Camp Creek, reached via Rock Bridge Road (FS Road 24) and Ky-715 in Red River Gorge Geological Area. Stocked in March, April, May, and June.

Muskellunge Streams

Big South Fork Cumberland River from Tennessee-Kentucky line to backwater of Lake Cumberland. Primary access via FS Road 706, Ky-92, and FS Road 630.

South Fork Kentucky River, from its mouth in Lee County to Oneida, Kentucky, in Clay County. Primary access Ky-11, Ky-399, and Ky-1571.

Allen County

Drakes Creek (see Simpson County).

Barren County

Barren River from Barren River Lake to Morgantown. Primary access roads are Ky-101, Ky-234, Ky-67, Ky-263, and Ky-79.

Bath County

Licking River (see Magoffin County).

Butler County

Barren River (see Barren County).

Green River (see Taylor County).

Carter County

Little Sandy River from Grayson Lake to Ohio River. Primary access is Ky-1 to Argillite, then Ky-2 to Greenup, Kentucky.

Tygart's Creek at Olive Hill on US-60, Ky-182, Ky-474, Ky-784, and Ky-7 from Kehoe to South Shore, Kentucky.

Clay County

Big Goose Creek, reached via Ky-2467 from Knox-Bell county line at Bright Shade, Kentucky; Ky-1524 and Ky-80 towards Manchester.

Sexton Creek, reached via Ky-577 and Ky-1350 at Chesnutburg.

Edmonson County

Green River (see Taylor County).

Nolin River from Nolin River Lake to mouth of Barren River in Mammoth Cave National Park. Primary access is Ky-728 at Nolin Dam and Houchin's Ferry Road in National Park on Green River, two miles above mouth of Nolin River.

Estill County

Station Camp Creek reached via Ky-1209 at Jackson line, then Ky-89 to Irvine, Kentucky.

Fleming County

Fox Creek, reached via Ky-158 at Ringos Mills, Kentucky, and Ky-111 at Old Covered Bridge.

Green County

Green River (see Taylor County).

Little Barren River; primary access Ky-218 and Ky-88.

Greenup County

Little Sandy River (see Carter County).

Tygart's Creek (see Carter County).

Hart County

Green River (see Taylor County).

Lee County

Sturgeon Creek, reached via Ky-587 and Ky-399 east of Beattyville, Kentucky.

Leslie County

Greasy Creek, reached via Ky-2008 and Ky-2009 from Leslie-Harlan county line to Hoskinston, Kentucky.

Lewis County

Kinniconick Creek, Ky-474, Ky-1149 at Tannery, Kentucky, and Ky-1306 at Garrison, Kentucky.

Magoffin County

Licking River from Salyersville (US-460) to West Liberty, Kentucky; Cave Run Lake; Ky-111 and Ky-11 and Ky-32 at Myers.

Menifee County

Beaver Creek, reached via Ky-1274; Ky-1240 at Scranton, Kentucky, and Leatherwood Creek Road.

Morgan County

Licking River (see Magoffin County).

Powell County

Red River (see Wolfe County).

Rowan County

Licking River (see Magoffin County).

North Fork Triplett Creek, Ky-32 and Ky-1722 (at Farmers, Kentucky).

Simpson County

Drakes Creek; native populations of musky are concentrated in lower section of creek below intersection of Trammel, middle and west forks, reached via US-231. Access downstream reached via Middle Bridge Road and Ky-234.

Taylor County

Green River; primary access via Ky-55, Ky-70, Ky-88, US-31E, US-31W, Ky-259, and Ky-185.

Warren County

Barren River (see Barren County).

Drakes Creek (see Simpson County).

Wolfe County

Red River; primary access Ky-191, Ky-746, Ky-715, Ky-77, Ky-213, and Ky-89 (on Estill and Clark county line).

Waterfowl hunter and floating blind on an oxbow lake. Photograph by Arthur B. Lander, Jr.

10
Hunting

INTRODUCTION

Long before the pioneer era of the late 1700s when the first "longhunters" crossed the Cumberland Mountains, Kentucky was known as a hunter's paradise. The Shawnee, Cherokee, and Chickasaw Indian tribes all claimed hunting rights to the incredibly rich land. Deer, elk, buffalo, wild turkey, and small game abounded in numbers that stagger the imagination. In fact, the work "Kentucky" is a derivative of an Indian term meaning the "dark and bloody ground," alluding to the dense forest cover and the fierce clashes between bands of young braves who encountered one another when hunting.

Although Indians in Kentucky practiced subsistence hunting, they were in effect the first game managers. They hunted to live, and thus had the utmost respect for their quarry. Their crude wildlife management techniques, such as burning over forest lands to encourage second growth to attract deer, prefigured what today is a highly scientific profession. The modern wildlife biologist shares the same respect for the land and seeks to manage game species wisely so that their numbers will be sustained.

Hunting has always been a treasured outdoor pastime in Kentucky. For the farm boy stalking squirrels with a single-shot .22 in the woodlot behind his house, hunting is part of growing up. For the city-bound worker, his two-week fall campout and bowhunt for deer is a respite from the rigors of traffic, noise, pollution, and regimentation. All hunters share a bond with the past, whether they realize it or not. Hunting fulfills a primitive but healthy need to "get back to basics."

There are more than one million acres of public hunting lands in Kentucky. Most of them are owned by or under license to the Kentucky Department of Fish and Wildlife Resources. These public hunting areas are especially important to hunters who do not have access to private property.

The key to Kentucky's abundance of game species is its varied terrain and extensive tracts of wildlife habitat. Waterfowlers, upland game hunters, and big game enthusiasts can all find acreage in which to pursue their gunning sports.

Each region of Kentucky has its own brand of hunting. Eastern Kentucky is a sparsely settled mountainous region. Its vast tracts of timber harbor grouse, deer, squirrel, and wild turkey. The ridges and hollows in the area offer solitude and breathtaking scenery.

Central Kentucky is characterized by gentle, rolling hills and limestone-rich soil. Upland game hunters find this section of the state especially attractive. Large populations of rabbits, squirrels, raccoons, doves, and quail abound there. Sleek, heavily-antlered whitetail deer live in the wooded fringes of many farms in this area.

Western Kentucky is a flat, expansive region bordered by the Ohio and Mississippi rivers, and is characterized by rich farmland and river bottom woodlands. Hundreds of thousands of ducks and geese swarm into this area annually. A large portion of the waterfowl that migrate down the Mississippi flyway winter on Kentucky refuges. Small game and deer thrive in the bottom woodlands which constitute most of the habitat in this region.

Kentucky's 10 primary game animals (including the 20 species of waterfowl) will be discussed in this chapter, which also includes a special section on wildlife management areas open to public hunting. Hunting areas are organized according to the game species most often sought there. To keep cross-references to a minimum, wildlife management areas will be listed only once, although areas that offer good hunting for several species will be mentioned in the respective sections on individual game animals.

Whitetail Deer

The whitetail deer *(Odocoileus virginianus)* is the backbone of Kentucky's big game program. Every year thousands of hunters prowl Kentucky's woodlands in hopes of bagging one of these magnificent game animals. Successful deer hunting calls for a unique combination of woodcraft, marksmanship, and cunning.

Kentucky has two kinds of whitetails: "farm" deer and "woodland" deer. Although they are biologically indentical, their habits differ widely. Each has developed its own behavior patterns based on its respective environment.

Farm deer are extremely wary. Because they live in close proximity to man, they have learned about the ways of humans. Farm deer are very adept at utilizing small patches of cover and may spend their daylight hours in woodlots smaller than one acre in size. The cover they use is often so sparse that you would never believe it could hide a deer. Overgrown fence rows, creek banks, and field edges are excellent places in which to hunt these ghost-like animals.

As a general rule, farm bucks are big, heavily-antlered animals. Their diet consists primarily of corn, soy beans, and winter wheat. Most of the deer in the Purchase Region of the state utilize farm crops, and 200-pound bucks are relatively common.

Because farm deer are often taken while going to and from feeding areas, flat shooting rifles are the best choice. Scope-sighted rifles in .243, .270, .308, or 30-06 calibers are popular choices because they will reach out and bring down deer at the long ranges this type of hunting calls for.

Woodland deer are less nocturnal and somewhat harder to pattern than farm deer. Although they often bed down in deep thickets, they prefer "edges" when moving and feeding. Most woodland deer will frequent the narrow belts of cover adjacent to open ground.

Woodland deer subsist on a variety of foods: acorns, beechnuts, and the tender shoots of herbaceous plants draw them like a magnet. Cutover woods of second-growth timber are good places to hunt early in the season. Most woodland deer prefer hilly terrain, brushy draws, and narrow ridges. The topography of the land usually determines the travel lanes deer will use. Deer trails will generally follow the contours of brushy hills, connecting the open areas where they browse at night and the thickets where they bed down during the day. Creek bottoms with adjacent wooded hillsides are always a good bet, especially in warm weather.

Woodland deer are most often taken with the so-called "brush-busting" calibers. Many hunters who still-hunt or stalk their quarry prefer semi-automatic rifles or the traditional lever-action 30-30. Shotguns loaded with slugs are another good choice in areas where heavy cover is a problem.

Deer may legally be taken from tree stands in Kentucky; in fact, more big bucks succumb to this time-proven technique than to all other methods of deer hunting combined. There are several reasons for the effectiveness of hunting from tree stands: the hunter has increased visibility in heavy cover; human scent is dispersed up and away from the deer's sensitive nose; and, because the hunter is elevated above the deer's normal line of sight, his movements are less noticeable. Regulations at all public hunting areas forbid the building of permanent tree stands or the use of portable climbing equipment or stands which are harmful to trees.

Gun and bow hunters are required to purchase a deer tag in addition to a Kentucky hunting license. Gun hunters are required to wear an article of "hunter orange." Archery season for deer usually runs about two months, October and December. In recent years, the Kentucky statewide gun season for deer has been split into two three-day hunts. Each hunter is advised to check regulations carefully before entering the field each year, since they are subject to change annually. Computer draws for hunting dates are held in the summer.

There are several key management areas for deer hunting. These management areas offer the best deer hunting opportunities and have their own separate registration procedures and season dates. Fort Knox, Fort Campbell, Bluegrass Army Depot, Land Between the Lakes, and the Ballard County Wildlife Management Area are usually the top deer-producing areas.

The statewide harvest for whitetail deer in 1977 was 12,422 animals. This represents a success ratio of approximately 10 percent. Fort Knox yielded 1,688; Fort Campbell, 506; Bluegrass Army Depot, 646; Land Between the Lakes, 967; and Ballard County Wildlife Management Area, 212.

Kentucky's deer herd is rapidly expanding. Current estimates place the statewide population at 100,000 animals. Either-sex hunts are currently being held in several counties, most of which are in western Kentucky. With the passage of new laws to restrict poaching, which has been a problem in many areas of the state, the future of the whitetail looks very bright.

Details on fallow deer hunting are discussed in the chapter on Land Between the Lakes.

Wild Turkey

The wild turkey (Meleagris gallopavo) is Kentucky's "big game" bird. These immense, regal-looking birds, which at one time almost became our nation's symbol, inspire the respect of sportsmen everywhere. The turkey gobbler, with its purple and red head, beard, and iridescent plumage, is the epitome of beauty in the wild.

Kentucky's wild turkey populations are confined to the more remote sections of the state, since turkeys require extensive tracts of mature timber which are isolated from human disturbance. Each turkey flock requires several thousand acres of range, and one huntable bird for every 200 acres of prime habitat is an excellent average.

At one time, turkeys were found in every area of the state. Destruction of habitat and hunting pressure are the main factors which caused their numbers to dwindle. In the late 1940s the Kentucky Department of Fish and Wildlife Resources undertook a determined stocking effort to bolster the small native flocks remaining.

Initial stocking efforts proved to be a dismal failure. Pen-raised birds from "pure wild stock" couldn't adapt to the rigors of the wilds. About the same time, however, wildlife biologists from other states found that live-trapped turkeys did very well when introduced into areas with adequate habitat. The good news spread to Kentucky's wildlife managers, and a comprehensive stocking program was begun. Kentucky's present day turkey population is a direct result of massive live-trapping efforts.

At the present time, turkey hunting is confined to approximately 20 Kentucky counties, 14 of which are located in eastern Kentucky's Daniel Boone National Forest. McCreary, Whitley, Pulaski, Laurel, Clay, Leslie, Rockcastle, Jackson, Lee, Owsley, Wolfe, Menifee, Rowan, and Bath counties are known to support small flocks. The Pioneer Weapons Hunting Area offers the best hunting in the national forest.

The state's largest turkey population is in the Land Between the Lakes in western Kentucky and Tennessee. Many of the turkeys used in the restocking program were live-trapped from this area.

Turkey hunting with shotguns is a spring sport in Kentucky. The gun hunting season dates coincide with the mating season. In addition, there's a special gobbler season for bowhunters in the fall at Land Between the Lakes. All turkey hunters are limited to one bird per season, gobblers only.

When the dogwood and redwood trees start to bloom in April, the gobblers start staking out their territories. Their loud, resounding gobbles carry through the forest, announcing to the world that they are in the mood for female companionship. A wild turkey hen usually responds to the gobbler's serenade. His frequent gobbles help her home in on his position. The seductive yelp of a hen turkey sends gobblers into fits of passion. Hunters that are handy with a call can turn the tables on these bearded monarchs. Tube calls, diaphragm calls, and box calls are all designed to lure the gobbler within gun range. A hunter who can effectively imitate the plaintive call of a hen looking for a mate greatly enhances his chances for success.

Turkeys are extremely wary birds and possess some of the keenest eyes in the animal kingdom. Hunters should camouflage themselves from head to toe, including the face and hands. If a wise old gobbler makes a hunter out or sees an unnatural movement, it will usually send him over the ridge and into the next county.

Most hunters use full-choke shotguns to bag their quarry because they throw such tight groups. Magnum or high velocity shells loaded with 7½ or 6 shot are preferred because of the large number of pellets which are needed for clean kills on big birds. Some hunters back up their first shell with #4's or 2's for a body shot in case the first shot fails to connect.

During the 1977 season, 1,409 hunters harvested 37 gobblers. The Land Between the Lakes area was the most productive; 26 of the bearded monarchs came from there. The rest were taken from eastern Kentucky counties and Fort Knox.

Although Kentucky's wild turkey populations will always be limited by the availability of suitable habitat, the future looks bright. Sound hunting regulations and progressive management practices will help insure the future of this magnificent Kentucky game bird.

Waterfowl

Kentucky is located in the center of the largest waterfowl migration route in the country, the Mississippi flyway. Every fall thousands upon thousands of ducks and geese travel down this age-old highway in the sky. Winter in Kentucky is a wondrous time for those of us who thrill to the reedy quack of mallards or the clarion call of majestic Canada geese.

Thanks to an extensive management program, ducks and geese stay here most of the winter. Swarms of waterfowl funnel into Kentucky's wildlife management areas, offering thousands of hunters a chance at these noble birds.

Even though large tracts of waterfowl habitat in western Kentucky are privately owned, there are extensive land holdings open to public hunting. Of the four public hunting areas in western Kentucky managed for waterfowl by the Kentucky Department of Fish and Wildlife Resources, the Ballard County Wildlife Management Area, located on the Ohio River west of Monkeys Eyebrow, Kentucky, is the largest and best. The area consists of 8,000 acres of river bottom fields interspersed with woodlands.

Roughly one-fourth of the management area is a waterfowl refuge closed to hunting. The refuge area is bounded by the Ohio River on the north and Mitchell Lake on the south, and includes Butler, Turner, Little Turner, Castor, Turkey, and Goose ponds. There are 75 field pits for goose hunting within the management area and 20 blinds over water for duck hunting. Regulations specify that a hunter must hunt either geese or ducks and may not take both from the same blind or pit. Reservations are assigned by a special draw held during the summer prior to the season. For information concerning waterfowl hunting on the Ballard County Wildlife Management Area write Refuge Manager, Ballard County Wildlife Management Area, Route #1, La Center, Kentucky, 42056.

A public hunting area nearby, open on a first-come, first-served basis, is the Peal Wildlife Management Area in southern Ballard County. The area encompasses 1,849 acres of marshland, river bottom fields, and oxbow lakes. There are two tracts—one, four miles west of Barlow, Kentucky, on highway Ky-118, and the other one mile west of Wickliffe on US-60. Both have permanent blinds and gravel access roads.

Just south of the Peal Wildlife Management Area is the newly-opened Winford Wildlife Management Area, consisting of 237 acres in Carlisle

County, six miles northwest of Bardwell, Kentucky, off US-62 in the May-field Creek bottoms.

The other major public hunting area in this waterfowl hotspot region is the West Kentucky Wildlife Management Area, 12 miles west of Paducah in McCracken County, on highway Ky-358. The 6,896 acres are prime waterfowl habitat with 50 miles of access roads.

Another public hunting area on the Ohio River is the Sloughs Wildlife Management Area, consisting of four separate units in Henderson County, Kentucky. The Sauerheber Unit, 2500 acres, is a refuge for Canada geese and is off limits to hunting. As many as 8,000 to 10,000 geese use the refuge during peak migrational periods.

The public hunting lands were recently bolstered with the purchase of 4,643 acres from the U.S. Army Corps of Engineers. The acreage has been divided into two management units. The Jenny Hole-Highland Creek area is good duck hunting land, mostly timbered sloughs. The second unit, two miles upriver, is the Grassy Pond-Powell's Lake unit, where more than 600 acres are planted in field crops for waterfowl. The Grassy Pond-Powell's Lake unit is adjacent to the Sauerheber Refuge, and is the best bet for goose hunting in the area.

The Jenny Hole-Highland Creek unit is northwest of Smith Mills, Kentucky, off highway Ky-136 at the junction of Gray and Aldridge roads. The Grassy Pond-Powell's Lake unit is north of Geneva, Kentucky, off Straight Line Road. The other public hunting area for waterfowl in Henderson County is the Ash Flats unit, across the county southeast of Henderson on Mason Landing Road, near Hebbardsville, Kentucky.

The largest chunk of real estate open to public waterfowl hunting in western Kentucky is the twin reservoirs, Lake Barkley and Kentucky Lake, which together comprise 216,000 surface acres of water. Mudflat islands, back bays, and specialized management units for waterfowl, operated by TVA and the states of Tennessee and Kentucky, are located along the 45-mile isthmus. Lake Barkley and Kentucky Lake lie in the path of migrating waterfowl who stop over to rest and feed in the shallow lakes and in the corn, millet, and buckwheat fields of Land Between the Lakes. During state-wide seasons, waterfowlers take Canada geese, buffleheads, American and hooded mergansers, scaup, goldeneye, gadwalls, widgeon, wood ducks, green and blue-winged teal, mallards, and black ducks. Pintails, redheads, and canvasbacks are also transient visitors, but in smaller numbers.

In 1977, hunters at the Ballard County Wildlife Management Area took 2500 waterfowl. The Sloughs Wildlife Management Area near Henderson yielded 311 waterfowl, and Lake Barkley Wildlife Management Area yielded 1303 ducks and 111 geese. Statewide, the 1977 duck and geese harvest figures stood at 48,000 and 16,000, respectively. These numbers include the figures from the state-operated wildlife management areas.

Although western Kentucky definitely offers the best waterfowl hunting, it certainly isn't the only part of the state where waterfowl may be found. Ducks and geese use all of the major river systems throughout the state, and farm ponds provide important resting areas along the way.

In the western part of the state, duck hunting is decoy hunting. Hunters select blinds in favorite feeding and resting areas, hoping to call their prey within range. Guide services are available in the Mayfield Creek bottoms, much of which is privately owned. A guide is a good idea for hunters who don't have access to posted lands.

Jump shooting is an exciting, highly productive method of hunting throughout the state. Although not as popular as the more traditional hunting methods, it often produces duck dinners when nothing else will.

Most jump shooters use binoculars to spot their quarry. Once the ducks are sighted, the hunter plans a route of attack that offers plenty of concealment during the stalk. By utilizing stands of cattails, a pond's dam face, or bends in the watercourse, it is often possible to eyeball a flock of ducks a scant few yards away.

Jump shooting enables the gunner to cash in on the wealth of waterfowl that frequent small bodies of water. Kentucky's small lakes, ponds, and streams are excellent places in which to practice this brand of waterfowling. Ducks feel safe in these areas, and are thus a real ace-in-the-hole for the smart opportunist.

Ducks like to loaf and preen themselves during midday. Small aquatic hideaways provide waterfowl with a welcome respite from the boat traffic and shooting pressures that they face on the larger bodies of water. Ducks are also attracted to the natural food sources that are present in these small wetlands.

Duck hunting is a purist's sport that demands hard work and dedication. A duck hunter's dog, boat, and decoys are much more than mere possessions; they are his reason for being.

Cottontail Rabbit

The cottontail rabbit *(Sylvilagus floridanus)* is one of the most important game animals in the state. Rabbits are present in every county in Kentucky, although the agricultural sections yield the highest numbers. With the possible exception of the gray squirrel, the rabbit is the most frequently hunted species in the state.

During the 1977 season, 114,500 hunters made 614,000 trips and bagged 567,000 rabbits. This figure is low in comparison with previous years' harvest due to severe winter weather the past two years. On a 12-year average, 113,000 hunters made 280,500 trips which yielded 950,500 rabbits annually.

Rabbits need cover in which to raise their young and escape from the long list of predators that actively feed on them. Adequate cover also provides a comfortable respite from harsh winter weather. Brush piles, honeysuckle thickets, and overgrown fence rows are favored shelters. Groundhog burrows are another important source of protection, especially during severe winter storms. Rabbits can last for a week or more without food, as long as they can retreat underground and escape from the elements.

Rabbits feed on a variety of foods. As in most other forms of hunting, finding the rabbits' favored food sources is an important part of a winning strategy. Alfalfa, clover, and goldenrod are staples of their diet, and bluegrass, honeysuckle, and farm crops are eaten whenever available. Berry patches, corn and soybean fields, and fruit orchards are also favored feeding sites.

Rabbits are extremely prolific, and it is not unusual for a doe to have four or more litters a year, each containing four or five young rabbits. The normal breeding season extends from March through September, although this varies considerably according to prevailing weather conditions.

Rabbits can be hunted with or without dogs, but many dedicated beaglers consider taking these fleet-footed rockets without dogs a sin. The best hounds have a good nose, the ability to seek the rabbits out, and the knack of unraveling the rabbits' twisting, circuitous trail.

For the most part, rabbit hunting is a shotgunner's game. Although it doesn't test the shooter's skills like some forms of wing-shooting, it's no easy sport. The element of surprise is ever-present, and rabbits can twist and turn on a dime. Light field loads with #6 shot are the best choice.

Because rabbits are such homebodies, finding them usually isn't much of a problem. Slow, thorough probing in the transitional edges of food and cover almost always puts rabbits in the bag.

Swamp Rabbit

The swamp rabbit (Sylvilagus aquaticus) is a cousin of the cottontail that inhabits about 15 counties in western Kentucky. Isolated populations have been substantiated as far north as Hancock County. The "swamper" is considerably larger than his cousin, weighing up to six and one-half pounds, although the average adult weighs about three and one-half pounds.

The numbers of swamp rabbits in Kentucky have declined in recent years because of the draining of wetlands. The swamp rabbit makes his home in woodlands and brushy areas along creeks, sloughs, and oxbow lakes, and on islands in the lower Ohio and Mississippi rivers. Swampers are adept at swimming and will sit out a flood on a pile of drift. They make their nest on the ground as do cottontails, or in a hollow log; but because they live where the ground is wet, they have little chance of finding holes in which to spend the cold winter months. Does produce two to five litters of two to six young each year, with a gestation period of 40 days. As with cottontails, the main population limiting factors are disease, predation, and lack of food and adequate cover.

Because swamp rabbits live in territory which is incredibly hard to hunt, gunning pressure has little effect on their numbers. The best swamp rabbit hunting technique is wading in hip boots and stomping brush piles. As in cottontail hunting, a pack of beagles may make the difference in taking game. Swampers aren't nearly as fleet of foot as cottontails, but will hold tight when in danger, quietly easing off once the hunter has passed. Slow methodic searching often rewards hunters with shots at sitting bunnies. Some hunters use .22 rifles on swampers. Small-gauge shotguns with number five shot are preferred; field loads are adequate.

Swamp rabbits can be hunted on four wildlife management areas in western Kentucky: Peal, Sloughs, West Kentucky, and Winford wildlife management areas. Biologists have been studying swamp rabbits at the West Kentucky Wildlife Management Area for years in hopes of learning more about their food habits, reproduction, and the effects of hunting and diseases, all of which are factors in the survival of this remarkable bunny.

Gray and Fox Squirrel

Two species of squirrels sought by hunters are found in Kentucky: the gray squirrel (Sciurus carolinensis) and the fox squirrel (Sciurus niger). Together, they provide countless hours of enjoyment for hunters throughout the state because of the long season and liberal bag limit. During the 1977 season, Kentucky biologists estimate that 103,500 hunters made 661,000 trips in search of bushytails. Their efforts netted a staggering total of 1,081,000 squirrels.

Although their ranges often overlap one another, each species has its own specific habitat requirements. The gray squirrel has a wider distribution and is more abundant than his larger cousin. Gray squirrels prefer large stands of mature timber like those found in the heavily wooded eastern and southeastern sections of the state.

Grays subsist primarily on the mast of oak, hickory, beech, walnut, and butternut trees. In late winter and early spring they utilize other foods as well. Tree buds, fleshy fruits, seeds, insect larvae, and bird eggs all find their way into the gray's diet; in fact, grays will eat just about anything that is available to them.

The fox squirrel is a larger, more chunkily-built animal than his cousin. While a big gray squirrel will tip the scales at a pound and a half, the average fox squirrel weighs two pounds or more. The fox squirrel's coat has a distinct reddish cast, and the underbelly is orange instead of white.

Fox squirrels are scarce in the eastern half of the state. Their range starts on the eastern border of the Bluegrass section and extends into western Kentucky. The tier of northern counties bordering the Ohio River is also a stronghold for the species.

Ideal fox squirrel habitat is composed of small wooded fringes and woodlots. The mast of mature hardwood trees usually makes up the bulk of their diet, but they show a strong preference for farm crops as well. Corn and soybeans are eaten whenever available, often to the exclusion of "natural" foods.

Early in the season, squirrels concentrate on the woods' edges and high ground. Hickory, walnut, and butternut mast dominate their diet. Early season hotspots are usually groves of nut trees located on the higher ground where they ripen most quickly. Stalking is a productive hunting method during that time of the year.

Many squirrel hunters use shotguns during the early season because of the dense foliage and restricted visibility. The small-gauge shotguns do well on squirrels, as long as they're tightly choked and loaded with shot no smaller than size 6.

In the late season, the squirrel's diet shifts to acorns and beechnuts. These soft-shelled nuts yield more calories per unit of expended energy than the hard-shelled nuts. This factor becomes increasingly important as the weather gets colder.

Hunting from a stand is more productive than stalking late in the year. The woods are bare and squirrels have notoriously sharp eyesight. This is the time when the skilled riflemen really shine. A scope-sighted .22 is the perfect firearm for late season hunting. Lowland areas and river or creek bottoms are excellent places in which to play the waiting game. It's not unusual to take a limit of squirrels from a single, well-chosen spot.

Squirrel hunting is a time-honored tradition in Kentucky. In Daniel Boone's time, squirrels provided an important source of food. Although the days of the "Kentucky Squirrel Rifle" and buckskin shirts are long gone, squirrel hunting is still very much a part of Kentucky's outdoor legacy.

Bobwhite Quail

The bobwhite quail *(Colinus virgianus)* is a popular game bird in Kentucky, particularly in the western part of the state. Quail is the second most popular game species taken during the winter months, pursued by nearly half of the licensed hunters in the state. Few moments in hunting are as satisfying and thrilling as bagging a double of quail on the rise, shooting over a good dog. Following a well-trained pointing dog in search of this elusive bombshell is a sport in a class by itself.

Based upon a 12-year average, 81,000 hunters harvested 1,070,000 quail annually. During the 1977 hunting season, 67,500 hunters made 433,000 trips and harvested 812,500 quail. In order to augment the wild bird population, the Kentucky Department of Fish and Wildlife hatched 88,949 quail last year and distributed them to various sportsmen's clubs throughout the state.

Although quail prefer fairly open land, they are heavily dependent upon adequate cover. Overgrown fence rows, brush piles, and weed fields are absolutely essential. Quail have many enemies. Hawks, owls, cats, snakes, and weasels all play havoc on their numbers wherever there is a shortage of cover.

Quail thrive wherever food and cover are provided for them. The quail is dependent upon a diversified habitat which is a combination of cropland, meadow, and woodland areas. Without any of these essentials, quail become scarce. They are primarily a farm species.

While western Kentucky is the quail's stronghold, "birds" can be found statewide wherever there is suitable food and cover. Several eastern Kentucky counties harbor excellent quail populations, especially those with small valley farms. The Bluegrass region also produces good quail hunting.

The best shotguns for quail shooting are light, open-choked, and point easily. Most shots are taken in close, and quail are notoriously easy to knock down. Light loads with #8 or #9 shot provide the pattern density needed to bag them. Late in the season some hunters switch to 7½ shot because the birds flush wildly. Although double barrel or over-and-under shotguns are the traditional favorites, more and more hunters carry semiautomatics every year.

Ruffed Grouse

Eastern Kentucky's portion of the Appalachian mountain range holds a special fascination for many hunters. That's because it's the home of one of

Kentucky's most challenging game birds, the ruffed grouse *(Bonasa umbellus)*. No other game bird so tests the wing shooter's skill.

To hit a grouse, one has to shoot at it. I know that sounds rather self-evident, but the fact is, since most of the good cover in this state is extremely dense, clear, open shots are a rarity. A grouse's quick evasive flush can put a tree between himself and the hunter in the blink of an eye.

The average beginner seldom sees the wisdom in shooting quickly. He finds himself looking for a clear shot and ends up doing just that: looking. Go ahead and blast away; one bird for every three shells fired is an exceptional average.

Although grouse are considerably larger than quail, they aren't much harder to bring down. Most experienced hunters use small-size shot for pattern density. A grouse gun must fit the hunter like a glove; there is no time for second guessing in this game. Most hunters prefer a light gun that handles well. Improved cylinder and modified are the most popular chokes.

All of the Kentucky counties east of Mt. Sterling harbor resident populations of grouse. The vast tracts of land located in the Daniel Boone National Forest encompass some of the best grouse habitat in this part of the country. During the 1977 season, 9500 hunters harvested 17,000 grouse in 74,000 hunts. The best counties for grouse are Letcher, Harlan, Bell, Whitley, Knox, Laurel, Clay, and Leslie.

Grouse prefer second-growth timber, and the lumberman's axe and saw help create favorable habitat. Mature stands of timber provide little food or cover and are thus a poor choice for the aspiring hunter.

Grouse are ground-scratching birds. They are members of the gallinaceous family of birds which includes the quail and wild turkey. As such, they are fond of all manner of seeds and berries. Acorns, beechnuts, wild grape, and sumac are favorite foods. After snow covers the ground, their food preferences change to the buds and emerging leaves of maple and dogwood trees. Skunk cabbage and ferns are other sources of sustenance later in the year.

Grouse prefer to roost in stands of conifers. In fact, grouse and pine trees are inseparable in this part of the country. Early morning and late evening hunting should be directed toward the edges of these preferred roosting sites.

The best areas in which to hunt grouse are those characterized by a balanced mixture of evergreens and hardwoods. Transitional edges of cover with abundant food sources nearby are a veritable gold mine. Abandoned farms, reclaimed mining areas, and old forest fire sites are all excellent producers.

Grouse hunting in Kentucky is a magnificent sport. It takes the hunter into some of the most remote and beautiful country in the western Appalachians. Any hunter who bags a limit of these wily, resourceful birds can puff out his chest and feel proud, indeed.

Mourning Dove

Doves are Kentucky's game bird of the future. The mourning dove *(Zenaidura macroura)* is one of the few game birds that actually thrive on modern-day agricultural practices. As a result, dove hunting is one of Kentucky's fastest growing gunning sports. During the 1977 season, 53,000 hunters made 253,500 trips and took home 1,263,000 doves.

Doves are seed eaters. The large open fields of wheat, corn, and soybeans so prevalent today serve their needs handsomely. Although large, fenceline-to-fenceline grain fields have proven to be the demise of other farm species gamebirds, doves love them.

Dove population dynamics are well suited to a high rate of harvest, since 80 percent of each year's dove crop dies from natural causes before the next breeding season arrives. Hunters normally harvest less than 10 percent of the total annual crop of doves.

Doves nest readily in close proximity to man. Parks, residential areas, and other urban retreats are heavily utilized. In the wild, doves nest in every type of cover imaginable, from dense, low-lying bushes to evergreens and tall hardwood trees.

In the early part of the season, the young of the year gather in large, loose flocks. Millions of birds converge on freshly harvested fields and are thus relatively easy to locate. Power lines and dead trees are preferred roosting sites between the morning and afternoon feeding periods, and a pair of field glasses is an invaluable aid while scouting these areas.

In Kentucky, doves may only be hunted from noon to sunset. During the early part of the season, open-choked guns and small shot are best for harvesting doves. Most of the shots are close, since the birds are not as wild and wary as they will be later on. Light loads in #8 shot are pure poison on these early season birds.

Later in the season, once the full-scale migration is underway, the doves act like different birds. They often fly in twisting patterns, and it takes an expert shot to score regularly. Late-season gunning calls for modified or full chokes and 7½ or 8 shot. Most veteran hunters lean heavily in favor of 7½'s in the late season.

Because doves are migratory gamebirds, dove hunting is regulated by the Federal government. Each year, the U.S. Fish and Wildlife Service issues a framework or guideline for season dates and bag limits, determined by the estimated dove population for the current year. Kentucky's dove season is usually about two and one-half months long, starting in early September and ending in October, with a 10-day bonus season in December.

Dove hunting is a sport with a long-standing tradition in Kentucky. Dove "shoots" are social as much as sporting occasions, the highlight of the fall season for hunters. Large groups of men, women, and children gather around freshly harvested fields. The large number of hunters keeps the doves on the wing, and the action is usually fast and furious. Impromptu picnics and barbecues often cap off the afternoon.

Raccoon

The raccoon (*Procyon lotor*) is a hound-dog man's dream-come-true. He's active enough to leave plenty of scent, smart enough to know when a pack of hounds is on his trail, and clever enough to extricate himself from all but the most impossible situations. He's also a terrific scrapper when cornered.

Raccoons are a popular game animal in Kentucky. They are found statewide, and often live in close proximity to man. During the past year, 14,000 hunters made 163,500 hunting trips after B'rer Coon, which accounted for a lot of sleepless nights! The total harvest was 80,500 of the masked critters.

If you include the training season, when the animals may be pursued but not taken, raccoon hunting is a year-round sport. In addition to the training season, there is a "shake out" season, during which the animals may be taken by dogs only. The "shake out" season usually occurs before the regular small game season.

Raccoons depend upon water for their sustenance and frequent nearly all of the state's woodlands along streams, rivers, and lakes. Fish, freshwater mussels, frogs, and crayfish make up the bulk of their diet. Raccoons are virtually omnivorous, however, and insects, bird eggs, nuts, and farm crops all find their way into their diet.

As every night-prowling hunter knows, the coon has a whole bag of tricks. The true sport in coon hunting comes in the chase. He'll circle in his own track, use the scent of domestic stock to throw off his own, take to the trees, then leap to the ground and run off. To a "coon hunting fool," there's nothing in the world to match him.

Furbearers and Varmints

Kentucky's annual trapping season for furbearers usually runs from late November until late January. Red fox, raccoon, mink, beaver, muskrat, opossum, weasel, and skunk are legal game. There's no limit and no special licenses are required.

Animals classified as varmints that can be taken year-round with no limit are gray fox, woodchuck, crow, coyote, English sparrows, and starlings.

Best Wildlife Management Areas For Waterfowl Hunting

Lake Barkley

Barkley Lake Wildlife Management Area is 2,400 acres in Trigg, Lyon, and Livingston counties. Public lands consist of a number of islands in Lake Barkley, one of which is maintained as a waterfowl refuge area. There is hunting for ducks and geese. Special regulations are in effect for waterfowl hunting. Mailing address: Barkley Lake Wildlife Management Area, c/o Frank Dibble, 320 Woodlawn, Murray, Kentucky, 42071. Telephone: (502) 753-3040.

Yellowbank

Yellowbank Wildlife Management Area is 4,055 acres in Breckinridge County 40 miles north of Hardinsburg on Ky-259, along the Ohio River at the Meade County line. The area contains steep to moderately sloping woods and flat river bottom farmlands. There is hunting for rabbit, quail, squirrel, dove, raccoon, fox, and waterfowl. The area is closed to deer hunting at this writing, but may reopen in the future. Mailing address: Yellowbank Wildlife Management Area, c/o Vernon Anderson, Route 1, Stephensport, Kentucky, 40170. Telephone: (502) 547-6303.

Ballard County

The Ballard County Wildlife Management Area is located in Ballard

County, 35 miles west of Paducah. From US-60 in Paducah, take Ky-358 at La Center, then turn left on Ky-1105 for four miles, then right on Ky-473 to the Headquarters Building. There are several roads within the area. The 8,373-acre area contains sloughs and agricultural bottomlands, with some stands of hardwood. There is hunting for waterfowl, squirrel, and dove. Special regulations are in effect for hunting, and fee and reservation are required for waterfowl hunters. For additional information, write Kentucky Department of Fish and Wildlife or Refuge Manager, Ballard County Wildlife Management Area, La Center, Kentucky, 42056. Telephone: (502) 224-2244.

Kentucky Lake

Kentucky Lake Wildlife Management Area consists of 3,274 acres in Calloway, Marshall, and Lyon counties. Public areas consist of islands, lowlands at back of the bays, and a narrow strip along much of the shoreline of Kentucky Lake. The area is accessible by boat and several TVA access points and rural roads. There is hunting for waterfowl, squirrel, rabbit, quail, deer, and doves. Mailing address: Kentucky Lake Wildlife Management Area, c/o Frank Dibble, 320 Woodlawn, Murray, Kentucky, 42071. Telephone: (502) 753-3040.

Peal

The Peal unit is 1,821 acres in Ballard County. Tract #1 is four miles west of Barlow on Ky-118; tract #2 is one mile west of Wickliffe on US-60. There are three roads within the area, but no trails. The area contains marshland and river bottom land. Rabbits, squirrels, waterfowl, and furbearers are hunted in the area. Mailing address: Peal Unit, c/o Refuge Manager, Ballard County Wildlife Management Area, La Center, Kentucky, 42056. Telephone: (502) 224-2244.

Sloughs

The Sloughs Wildlife Management Area encompasses 3,016 acres in Henderson County. This area is composed of three separate units. *Sauerheber Refuge* is located 5.5 miles northwest of Geneva on Ky-268. To reach *Jenny Hole,* turn left off Route 136 one half mile northwest of Smith Mills onto Burbank Road, then follow signs from junction with Gray-Aldridge Road. *Ash Flats* is reached via Mason Landing Road northeast from Hebbardsville; follow signs to area. Sauerheber Unit has two interior roads; the other units require four-wheel drive vehicles on interior roads. The area contains alternating ridges and sloughs, woods, brush areas, and cleared fields. Species hunted include ducks, geese, cottontails, swamp rabbits, squirrel, quail, raccoon, woodchuck, and dove. Sauerheber Unit, a wintering area for over 20,000 Canada geese, is closed to the public from October 15 through March 15 each year. The other units are open year-round. Mailing address: Sloughs Wildlife Management Area, c/o Ben Burnley, Route 2, Box 230D, Old Corydon Road, Henderson, Kentucky, 42420. Telephone: (502) 826-9507.

West Kentucky

The West Kentucky Wildlife Management Area is 6,896 acres in McCracken County, 12 miles west of Paducah on Ky-358. There are 50 miles of roads within the area, which consists primarily of flat terrain, old farms, and small wood lots, in addition to 500 acres of woodlands. Deer, squirrel, rabbit, quail, dove, ducks, and raccoon are commonly hunted. Special regulations are in effect for most hunting. For more information contact Tom Young, Kevil, Kentucky, 42053. Telephone: (502) 488-3233.

Winford

Winford Wildlife Management Area consists of 237 acres in Carlisle County, six miles northwest of Bardwell on US-62. There are no roads or trails within the area, which consists of flat creek bottom land with several lakes. There is hunting for waterfowl, rabbits, deer, and raccoon. Mailing address: Winford Wildlife Management Area, c/o Joe Bruna, Division of Game Management, Kentucky Department of Fish and Wildlife Resources, 592 East Main Street, Frankfort, Kentucky, 40601. Telephone: (502) 564-4406.

For more information on commercial outfitters in the western Kentucky area, contact Martin Flournoy, Route 1, La Center, Kentucky, 42056. Telephone: (502) 224-2617.

Best Wildlife Management Areas For Deer Hunting

Fort Campbell

Fort Campbell encompasses 34,000 acres in Christian and Trigg counties, 15 miles south of Hopkinsville on US-41A. Hunting permits ($7 fee) and information are available at Rear Area Military Police Station near the intersection of Woodland and Old Lafayette roads. The area contains a vast system of interpost roads, several of which are hard-surfaced. The terrain varies from gently rolling to steeply hilly, with a variety of both forest-game and farm-game habitat, sinkholes, and beaver lakes. Deer, squirrel, rabbit, quail, and raccoon are the common game species. Mailing address: Fort Campbell, Outdoor Recreation Branch, Hunting and Fishing Unit, Fort Campbell, Kentucky, 42223. Telephone: (502) 798-2151.

Higginson-Henry

Higginson-Henry Wildlife Management Area is 5,420 acres in Union County, two miles east of Morganfield on Ky-56. The area contains rolling hills with patches of hardwoods, numerous small clearings, and some large fields in crops. Common game species are dove, deer, rabbit, quail, squirrel, raccoon, groundhog, woodcock, and fox. Special regulations are in effect for deer hunting. Mailing address: Higginson-Henry Wildlife Management Area, c/o Larry Sharp, Route #3, Morganfield, Kentucky, 42437. Telephone (502) 389-3580.

Daniel Boone National Forest

The Daniel Boone National Forest runs from the Tennessee line in McCreary County north to Fleming and Lewis counties, south of the Ohio River. There are gravel Forest Service roads, marked hiking trails, and numerous unmarked logging roads in the more than 630,000 acres. The terrain is primarily mountainous and rugged, but contains some fairly flat river and creek bottoms and ridge tops. There is hunting for deer, squirrel, rabbit, grouse, fox, raccoon, and quail. Generally, the best hunting is in the sparsely populated southeastern counties. Letcher, Harlan, Bell, Whitley, Clay, and Leslie counties are best for grouse and squirrels. Much of the land within the boundaries of the national forest is still privately owned, and permission should be obtained before hunting on these private holdings. Redbird Unit is temporarily closed to all hunting by the Kentucky Fish and Wildlife Commission as part of a program to increase the size of the deer herds in eastern Kentucky. This area will be stocked with deer and used to study the population growth, availability of food, and other habitat requirements. As the herd increases, the deer will be used to stock adjoining areas. For information on the Redbird Purchase Area in the Daniel Boone National Forest, contact George Wright, Route #2, Box 110A, Campton, Kentucky, 41301. Telephone: (606) 668-3285.

Knob State Forest

Knob State Forest consists of 4,000 acres in Nelson County reached via Hardin Leslie Road off US-62 between Bardstown and Elizabeth. The area contains slightly rolling to steep terrain and is primarily forested. There are several dirt roads that are impassable to all but four-wheel drive vehicles. Squirrel and deer are the species most commonly sought. Mailing address: Knob State Forest, c/o Joe Bruna, Division of Game Management, Kentucky Department of Fish and Wildlife Resources, 592 East Main Street, Frankfort, Kentucky, 40601. Telephone: (502) 564-4406.

Pennyrile State Forest

The Pennyrile Forest is 15,200 acres in Christian County, eight miles south of Dawson Springs. There are many roads and trails within the area, some of which are paved. The area contains hilly terrain which is heavily timbered, with hunting for deer, quail, and squirrel. Mailing address: Pennyrile State Forest, c/o Frank Dibble, 320 Woodlawn, Murray, Kentucky, 42071. Telephone: (502) 753-3040.

Best Wildlife Management Areas For Wild Turkey Hunting

Land Between the Lakes

Land Between the Lakes is an area of 175,000 acres in Trigg and Lyon counties, between Kentucky and Barkley lakes. It is reached by Ky-453 (the Trace) and Ky-80. There are many secondary roads and trails within the area. The terrain varies from gently rolling to fairly steep, and much of the area is forested. There are many clearings, old farm sites, and wildlife food plots. Hunting is available for deer, squirrel, dove, quail, rabbit, raccoon, opossum, and fox. Special regulations govern seasons, weapons, and hunting areas. For specific information, write TVA, Land Between the Lakes Information Office, Golden Pond, Kentucky, 42231. Telephone: (502) 924-5602.

Fort Knox

Fort Knox consists of 20,000 acres in Hardin and Bullitt counties, 30 miles south of Louisville on US-31W. Take US-60 to Grahampton Outdoor Recreational Center, where all users of the area must check in at Hunt Control Headquarters, Building 9210. Since this is an active military reservation, access is available only by a strictly controlled and rigidly enforced system. Approximately 120 miles of roads traverse the area, and a map is furnished to each hunter. The area contains rolling uplands, broad ridge tops, and narrow valleys with steep to sloping cliffs. There are hardwood forests with associated open areas. Species commonly hunted include deer, squirrel, quail, rabbit, dove, turkey, raccoon, waterfowl, and woodchuck. Mailing address: Fort Knox, Fort Knox Conservation and Beautification Committee, P.O. Box 1052, Fort Knox, Kentucky, 40121. Telephone: (502) 624-1181.

Pioneer Weapons Hunting Area

Pioneer Weapons Hunting Area, one of the few areas in the United States where crossbow hunting is permitted, is 7300 acres in Bath and Menifee counties, five miles south of Salt Lick. It can be reached by FS Road 129 or by boat on Cave Run Lake. FS Road 918 (Tater Knob Road) provides access to the center of the area, and there is also a series of marked hiking trails. Mainly hilly and quite steep, the area contains gently sloping spots in ridgetops and creek valleys, and is almost completely forested. Species commonly hunted include deer, turkey, grouse, and squirrel. Hunting is limited to longbow, crossbow, and muzzle-loading firearms only. State-wide seasons and limits apply to all species except deer and turkey. Mailing address: Pioneer Weaspons Hunting Area, c/o Harold Barber, P.O. Box 115, West Liberty, Kentucky, 41472. Telephone: (606) 743-4481.

Best Wildlife Management Areas For Small Game Hunting—Rabbit, Squirrel, Grouse, Dove, Quail, or Raccoon

Buckhorn Lake

The Buckhorn Lake Wildlife Management Area is 2,580 acres in Perry County along the lake shoreline. To reach the area, take Ky-15 and Ky-28 west from Hazard and Ky-257 north from Hyden, where two old roads follow the lake shore. Some parts are passable in four-wheel drive vehicles. The area consists of mountainous terrain, primarily forested with hardwoods, but with some open land in the bottoms. Common game species are squirrel, grouse, and deer. Mailing address: Buckhorn Lake Wildlife Management Area, c/o George Wright, Route 2, Box 110A, Campton, Kentucky, 41301. Telephone: (606) 668-3285.

Clay

Clay Wildlife Management Area is in Nicholas County, eight miles northeast of Carlisle on Ky-32. From there take Cassidy Creek Road to the area. The area contains 1,700 acres of woodland and 3,074 acres cleared, with some in wildlife food plots. Steep to rolling terrain predominates. There is hunting for squirrel, deer, dove, quail, rabbit, raccoon, woodchuck, and fox. Mailing address: Clay Wildlife Management Area, c/o Charles Wilkins, Route 4, Carlisle, Kentucky, 40311. Telephone: (606) 289-2564.

Cranks Creek

The Cranks Creek Wildlife Management Area consists of 1,288 acres in Harlan County, 15 miles southeast of Harlan on Stone Mountain Road (off US-421). There is a jeep trail through the area, which is mountainous, extremely rugged, and heavily forested, primarily in hardwoods. Squirrel, deer, and grouse are commonly hunted. Mailing address: Cranks Creek Wildlife Management Area, c/o George Wright, Route 2, Box 110A, Campton, Kentucky, 41301. Telephone: (606) 668-3285.

Dale Hollow

Dale Hollow Wildlife Management Area is 3,000 acres in Cumberland and Clinton counties, along the shoreline of Dale Hollow Lake. There is access by several state and county roads and by boat. Terrain varies from gently rolling creek bottoms to steep ridges. There is hunting for deer, squirrel, rabbit, and raccoon. Mailing address: Dale Hollow Wildlife Management Area, c/o Joe Bruna, Division of Game Management, Kentucky Department of Fish and Wildlife Resources, 592 East Main Street, Frankfort, Kentucky, 40601. Telephone: (502) 564-4406.

Dewey Lake

Dewey Lake Wildlife Management Area consists of 8,650 acres of lake shoreline and ridgetop woods in Floyd County, six miles east of Prestonsburg on Ky-194. It is also accessible by boat. The area is extremely steep, rugged, and completely forested. This area is temporarily closed to all hunting by the Kentucky Fish and Wildlife Commission as part of the program to increase the size of the deer herds in eastern Kentucky. Mailing address: Dewey Lake Wildlife Management Area, c/o Harold Barber, P.O. Box 115, West Liberty, Kentucky, 41472. Telephone: (606) 743-4481.

Fishtrap Lake

Fishtrap Lake Wildlife Management Area encompasses 10,000 acres of the lake shoreline in Pike County south of Pikeville on US-460. The dam area is accessible via Ky-1789, and the upper end of the lake via Ky-1499. There is also access by boat. The area has very steep, rough terrain with narrow ridges and valleys, and is completely forested in hardwoods. There is hunting for squirrel, deer, raccoon, and grouse. Mailing address: Fishtrap Lake Wildlife Management Area, c/o Joe Bruna, Division of Game Management, Kentucky Department of Fish and Wildlife Resources, 592 East Main Street, Frankfort, Kentucky, 40601. Telephone: (502) 564-4406.

Grayson Lake

The Grayson Lake Wildlife Management Area includes 6,350 acres of lake shoreline in Carter and Elliott counties, seven miles south of Grayson.

It can be reached by Ky-7, Ky-409, and Ky-1496, and by boat. The area has a few primitive interior roads. It is mainly hilly and steep, with some gently sloping upland areas and fairly flat creek bottoms, and is mostly forested, with some abandoned fields and food plots. This area is temporarily closed to all hunting by the Kentucky Fish and Wildlife Commission as part of the program to increase the size of the deer herds in eastern Kentucky. Mailing address: Grayson Lake Wildlife Management Area, c/o Harold Barber, P.O. Box 115, West Liberty, Kentucky, 41472. Telephone: (606) 743-4481.

Jefferson National Forest

Two portions of this national forest extend into Kentucky—845 acres in Letcher County on Ky-932 and 116 acres in Pike County, which can be reached by a trail up Vanover Hollow from Ky-197. Both tracts are on the Kentucky-Virginia border and both offer extremely steep and mountainous terrain with hunting for squirrel, deer, grouse, and raccoon. Mailing address: Jefferson National Forest, c/o Joe Bruna, Division of Game Management, Kentucky Department of Fish and Wildlife Resources, 592 East Main Street, Frankfort, Kentucky, 40601. Telephone: (502) 564-4406.

Kentenia State Forest

Kentenia State Forest consists of 3,624 acres in Harlan County. Take US-421 three and one-half miles north from its intersection with US-119 to Ky-1679 (Little Shepherd Trail), which runs through the center of the area. The area contains mountainous, steep terrain, with narrow ridgetops and numerous rock outcroppings. It is completely forested, primarily in hardwoods. There is hunting for grouse, deer, squirrel, rabbit, raccoon, and fox. Mailing address: Kentenia State Forest, c/o Joe Bruna, Division of Game Management, Kentucky Department of Fish and Wildlife Resources, 592 East Main Street, Frankfort, Kentucky, 40601. Telephone: (502) 564-4406.

Kentucky Ridge State Forest

Kentucky Ridge State Forest is an area of 11,600 acres in Bell County five miles southwest of Pineville on Ky-190. Fire trails provide limited access to the interior of the area, which is predominantly forested and mountainous. There is hunting for squirrel and grouse. Mailing address: Kentucky Ridge State Forest, c/o Joe Bruna, Division of Game Management, Kentucky Department of Fish and Wildlife Resources, 592 East Main Street, Frankfort, Kentucky, 40601. Telephone: (502) 564-4406.

Mead Forest

Mead Forest is an area of 6,600 acres in Lewis County 15 miles south of Vanceburg. It can be reached by gravel roads off either Ky-377 or Ky-1068. There is a dirt road through the area passable by car in dry weather. Steep slopes, narrow creek valleys, and ridgetops predominate. The area is completely forested, mainly in hardwoods. Common game species are deer, grouse, and squirrel, with some fox and raccoon hunting. The area is owned by the Mead Corporation. Mailing address: Mead Forest, c/o Harold Barber, P.O. Box 115, West Liberty, Kentucky, 41472. Telephone: (606) 743-4481.

Olympia State Forest

Olympia State Forest is 780 acres in Bath County and can be reached by unimproved road southeast from Olympia Springs (between Olympia and Sudith on Ky-36). There are no established roads or trails within the area. The area is completely forested and contains steep, mountainous terrain. Hunting for squirrel, deer, grouse, and raccoon is available. Mailing address: Olympia State Forest, c/o Joe Bruna, Division of Game Management, Kentucky Department of Fish and Wildlife Resources, 591 East Main Street, Frankfort, Kentucky, 40601. Telephone: (502) 564-4406.

Pine Mountain

Pine Mountain consists of 5,018 acres in Letcher County. Take US-119 five miles southwest of Whiting to Little Shepherd Trail (Ky-1679), then travel 10 miles west to the Letcher-Harlan county line. The area is mountainous and steep, with narrow ridges and numerous rock outcroppings, and is entirely forested in mixed hardwoods. This area is temporarily closed to all hunting by the Kentucky Fish and Wildlife Commission as part of the program to increase the size of the deer herds in eastern Kentucky. Mailing address: Pine Mountain, c/o George Wright, Route 2, Box 110A, Campton, Kentucky, 41301. Telephone: (606) 668-3285.

Stearns

Stearns Wildlife Management Area encompasses 10,000 acres in McCreary County. Go west from Stearns on Ky-92, then south on Rock Creek Road (Ky-1363) to either Koger Hollow Road (FS Road 582) or Peters Mountain Road (FS Road 566). A jeep trail circumscribes the area and there are numerous side trails on the ridge tops. The area contains extremely mountainous terrain with flat narrow ridges, deep gorges, and many high cliffs. It is almost completely forested. Hunting for squirrel, deer, and grouse is available. Mailing address: Stearns Wildlife Management Area, c/o Chester Stephens, Route 1, Box 662, Whitley City, Kentucky, 42653. Telephone: (606) 376-2688.

L.B. Davison

L.B. Davison Wildlife Management Area is 150 acres in Ohio County, between Dundee and Hartford on Davidson Station Road (off Ky-878). There are no roads or trails within the area. The terrain is hilly with some steep cliffs. The area is almost completely forested, much of it in virgin hardwoods. There is hunting available for squirrel, rabbit, deer, and quail. The area around the home site is a wildlife refuge where hunting is prohibited. Mailing address: L.B. Davison Wildlife Management Area, c/o Lee Nelson, Route 3, Owensboro, Kentucky, 42301. Telephone: (502) 683-0789.

Tygarts State Forest

Tygarts State Forest is an area of 800 acres in Carter County west of and adjacent to Carter Caves State Resort Park off Ky-182. A county road (Oakland Ridge Road) runs along the western edge of the area. It is also accessible by short hike from the state resort park. The area is hilly with some gently sloping ridge tops and is forested in hardwoods. This is primarily a squirrel hunting area, with some deer, raccoon, and grouse hunt-

ing. No developed or marked roads or trails are in the area. Mailing ad-
dress: Tygarts State Forest, c/o Joe Bruna, Division of Game Management,
Kentucky Department of Fish and Wildlife Resources, 592 East Main Street,
Frankfort, Kentucky, 40601. Telephone: (502) 564-4406.

Barren Lake

Barren River Lake Wildlife Management Area is in Barren and Allen
counties. Access is gained from US-31E and Ky-87, Ky-98, Ky-100, and
Ky-252, as well as by lake. The 5200-acre area contains hilly to gently
sloping terrain, with woodlands and cleared bottom lands maintained for
wildlife. Deer, squirrel, rabbit, and quail are commonly hunted. Mailing
address: Barren Lake, c/o Pete Troublefield, 112 Cubbage, Leitchfield, Kentucky, 42754. Telephone: (502) 259-3352.

Central Kentucky

The Central Kentucky Wildlife Management Area consists of 1,323
acres in Madison County. Go nine miles southeast of Richmond on US-
421, then take Dreyfuss Road at Kingston, Kentucky. There is a gravel road
through the center of the area which contains rolling to flat terrain with
wooded areas and several wildlife food plots. Hunting is permitted for
squirrel and dove only. Mailing address: Central Kentucky Wildlife Management Area, c/o Dewey Mullins, Route 2, Berea, Kentucky, 40403. Telephone: (606) 986-4130.

Curtis Gates Loyd

Curtis Gates Lloyd Wildlife Management Area is in Grant County,
one-half mile southeast of Crittenden. Dirt roads provide access to all
portions of the 1,179-acre area. The terrain is level to rolling, with some
steep hills, farmland, brush, and woods. Species hunted include dove,
squirrel, rabbit, quail, and woodchuck. Mailing address: Curtis Gates Lloyd
Wildlife Management Area, c/o Dale Duley, Route 1, Box 9, Crittenden,
Kentucky, 41030. Telephone: (606) 428-2262.

Green River

Green River Wildlife Management Area consists of 14,625 acres in Taylor and Adair counties ten miles south of Campbellsville along the shoreline of Green River Lake. The terrain is gently rolling with flat bottoms and ridge tops. There are mixed hardwood sections with cleared areas in food crops. Common game species include deer, quail, rabbit, squirrel, and dove. Mailing address: Green River Wildlife Management Area, c/o Robert Kesller, P.O. Box 22, Lebanon, Kentucky, 40033. Telephone (502) 692-2419.

Lake Cumberland

The Lake Cumberland Wildlife Management Area encompasses 23,000 acres in numerous tracts along the shoreline of Lake Cumberland in Pulaski, Russell, Wayne, and Clinton counties, along Fishing, Poynter, Clifty, and Coldwater creeks. There are also tracts 10 miles west of Somerset on Ky-80, then 8 miles south on Piney Grove Road, and along Caney Fork Creek 8 miles northwest of Jamestown on Ky-619. Access points, roads, and trails around the lake are designated by signs. The area contains gently sloping creek bottoms and steep ridges, hardwood forests, old farmlands, and wildlife food plots. There is hunting for deer, squirrel, rabbit, quail, fox, raccoon, and dove. Mailing address: Lake Cumberland Wildlife Management Area, c/o Chester Stephens, Route 1, Box 662, Whitley City, Kentucky, 42653. Telephone: (606) 376-2688.

Mullins

The Mullins Wildlife Management Area is 267 acres in Kenton County a mile north of Crittenden along Interstate-75. There is access by dirt roads. The area contains level to rolling land with some steep hills, woods with some grasslands, and food plots. Dove, squirrel, rabbit, quail, and woodchuck are commonly hunted. Mailing address: Mullins Wildlife Management Area, c/o Dale Duley, Route 1, Box 9, Crittenden, Kentucky, 41030. Telephone: (606) 428-2262.

Nolin Lake

Nolin Lake Wildlife Management Area consists of 6,500 acres along the lake shoreline in Grayson, Edmonson, and Hart counties, and can be reached by Ky-88, Ky-1214, Ky-694, and Ky-728. The terrain is rolling to rugged, with a mixture of wooded areas and cleared fields, some in wildlife food plots. Deer, squirrel, rabbit, and quail are the most common game animals. Hunting is permitted in small isolated areas, mostly accessible by boat. Mailing address: Nolin Lake Wildlife Management Area, c/o Pete Troublefield, 112 Cubbage, Leitchfield, Kentucky, 42754. Telephone: (502) 259-3352.

Rough River

Rough River Lake Wildlife Management Area includes 2,999 acres of lake shoreline in Breckinridge and Grayson counties. Access is available via Ky-737, Ky-259, Ky-108, and Ky-79, and by boat. The area contains rough terrain and high banks with limited access to established areas, and is wooded, with a few cleared fields. Hunting is available for deer, squirrel, rabbit, and quail. Areas surrounding the public lands are heavily developed; care should be used by hunters. Mailing address: Rough River Wildlife Management Area, c/o Pete Troublefield, 112 Cubbage, Leitchfield, Kentucky, 42754. Telephone: (502) 259-3352.

Twin Eagle

Twin Eagle Wildlife Management Area is 166 acres in Owen County four miles northeast of Perry Park on Ky-355. There are adequate roads and trails within the area, which contains steep Kentucky River terrace terrain with some woods, croplands, grasslands, and sloughs. Game species include dove, rabbit, quail, squirrel, and deer. Mailing address: Twin Eagle Wildlife Management Area, c/o John Phillips, Route 1, Williamstown, Kentucky, 41097. Telephone: (606) 824-4688.

John A. Kleber

John A. Kleber is an area of 1,088 acres in Owen County on Ky-368 (Cedar Road) between US-127 and Ky-227. There are abundant jeep and hiking trails within the area, and the main trails are passable by pickup in dry weather. The terrain consists of steep hillsides, narrow ridgetops, floodplains, and a combination of woods, brush, grasslands, and wildlife food plots. There is hunting for quail, deer, squirrel, rabbit, groundhog, and raccoon. Mailing address: John A. Kleber Wildlife Management Area, c/o Doug Marshall, Route 1, Owenton, Kentucky, 40359. Telephone: (502) 535-6335.

Jones-Keeney

Jones-Keeney Wildlife Management Area consists of 1,604 acres in Caldwell County between Princeton and Dawson Springs on US-62. There are very few trails or roads within the area. The terrain is hilly, with forested uplands and some clearings in the bottoms and ridges. Hunting is available for deer, squirrel, quail, raccoon, and rabbits, and there are bow and rifle ranges in the area. Mailing address: Jones-Keeney Wildlife Management Area, c/o Frank Dibble, 320 Woodlawn, Murray, Kentucky, 42071. Telephone: (502) 753-3040.

West Kentucky 4-H Camp

West Kentucky 4-H Camp consists of 125 acres in Hopkins County one mile north of Dawson Springs off Ky-109. Steeply hilly to rolling terrain predominates. Hunting for deer, squirrel, and raccoon is available. Mailing address: West Kentucky 4-H Camp, c/o Joe Bruna, Division of Game Management, Kentucky Department of Fish and Wildlife Resources, 592 East Main Street, Frankfort, Kentucky, 40601. Telephone: (502) 564-4406.

Tradewater

Tradewater Wildlife Management Area consists of 728 acres in Hopkins County one mile south of Dawson Springs on Ky-109. There are access points on both sides of the road one-half mile south of Tradewater River Bridge. The area adjoins the Pennyrile Forest. The steep, hilly terrain is almost completely forested. There is hunting for deer, squirrel, and raccoon. Mailing address: Tradewater Wildlife Management Area, c/o Frank Dibble, 320 Woodlawn, Murray, Kentucky, 42071. Telephone: (502) 753-3040.

Reelfoot Lake

Reelfoot Lake is an area of 2,040 acres in Fulton County on Ky-94 west of Hickman. There are adequate trails within the area. Flat riverbottom land and a mixture of woods and cleared areas predominate. Hunting is permitted for squirrel and raccoon only, and raccoon hunters must check in and out. Hunting is restricted to special seasons and areas. Groundhog and gray fox may be taken while squirrel hunting only. Mailing address: Kentucky Department of Fish and Wildlife Resources, 592 East Main Street, Frankfort, Kentucky, 40601. Telephone: (502) 564-4336.

Menasha Ridge Press Guide Books

Carolina Whitewater
by Bob Benner $9.95

A Guide to the Backpacking and Day-Hiking Trails of Kentucky
by Arthur B. Lander, Jr. $9.95

A Fishing Guide to the Streams of Kentucky
by Bob Sehlinger and Win Underwood $9.95

A Guide to Kentucky Outdoors
by Arthur B. Lander, Jr. $9.95

Northern Georgia Canoeing
by Bob Sehlinger and Don Otey $9.95

Southern Georgia Canoeing
by Bob Sehlinger and Don Otey $9.95

Wild Water West Virginia
by Bob Burrell and Paul Davidson $7.95

A Canoeing and Kayaking Guide to the Streams of Kentucky
by Bob Sehlinger $12.95

Whitewater Home Companion Southeastern Rivers Volume I
by William Nealy $7.95

A Canoeing and Kayaking Guide to the Streams of Tennessee,
Volume I
by Bob Sehlinger and Bob Lantz $9.95

A Canoeing and Kayaking Guide to the Streams of Tennessee,
Volume II
by Bob Sehlinger and Bob Lantz $9.95

**The books are available at outdoor shops, better bookstores and
directly from Menasha Ridge Press, Route 3 Box 58G,
Hillsborough, NC 27278**